DATE DUE			
DEC 2 8 1998			

Whatever Happened to Cinderella?

Whatever Happened to Cinderella?

Middle-aged Women Reveal Their True Stories

by FLO FRANKEL
and SALLY RATHVON

St. Martin's Press • New York

Library of Congress Cataloging in Publication Data

Frankel, Flo.
    Whatever happened to Cinderella?

    1. Middle aged women—United States—Biography.
2. Women—Psychology—Case studies.   3. Middle aged
women—United States—Family relationships—Case studies.
I. Rathvon, Sally, joint author.   II. Title.
HQ1412.F7   155.6   79-28499
ISBN 0-312-86591-10

Our thanks and love to the fifty-six women we interviewed who gave their time so generously and their memories so thoughtfully.

Table of Contents

Though we would like to live without regrets, and sometimes proudly insist that we have none, this is not really possible, if only because we are mortal. When more time stretches behind than stretches before one, some assessments, however reluctantly and incompletely, begin to be made. Between what one wished to become and what one has become there is a momentous gap, which will now never be closed. And this gap seems to operate as one's final margin, one's last opportunity, for creation. And between the self as it is and the self as one sees it, there is also a distance, even harder to gauge. Some of us are compelled, around the middle of our lives, to make a study of this baffling geography, less in the hope of conquering these distances than in the determination that the distances shall not become any greater.

James Baldwin

(From a review of *The Arrangement,* by Elia Kazan, in *The New York Review of Books,* Vol. 8, No. 5, March 23, 1967, p. 17.)

Introduction

ONCE UPON A TIME when we, the authors, were little girls, we dreamed of becoming Cinderella. Our task was to be pleasing and good, and our goal was to find Prince Charming, marry him, and live happily ever after in the glow of romance.

After marriage we put aside our teaching careers and bought the feminine mystique that being a full-time wife and mother would be our fulfillment. As wives, we often found that being a mistress in the bedroom was more difficult and less exciting than our backseat necking had led us to believe. As mothers, we never questioned Dr. Spock's claim that our maternal dedication would produce well-adjusted, successful children. The anticipated pleasures and satisfactions of motherhood turned out to be indeed great, but, alas, temporary.

Now middle-aged, we are feeling less like Cinderella and more like the stepsisters. Instead of looking forward to a fairy-tale future, we are querulous about the present. We are sometimes caught between the demands of our grown, indulged, not always successful children and the demands of our parents, who are sometimes sick, lonely, or just demanding. We are occasionally caught between the needs of our husbands and our own need to respond to a changing society. And, having read Masters and Johnson, we are also caught between amusement and concern over the finding that we are capable of infinite orgasms but our husbands are not.

As for the future, we are ill-prepared for it. We failed to understand that a good mother puts herself out of business—and we are out of business. Neither our fantasies, our education, nor our domestic skills are sufficient to project a meaningful future for us.

In the hope that other middle-aged women might shed light on aging and role loss, we decided to ask them about their past and present circumstances and their plans for the future. Accordingly, we placed the following advertisement in local newspapers:

WANTED

Women, 40–55, to supply physiological, psychological, sexual, social, mental, and emotional histories in taped interviews. Purpose: understanding successes and failures of passage through middle age. Goal: a book. Anonymity guaranteed.

Phone _____.

As a result of this advertisement, we were able to interview fifty-six women. We tape-recorded each woman's life story during a three- to-six-hour session conducted either at her home or at one of ours.

We worked out a lengthy questionnaire to discover what is happening to other middle-aged Cinderellas. Our questions were designed to identify their solutions to the problems of aging and role loss. Our assumption was that a woman's relative successes and failures would be related largely to the amount of self-esteem that she possesses. We defined self-esteem as having three aspects: the feeling of personal lovability, the feeling of competence in handling life's challenges, and a confidence that the gap between expectation and fulfillment can be narrowed. For example, one woman was the sole financial support of her family through two marriages and divorces. Instead of taking pride in her enormous accomplishment, she said only, "The fact that I'm still hanging in there is the best that I have right now." We judged her self-esteem as relatively low, and her expectations as high.

The women we interviewed show enormous variety in the levels and sources of their expectations and their self-esteem. Sources include parents, lovers, husbands, children, and friends, as well as roles played and work done.

The women also vary widely in experience: happily and unhappily married suburbanites; a divorced hillbilly whose father assaulted her; a writer who has survived desertion, alcoholism, and more; a salty lesbian who has turned tragedy into humor; and a widow crushed by self-pity and despair.

They differ economically from rich to poor, sociologically from high society to first-generation immigrant, educationally from a Ph.D. to a high school dropout, bodily from svelte to fat, and sexually from passionate to cold.

They also vary in the concerns they are facing: Some lack a sense of purpose; they have no useful activity, work, or interests. Others keenly feel the lack of a sexual partner, a loving partner, or a friend. A few fear poverty or poor health. Less serious, but most common, are the complaints about physical aging: wrinkles, sagging flesh, and, especially, excess weight. Nevertheless, we are impressed that almost every woman found one or more solutions to one or more of her problems.

To our surprise, we find that these concerns, fears, and complaints are not mysterious psychobiological problems caused by menopause. They result from a combination of early childhood deprivation, role loss, aging, failed expectations, and the vicissitudes of life in general. Our society contributes to the fears of aging women by providing them with neither status nor support.

In exchange for our interviewees' gifts of intimacy, we offered only anonymity and the hope that the transaction would provide mutual enlightenment. We received more than we gave. We regret that space does not permit us to reproduce all of the interviews that we have.

As you read these interviews, you may recognize yourself, especially if you are over forty and female. In that case, you are like the women we interviewed in one respect: You and they are all experiencing or are about to experience menopause, that "animal birthday" that represents decline. No matter how gentle or severe the decline, it can be a blow to self-esteem. When menopause coincides with the loss of one or more of your roles, it is a dramatic signal of the need to stop and look at yourself, assess your present and future, and decide whether your relationships and activities make you feel useful, happy, and, most of all, worthwhile.

Granted that, as Carl Becker might say, every woman is her own historian, and that, as the central heroine in her life story, she will select the facts and emphases that suit her, each of these interviews has validity in the study of human nature. They may help you to find solutions to some of your problems. They may help you to reassess your own standards, your own self-esteem, and your own future. You may laugh, cry, identify with these women, or reject identification, but you will learn something about yourself. We did.

Whatever Happened to Cinderella?

CHAPTER 1

Lillian–The Helpless Lion

My idea of myself always related to the question: "Am I desirable to a man?" . . . My whole life has been wrapped up in me as a woman, and the only success I thought I had was that men desired me. The fear of losing that is what's bothering me now.

Lillian has gained and lost hundreds of pounds in her lifetime. She still eats and diets with passion. She is forty-eight years old and has long, platinum hair and a slow, mellifluous drawl. For the interview in her small, attractive home she wore glamorous, flowing pajamas with a revealing top. Conscious of the lower-class background she shares with her husband, and regretting their lack of education beyond high school, she is nevertheless proud of her self-taught taste in clothes, furniture, and reading matter. She is humorous and self-aware.

Lillian, a child of immigrants, was barely out of high school when she married. She has been married for thirty-two years. She is childless—happily so. She has worked at a number of part-time jobs during her marriage, none of them important to her. At the age of forty, to prove that she could still get attention from men, she began to frequent bars. At the same time, she established a relationship with a lover. However, her father is still number one with her, and she with him.

* * *

LILLIAN

I'VE NEVER BEEN PREGNANT, to my knowledge. For years I felt I *should* have a child, but I didn't really want one. I felt that society expected me to, my mother and everybody around. I was sixteen when I got married. My husband, Jack, is six years older, but he is not a responsible person. I was afraid of childbearing and I was afraid of taking care of a child, and I didn't think our marriage was going to last. That wasn't too happy a time. I used to keep a straight face, but I really felt like crying when the subject of children came up. Both Jack and I were checked out and were told there was nothing wrong with us. We didn't use birth control at all. I guess I just decided that motherhood was not for me. I wanted it from time to time because I thought I was doing my husband out of something. I think he wanted a child, even though the marriage was too much for him. Jack sometimes asked me if I wanted to adopt, and I wouldn't do it. I don't think I was interested in the motherhood bit, and now I'm very happy that I don't have any.

I didn't want to recognize it until now, but it's beginning to get to me that I am no longer young. Lately I find that every man that I'm attractive to or is attractive to me is six, seven, eight years younger than me. And in my consciousness-raising group I'm the oldest one. It bugs me. I feel like sixteen. I do. It's confusing. I feel unsure and unsettled, but I don't feel old. I don't see myself as old. Everybody that I don't see for a long time, and I see them, I go, "Oh God, they look horrible!" And I get scared, and I come home, like after a funeral, and I say, "Jack, do I look like that?" I know he doesn't see me right because he says I look great.

I've taken great pains with my skin, and I don't want it to dry up. I'm concerned that my looks are going to go, and that will make me know I'm old, so I'm hoping I don't get much of what I've been hearing about the menopausal years. The hysteria and the dryness—that's what worries me. As long as the price isn't too high, I'd do anything to help myself be as attractive as I possibly can. My husband says, "Go ahead, do what you want." I could use a tightening up, but I can't afford huge lumps of money for that sort of thing. A couple of thousand dollars is holding me back. Right now I'm dieting—I've had a weight problem off and on for years— and when I get some more loose flesh hanging around, I'll follow up on this thing. I'm *sure* I won't go to my grave without having had cosmetic surgery. If it makes you feel good, it's worth it. There's nothing else.

I don't know if it could be my age, but I think I have just started to have a little less sexual desire. I had no sexual experience before I was married, unfortunately. Jack was my only fella. I had a terrible honeymoon, really bad, and it took years and years before a pattern was established that was rewarding to me and I was able to have orgasms. It's so different now. I would never worry about premarital sex now or think these foolish things. It's more natural now. It was just something you were socialized into. But I was very sensual and intercourse was terribly disappointing to me. The petting before marriage was very rewarding and very heavy, and I could think of nothing else but that. I didn't want to go to school; I didn't want to think. Just get all the pleasure I could. I could think of nothing but this guy who was always after me, and I was tremendously pleased by the whole thing. So marriage was a tremendous letdown because there was no satisfaction. I kept trying and demanding. I'm a fighter. I did everything I possibly could to work it out, and I worked it out. But it was all me, because Jack couldn't even conceive that things were not all right. He didn't want to think that. Maybe he was so unsure of himself. I don't know. Things I suggested or demanded seemed not right to him. My sex drive was always stronger than his. I was always the active one, the motivator. I needed sex much, much more, and the fact that I wasn't getting it made me want it even more. It was a suffering. It was bad. Now we're more equal, and sometimes Jack will even offer me more than I really require in an effort to please me. In the last year or so I find myself even saying no to him! I never refused any offer before. I was always at it.

I was never inhibited, but there was a time when I thought I was weird because the things I wanted were considered no-nos. Oral sex is my thing. It's important to me. My husband called me perverted, and he wasn't joking. Today it's so different. I'm mild compared to what I hear about. I just like one-to-one relationships. I don't go for the two- or three-to-one stuff, or dirty movies.

Jack and I have a very close relationship. We hug and kiss and hit and kill. He says it's so close, it's too close. It's an intense relationship. It's either very good or very bad. It's unpredictable, you never know what's going to happen. After thirty-two years it's just the same. What can I tell you? We had a fight this morning. I'm always looking to change things. You know nothing ever changes. It's me, it's me. I talk so much about myself that if he doesn't understand me, he's not listening. He's a very closed person. We're almost opposites, and probably a person like me couldn't take me. I have great needs. The time we have bad problems is when we both need at the same time. Jack's going through a bad period right now with a lot of things, and I'm not feeling that great either. I need him, and he screams. I want the attention. So we're playing all kinds of roles to one another. Sometimes he's Daddy and sometimes, most of the time, I'm Mommy, know what I mean? And if we both need each other at the same time, it's rough.

I don't believe my husband has had any extramarital affairs, from what it looks like. He is a knocker of it. I had a couple of little affairs, and then about ten years ago I began to go out and I was really looking for a guy. I'll tell you why. I was about to hit my fortieth birthday. So, by strenuous diet I went from 300 pounds to 150 pounds. I had been very unhappy. It had a lot to do with the sex thing, my age, and my divorced sister who has having a lot of fun. The end of the rainbow was that I was going to make myself into a glamorous lady. But it didn't do anything for me. It was still the same old shit, you know? I wasn't any more attractive to my husband—he always thought I was very beautiful. Of course he did mind when I was fat, but he didn't say anything.

We were pretty much estranged at the time, and so I started going out with some single women. We used to frequent a cocktail lounge, a place that became my home. I was in the city more than I was at home in those days. I had a lot of purely sexual relationships, but I never had an orgasm outside of my home. I told myself that if I hadn't been having those affairs I would have been eating. I was really afraid to ever give it up. I sometimes think that if I were left by my lonesome, I might develop into an extremely promiscuous person. How do I know? I never went out for sex, you know. That was my reward to someone. Never did I expect to get anything. As a matter of fact I came close to enjoying the sex with one guy and I ran away from it. When I realized I was doing things that were different from the usual me, I got scared. I told myself that I didn't want to be seen as a sexual thing. I just wanted to give to the man. Definitely it was for my ego, for making me feel like a desirable woman, and when the guys come on, that's what makes me happy. At one time I would, like, pick up on the first one that flirted. It was very important to me. I would be depressed if it didn't happen.

But now I can't be bothered. I don't enjoy looking for guys any more. Sometimes I think I do. I threaten myself with it. I say to myself, "Oh shit. I'm going to go out and see if I can find something to do," you know? The other day I was in the city and I figured I had the time, I was all made up and everything, but I really didn't want to. It offers me nothing now, but for a long time I was afraid to even stop picking up guys.

There's one guy that I've been seeing for several years. Right now it's a sexual relationship with no sex. It was pure sex, and then it became a tremendous involvement. For a while I could think of nothing but him. He is married and has a child and he's never going to divorce his wife, but we can't seem to break this off. I'm going to see him tomorrow. I talk to him every day, but we don't go to bed. I wonder what he's doing with me and what I'm doing with him. If he would fade away right now, I'd let him go. Definitely. But, I tell you, there was a time when I opened and closed my eyes with that man and every spare moment of my life I didn't want to think of anything but him. He was as important to me as my husband was when I first met him. He gave me a sense of something that I thought I was missing.

I'm the takeover type. I take over and manage people and situations; like I worry about what you're ordering or where the waiter is, or what you're tipping, or what you're doing. I always put myself into a trap and then cry because I'm in it. But *he,* my lover, took care of everything; *he* managed everything. I had nothing to do but sit there. It was just my time to be irresponsible and silly. It was beautiful, but it didn't last. I got very involved, and he became the same pressure to me that everything else did. It sounds stupid, but this man is, like, mine. I feel the same about my husband. He isn't a separate person; he's part of me. I love them both very much. Right now the relationship is like the one with my husband, and I don't think it will change really. I do like seeing him. I'm not me when I'm with him. Maybe it's part of a dream, who knows? Maybe it's just a big fantasy. When I see him tomorrow, if he grabs me or says something, I'll do it. I think I still need it. My ego needs it. But I want something more. I don't know what.

I've been doing some thinking about Jack and myself. I never realized how dependent we are on each other. I suddenly thought that if Jack left me I wouldn't know how to take out the garbage. I'm childish. I thought I was doing him a favor by living with him. I just loved him and hated him. I've thought about divorce all these years. I considered divorce once this week. Once today! I'll consider it again tomorrow. He mentions it, too, but I think he's very happy with me. The main problem is me. I know how to make life absolutely miserable for him. He would like me to stand under his armpit, you know what I mean? Just be dependent on him. But he doesn't treat women as inferior. He likes women and he likes me. I feel very physical about him. When he's in the room, I know it and it's good. He's the only man I ever had sexual satisfaction with.

Jack wouldn't accept my affairs at all. I've even tried to throw it on him and then stopped. He may think of it and then throw it aside. After all, there was a period when I wasn't home much, when I was asking him to move out. But it's not fair to pile my guilt on him. Why should I hit him with it? He doesn't really want to know.

I guess the biggest satisfaction in my life is my father. He was always my god, my lover, my everything. It's still going on; it's still my strongest relationship. I still kiss my father on the mouth. He admires me; he really digs me as a woman. I used to vie for his attention. I used to disrupt my mother for it, and I won out over her and over my sisters. But I gave plenty for it, to be his favorite, and I still am giving. I gave him whatever he wanted. I made him very important. I found his weaknesses and made strengths of them. I went to ball games with him—I didn't like ball games, but he never knew. I was his friend, his mentor. I just adored him.

My father was a frightened man. He came from the old country. He had a rough time making it. He was sent into a factory to work a sewing machine and he bemoaned his fate every day of his life, and he did it loud, like I do. That I inherited. And I also inherited this bit about not looking at the good things. There are many good things in my marriage. I never see them. I only see what I'm *not* getting. My father's eighty years old, healthy, and he takes care of his apartment better than I do my house. I was with him yesterday, brought him a lovely dinner, and he walks around complaining and moaning. I tell him he's lucky. There are very few people who reach his age, in the full sense of the word. He's a beautiful man. He looks great, he dresses great, and he's looking for someone as pretty as my mother was years ago. It's ridiculous.

My father wasn't too happy to have me get married at sixteen. He was always in competition with Jack, at least I recognize that now. He would sit in my husband's chair, just like deliberately. After all, he lost something that was very important to him. I mean, I doted on him. I still call him every morning, and I still give him everything. After my father had a heart attack, he and my mother moved in on me. My marriage was very bad at the time, but forget about it, it was just impossible, frustrating like you never saw. I was always trying to satisfy my father; my husband was turning into a brother. My mother would walk into the bedroom and sit down and watch TV, not thinking of me as a sexual person. It was very bad. I had to throw them out. They fought very hard to stay, my father especially, but they went. That was the reason for the 300 pounds I had at the time. But it was either throw them out or go crazy.

At the beginning of my life, my mother was the enemy. I was always trying to be the big, important thing to my father, so my mother and I were always fighting. It was very aggressive. I have a scar in my head from an ashtray she threw at me, and another in my foot, from a knife. I just would not do the things she wanted me to do. I was very forceful. One time I said, "If you don't let me go to the game with my father, I'm throwing myself out the window." She said, "Oh yeah," and she pushed me toward the window with one hand and held me with the other, you know, to teach me a lesson. I never pulled that again. She was aware of what a bitch I was. But the thing is, she could never rule me. There was no way possible.

My mother also thought I was great. When I got married at sixteen, she was proud of me. It was a sign that her daughter was something. She liked my husband a lot. She said he was the most beautiful man she ever saw. And when I was getting heavy, she was ashamed of me and said I should lose weight to be acceptable to my husband's friends. I bought that hunk of bullshit at the time.

The positive side of me is my mother; the negative side is Dad. My mother was a very strong lady. She just did what she had to do. She never cried about anything. She just picked herself up and she did it. She was like me in that she liked men better than women. She was flirty, like me, and she always picked women friends who were less than her; that was a need of hers. In her old age, I took her places and spent time with her and was good to her. But I was the kingpin. The family revolved around me. From the age of eleven, I think, I was the mother of my parents. I took care of the bank account, the checking; the phone was in my name. When we used to go somewhere, it was "Lily's mommy, Lily's daddy, Lily's sisters"—that's the truth, I was the important person. My father and mother always depended on me. But my father manipulates me, too. Don't forget, I pay for all I give him.

Let me tell you the difference between my mother and father. During the war my mother got a job in a dress factory doing piecework; you get paid by the piece. She was doing bathrobes. So she put pockets all over the place. The supervisor came up and said, "These bathrobes are going to a mental institution, but even they know the pockets don't belong down here somewhere." But she didn't care. My father, on the other hand, was in the needle trades too, but he used to spend Sundays in the hallway, crying, praying that he should die before he goes to work Monday. It was too much for him. He was a pieceworker, too, and he'd do the garment over and over and over to the point where he couldn't even make a living at it. It had to be perfect. Nobody should bring back one piece of work to him. There should not be an error. And he was always afraid of tomorrow. I'm the same. I'm afraid of middle age. That's why I'm talking to you.

Actually, I have had no faith in my ability to do anything in this world except please my parents, especially my father. But I knew that my father was a very insecure man, so his and my mother's approval didn't mean the world's approval. I think I'm a very intelligent person and a good person. I've never done anything to a person that I'm ashamed of. But my accomplishments I'm ashamed of. There's nothing that I've accomplished. I do a lot of things. I work part time in a store. I read a lot. Every morning at 6:30, after I finish my fight with Jack, I read. I do volunteer work at the mental hospital. I help my husband: I type minutes for his union; I discuss with him whatever he wants. I have enough to do. The thing I'm worried about is winding up in a home for old people, and I'm going to be very unhappy because I'm not the kind of person who likes to be told anything. It scares me. It brings tears to my eyes right now, thinking about it. People think I'm fine. When I tell someone I'm frightened, they look at me. Jack says I'm like a lion, a lion roaring "Help!" You see, my self-esteem is still related to the question: "Am I desirable to a man?" I sound very shallow, don't I? I'm really not, I think, but my whole life has been wrapped up in me as a woman, and the only success I thought I had was that men desired me. The fear of losing that is what's bothering me now.

CHAPTER 2

Judy–Down but Not Out

I came from a family where you woke up in the morning and said,
"Now who am I not talking to today?" We were a very distant family
. . . sometimes it can destroy a person mentally.

*Judy was married at eighteen and divorced at forty. Her husband left her six
years ago. Now forty-six, she is living with five of her six children, who range in
age from fifteen to twenty-five.*

*Judy is very much overweight. She has battled this problem all her life. Her face
registers all her moods dramatically. She is a breathless, headlong talker, virtually
a monologuist, enacting many roles, providing voices for her mother, father, and
husband.*

*Judy quit high school after two years and has not had a job since her teen years.
Money for this family comes from the children's jobs, from Judy's babysitting, and
from her father. It adds up to less than $10,000 a year. Emotionally,
educationally, and financially, she is a child of poverty. Her small house is the
only one in the neighborhood still occupied by whites. There are "funny" signs on
most of the doors, walls, and windows.*

*Judy's daughter arranged for the interview, hoping it would help her mother.
While talking, Judy exuded warmth, and at the end of the interview she said, "I
feel I have known you all my life."*

* * *

JUDY

I GO TO Overeaters Anonymous. Weight has always been my big
problem. I lost weight to get men and then men hurt me, so I
gained weight. Then I wanted men, so I lost weight again. That's
the story of my life: up and down in weight and trying to spite men
through my weight. I'd say, "They'll love me fat or they won't get
me at all." Right? And now I can say that's not the point. The
point is I don't like myself very much. This OA organization is
exactly like Alcoholics Anonymous. It's been a lot of growing for
me. You don't sit and talk diet at the meetings. This is a spiritual

program. What they're doing is they're giving me therapy, actually, so it has seeped into other areas of my life, which is probably the greatest godsend of my life.

Sometimes I get very apprehensive about things, very scared. I tell my kids it's all downhill now. I joke and laugh about the declining years, but inside I know I have to have strength from somewhere. That's why I say this OA has done more for me than just help me lose weight. You write things down and then you burn them. It helps me keep from doing nasty little things. I write the awful things I feel, and then, if I can, I write that I forgive myself, and then I burn it. Now I can say that I hated my father. That word was stricken off the list when I was growing. You couldn't hate anyone, especially your mother and father. And I can diet now, if I just don't cheat. I rebel because I'm stubborn and unmanageable, and I go on binges. I'll eat three Big Macs and three chocolate milkshakes while you're picking at your potato chips. I have to say, "OK, God, I'll do it Your way. I'll stay on the diet."

But as I say, I get depressed and scared. I sleep with a little light showing. I don't want to die, you know? It's a vague panic. I chalk it off to this time of life because I didn't have it before. I'm getting old. Even if I'm not so bad, you know, walking on crutches or anything, even so, I'm getting old. My joints are tightening up, and my face and my hands are not the same. I want to take pride in growing old, but certain times I feel this way, scared to be alone. I want to cater to myself now, which I feel I deserve after all these bad years.

When my husband and I separated a few years ago, I found a whole new world of married men. I went out searching for them. I was frantic. I'd say, "I have to have that physical contact with a man. That's a positive." Because I didn't think too much of myself outside of the sex. Then two years ago I joined OA and started on all this new thinking, and I thought, "No, I don't want married men. They give you a few minutes, they give you an hour, they don't really care about *me,* so why should I give myself away like that? They wouldn't leave their wives, and I couldn't take them away." To tell you honestly, the ones I could take away, I didn't want.

So I went to single men, and of course I got stomped on, demolished. I always picked out ones who were wrong for me, like my compulsive gambler. Who picks out a compulsive gambler that's been to prison and lives with another woman? I thought I really liked him. He borrowed money. He never returned it. He lied about his girl friend; he lied about everything. Finally, he threatened me.

So I found out the single guys wanted me for the same reason the married guys wanted me. Just the sex, and they weren't as nice to me. So I quit going to those places where you meet men. I don't dance, and the people there make me feel old. Even Parents Without Partners is not for me, I think. I had one episode of that, and the man I met was only out to toss everybody in bed. He told me that. So I said, "I can't go through this. I have to quiet my mind down." To be honest with you, there's only one man that calls now, now that I've stopped looking for men. I could easily get laid. I could call up a dozen guys and say, "Hi, how about it?" But I haven't been with a man—it's very unusual—for three months. I'm absolutely amazed. I'm a very sexual person. But there are other things that I'm busy with now, and I find it's not that bad. I *can* live without sex. Well, I'm not sure how much *longer*, honey! But I'm settling down to a nice, peaceful resignation, and I'll wait for somebody nice to come along. There's got to be somebody. Maybe through the sex I was looking for approval, and now I've found a little more approval of myself, you know?

I have to be honest and say that I think I'm pretty good in bed. Otherwise I would have just thought of myself as a *complete* failure. There, at least, I was something. I give and I take. I never give without taking, but I never, never could just take. I make sure I give as much pleasure as I get. I was told through the years what a great sex experience I was, and this was by people who had other women and everything, and they would come back to me, so I must have been halfway decent. For years I didn't have any other idea of myself as any good. I mean, I'm a dummy; I don't know anything. But I was worth something in bed, taking off my clothes. Somebody liked me and wanted me. If I didn't think that, I would have just felt down in the gutter someplace.

I never fell in love till I met him, my ex-husband. We petted and necked, but we never actually had intercourse till after we were married. I never stopped to think—I was a virgin! I was not too well-informed and I would not have oral sex with him; and it was always the same with him, one position and no variations. I used to think we should do something different, but he settled for whatever happened because the sex was good. In the beginning I took my sexual feelings as love. I still have a problem there. If you want to be with somebody twenty-four hours a day and you're filled with this nice feeling, that must be love.

I came to the conclusion after we had been married about five years that it was strictly physical, maybe with both of us. He was exactly different than me. He was an introvert; I was a big-mouth extrovert. He didn't appreciate a lot of my sense of humor, like these crazy signs I have all over the house. Look, here's my favorite: "Candy Is Dandy but Sex Won't Rot Your Teeth." And he thought I was too friendly. I embarrassed him, and I guess I was ahead of my time in my tolerance of black people. He was a bit prejudiced and I'm not. He was a volunteer fireman, and I wrote a letter, a nice letter to the newspaper about blacks getting into the firehouse, and I signed my name. But I hadn't talked to my husband about this and he hit the roof. I got phone calls. I thought these callers were going to kill me.

But in the beginning my husband was a strong anchor to hold onto. I said, "Oh, boy, someone to lean on!" because I was a spendthrift, no good, rotten with money. I always went out and bought stuff he had to take back. I bought the babies every toy in the store and beautiful clothes to dress them up in. Then I probably started to grow up a little and take some responsibility for the home and the kids, and I wanted more money. I started caring, and he stopped caring. We were both spending too much, and the responsibility got too much for him. He never really left us penniless. He was an auto mechanic. He always had work, but he would quit one job after another. It was a pattern. So they would come and turn off the water, or say we couldn't have any more oil because the bills weren't paid. The house was falling down neglected, and we were having too many children. Six in ten years.

I was forty years old with six kids, and I felt self-pity—poor me, stuck in the house, too broke to go out. So I lost a lot of weight and I flew crazy. Crazy, crazy bird. I found someone in the neighborhood and had myself an affair. I guess you send out vibrations when you're having an affair. Everybody knew. My husband knew. I was so indiscreet it was absolutely amazing. I couldn't talk about anything but this man. I was just a stupid thing, not old enough or smart enough to have an affair. My husband had one too, with my best friend. Believe it or not, that didn't affect my friendship with her because I didn't care for my husband at the time. After we confessed to one another we should have started off clean from there, but the relationship was gone. The marriage had been on the rocks for years. Maybe if there had been the openness then that there is now we would have made it, but we never discussed things. It was partly his fault, but when we started out my husband could have been worked with. I was the one who nagged and screamed until he probably said, "The hell with her. I can't do anything to please her."

We fought plenty. I mean, I went at him with a knife, terrible things. But never in front of the children. I was really a bitch though. He was easygoing and loving and helped take care of the children, but I didn't appreciate him. There were times when I really treated him like garbage. I'm ashamed of it now, but I served him real garbage for dinner once. I arranged it like on a dinner plate. I'll never forget him looking at the potato peels and the greasy chicken bones!

I had a terrible temper. I used to think I was going crazy, the way I could throw things! And at my children when they were young. I'm convinced I should have had therapy a long time ago. Nobody ever told me I was sick. I thought everybody else was sick. I was so stupid and spoiled and selfish, and I yelled and screamed at my poor kids. I loved them too, and I took pride when I showed them off to people, all clean and neat, but I sure wasn't the best mother. I resented all the time they took, and I was impatient. I'd think, "What are they crying for?" I was at that time cleaning my house really good, washing the floors once a week, tearing down the blinds, all that. I was painting and papering and while the Red Devil was dripping down on the kids I was yelling, "Shut up!" One time all I remember was bending over the toilet. Of course the oldest, the retarded boy, was not trained. And the second was bad that way, a late trainer, and the third was too young to be trained. And I thought, dipping the diapers in the toilet, "This is my life."

When I finally came to the conclusion that I had to get help and went to our pastor, it was too late. I had pushed my husband too far. He said, "No. Nobody's going to know our business." So then I asked him to leave, and he wouldn't. We were fighting terribly, and I was sleeping in different rooms and on the floor. Finally I cut up his side of the mattress, and I guess he thought I was really going off. And I was; I was going totally berserk, threatening awful things. He thought I might kill the children. Se we separated, and within a month he was living with somebody.

My husband used to say, "We don't communicate," and he was right. I wouldn't talk to him. See, I came from a family where you woke up in the morning and said, "Now who am I not talking to today?" It was mostly my father. My mother and father, would you believe, used to not talk for two months. I never in my life saw my parents kiss. My mother took care of my father but without love or pleasure. She would get up in the morning, serve him his breakfast, give him his nice dinner, wish him bad in her heart, I know, never speak a word, and then on Friday nights she would go upstairs to my father, saying to me, "This is my duty. I can't deny him his sexual pleasure. He supports me and takes care of us." She'd go up, lay down, one, two, three, saying, "Do it quick. I can't stand it. Get the stuff away from me." She said to me, "Maybe you'll be different. Maybe, even, you'll like sex, but I hate it." She used to describe it, "Him sticking that thing." I thank God I didn't get her attitude. Much later I remembered what my mother said and I thought, "What do you mean—'duty'?" I never felt it was a duty to lay down for my husband. I thought it was for my pleasure.

We were a very distant family. From my father it was: "Keep an arm's distance, do not kiss me, and don't touch me." He never abused us physically, but sometimes it can destroy a person mentally. He never touched us, but he opened his mouth. I keep telling this funny little story, and it isn't really funny. He used to call me "fuckingsonofabitchbastard." Honest, by the time I hit kindergarten I was amazed to find out that my name was Judy.

My father was hate. That's all I remember. He was hateful to my mother, too. They had the most miserable fifty years I have ever seen. I remember when I was little my mother was going to leave him. She came right back. Where could she go? She just became a "yes, dear, be quiet, be good children, be nice to your father."

I hate to blame because I still have the feeling I'm not supposed to criticize, but my parents did nothing for me. I wanted to be a vet. I know I have brains inside this head, but they were just laying there all these years. Nobody did anything to encourage me. I saw my brother getting the violin lessons, and I used to say, "I want to take piano lessons. I really would." I kept on saying this even till I was fourteen, and nobody answered me. When I was sixteen I said, "I'm leaving school. I have no use for it. I don't really care." And my parents said, "You can't do that. You have to get a diploma." I said, "I don't want it. What's it for? Nobody said I could go to college. Nobody said I could be a vet. You always said not to talk about it. I'm sixteen. When *do* you talk about it? I'm getting the idea nobody gives a damn. I'd rather make money." They couldn't make me finish school. So I got a job at the telephone company, and I made out good. But then I got married.

My parents didn't like my husband's religion so they didn't speak to me for ten years. Then my mother had a dream that her father told her to speak to me again. She was a very superstitious woman, so I got a call to come over with my husband and children. We went, and we were friends again. My parents acted like grand-parents to our kids and all that, but to me it was the same old thing: my mother always saying, "Go and kiss your father." And he'd say, "Keep away from me. Don't touch me. I don't need that and stay the hell away from me." I don't know how many presents he threw at me. "Keep your goddamn present," he'd say. So I finally got to the point where I said, "I'm a woman. I don't have to take this." I said to my father, "You will not make me cry anymore. I'm a person, and I don't care if I ever see you as long as I live. I will come and see my mother, but you will not turn me away again." He didn't answer, but he toned down after that.

Well, my mother died and my father had a stroke and is in a home now. When he came to after his stroke, the first thing out of his mouth was, "I love you." And he hugged me and kissed me and all this baloney, and I didn't know what's happening. I couldn't believe this. So he loved me, and not only that, he needed me and wanted me. He had never thought much of women, you know; they should stay in the house and shut up; don't drive a car. He was an Archie Bunker when it comes to females; I forgot to say that.

Now I had to make all the decisions. I got power of attorney and managed all his money. I said to him, "I either work or I come to see you. I can't do both. I need to work for this family of mine." And he said, "No, don't work." So I put him in a nursing home and after about three months I began to enjoy him loving me. But then one day he turned on me: "You son-of-a-bitch, you stole all my money!" And the next time he was going to kill me. My daughter, she's my lifesaver, she went and put him in the bedroom there and slammed the door and said, "You will not treat my mother like this; you will not treat anybody like this; you will not yell and scream. We all do the best we can and all we ask is that you treat us like human beings, that's all. Now if you don't, we're not coming back to see you ever again, and I will not let my mother come." And that was it. He was OK again, and I go to see him nearly every day and take him food and take him and some other inmates out for little jaunts. But I'm afraid he'll have more and more, these little spurts of hate.

It's become easier over the years. My ex-husband has always been very kind to me. Those kids made out like crazy—we both tried to buy them; you know what happens. I like to believe they love me best, and I feel a little bit of sorrow for my husband because he doesn't have them. But they see him and his side of the family. At Christmas we were all invited for dinner with his new wife, and I felt I just couldn't handle it. He keeps telling me I should be able to do this, but I said, "What are we going to talk about? The days gone by? Remember when the kids did so and so? Or do we talk about what you've given her, or just what do we have in common?" So I can't be friends with his wife. I think I've stopped calling him names when he calls. The last time he hardly knew me, I was so nice. We're both nice people, but not together. I don't dare look back at what might have been. I just couldn't bear it. But can you believe that I have fantasies that maybe he'd leave his wife and come back? Look at all the years and the money wasted. It's because I get so dreadfully lonesome, because I want a man. I want everything. I'm that kind of compulsive person.

I think I'm more patient now, and my temper is better. I enjoy my children more now, and I thank God they have not brought me real problems. My oldest daughter is not really happy, but she's aware, she's searching. I was never aware. I never used to dig inside myself. It was too painful. I thought that if everybody would stop picking on me I could get skinny; if they'd stop throwing all these obstacles in my way things would get better, and tomorrow I could start on the diet, and after the diet I would become more reasonable because my trouble was either the weight or the smoking—I was smoking three packs a day—or was it something else? No. It was all my ex-husband's fault. In other words I was in such a confused state of mind I never could see myself. The people I met at OA have made me look at myself and admit that I was wrong in a lot of things.

The one thing I'm right now telling my fifteen-year-old daughter is that she'll have to give up her adolescence or I'll have to give up my menopause, because we can't go through them together. She's going through a bad period. She's saying some of the things I'm feeling. So I tell her, "Here I am, forty-six, you're fifteen; you're feeling that people are no good, they let you down, it's a bad time of your life." She feels apprehensive, like me. What's the purpose of the whole thing? I don't want to die, but what's the use of living? She feels those same things. We had a good talk yesterday about our worries and problems. But mainly, we sort of drift.

CHAPTER 3

Irene—A Nurturer

My father raised us completely, by himself. . . . He was a very gentle man with old-fashioned manners, and he was devoted to us.

Irene's clothes are conventionally styled in soft colors. Everything about her appearance is muted, but her friendliness and concern about others is strong and conspicuous. She was serious and thoughtful during the interview.

Irene was married at twenty and divorced at forty. Now fifty-five years old, she lives alone in a small, rural house. Her grown children live in distant states. Unprepared for anything more than domesticity, she wisely saw a need for financial independence after her husband became estranged from the family. She went to college, graduated at forty, became self-supporting, and left her husband. She has been single and a high school music teacher for fifteen years. She values education and continues to explore new subjects through lectures, courses, and books.

* * *

IRENE

MY MOTHER was orphaned when she was six, and after being farmed out here and there she was finally able to live with her father. But her stepmother treated her badly. She wasn't allowed to eat at the same table. She had to eat the leftovers afterwards.

I remember my mother as a very quiet, reserved person. I remember her being very melancholy, depressed. My brother and sister and I were never physically punished. Mother would wait until Dad got home to tell him if we were naughty, but he never punished us either. I think we just absorbed their values. I don't remember that they ever told us what they believed. I know we had to have good manners and work hard and be honest. That's the way my father was. We were very close to him because my mother passed away when I was eight, and my father raised us completely, by himself. My grandfather's sister told him to put us in an orphanage when my mother died, but my father refused to do that. He would have dated, but it was during the Depression, and there wasn't much money. I remember he would take a walk with a lady friend, but the little money he had went for us. We never went hungry, although my father lost his job in 1932. He hocked his winter coat, his gold watch, and other things. He was a very gentle man with old-fashioned manners, and he was devoted to us. When I first moved out here in the country, there was a water pump on the corner for the homes that didn't have water, and I can remember my father running out and getting the women's pails and carrying their water back. When he was around, a woman didn't have to lift a finger.

My sister and I didn't get along too well during that time. She was four years older and was supposed to be in charge after Mother died. We were supposed to split up the housework, but it seems that I really got more than my share. We had a four-room flat, no hot water, and the two rooms I had to clean were the kitchen and the first bedroom. She got the other bedroom and the living room. We didn't use the living room much because there was no heat back there. We had a coal stove in the kitchen. I did the shopping and took care of the cooking—this was when I was about eleven—and she was out having a good time. She was what we called "wild" then. I know now that she just wanted a normal good time.

My father went to the Bureau of Charities in our city to ask for help in raising us. We were assigned a social worker, a wonderful woman who became a part of our lives—getting us to the doctor, things like that. I really had a crush on her. She remained a family friend even after we grew up and no longer needed her services. I think she was a big influence in my life. She is still a friend.

Another woman made a big difference in my life too. I had a wonderful black high school teacher who paid special attention to me. She always encouraged me. At that time in order to graduate you had to have your teeth fixed. I had an after-school job, but there just wasn't enough money. The only reason I was able to graduate was that this very nice teacher spent the thirty dollars to have my teeth fixed. That's why I really get angry with people who discriminate because of color. Here I was, a white person, and she did all this for me.

Somewhere along in my school life, the IQs came out. I was in the average range, but I felt more stupid than that because my brother and sister had much higher scores than I did. So I never thought about college or a career. I did go to college when I was forty, and I did all right. I don't think I'm really very bright, but I've done better than I ever expected to.

Somehow my father and I were on the same wavelength. We understood each other very well. The unhappy part was that after I got married I couldn't invite him to stay with us very much, because it hurt him to see the way my husband behaved. He didn't understand my husband. He said to me and to my neighbors that my husband had a good wife and two nice children and why was he angry all the time? I didn't talk to my father about it, because I didn't want to hurt him. I didn't want him to know how bad it was. My husband was—they have an Irish saying—a house devil and a street angel. Not many people were aware of how unpleasant he was.

My father was a chef, and I always enjoyed cooking and trying out new dishes. At home when we sat down to eat, we always discussed how good this tastes and how good that tastes, and my poor husband was always left out of that. He wasn't interested in food. I read someplace that people who have problems are sometimes like that. They only eat to live. I complained once to my father that my husband never says anything is good, and my father, who was sort of a philosopher, would say, "Don't feel bad. He's eating it, isn't he?"

My husband was twenty-six and I was twenty when we got married. I didn't realize then how much difference there was between us. He had had an unhappy childhood, an alcoholic father and a mother who didn't do much to protect him. So when I came along with all my love and affection and fussed over him and took care of him and loved him as much as it's possible to love another human being, that was great for him. Then when the children came along, he was jealous. He felt that my attention was going to them. Of course, my expectations, having had a wonderful father, were that he would be a better father, and he wasn't. He wasn't the father that I wanted for my children. He used to get angry with them all the time, and I used to run interference. If they did anything naughty, I sort of kept it from him so he wouldn't get angry. I always taught the children to come and tell me if they did something wrong. Then, I wouldn't punish them, I'd explain why they were wrong. If he ever found out that I had punished them in my way, he would double-punish them.

The problem with our son was the biggest one. There were times when I was afraid, because my husband had such an awful temper. The children were very upset when he was around, but we had a calm relationship when he wasn't. Interestingly enough, although my husband wasn't violent with our daughter, she is now the one who feels most hostile toward him. She still retains the anger. But my son, though he took the brunt of the violence, sort of blamed me for the divorce, even though I got the divorce partly so that his father wouldn't beat him up and so I wouldn't have to see my son either hitting his father back or else leaving home. I think my son felt that his father should love him, and he kept trying to do things to make his father love him. He sort of gave up about three years ago. He kept trying to see his father and reestablish something, but his father is too self-centered.

When my son was ten, he asked me, "Are you afraid of Daddy?" I was always trying to keep peace. I didn't fight back. Another time he said, "Wouldn't it be nice if we had company all the time because Daddy is so pleasant when we have company." The social life we had was my doing. I wanted to have things for the children to do so we were very involved in church activities. I was a Sunday school teacher, in the choir, and so forth. And we dragged my husband along although he didn't like to be with people. We had an understanding minister, and he tried to get my husband to do things around the church to give him a sense of importance. I think his big problem was his lack of feeling of worth about himself, and he projected this onto other people. He took everything I might say as criticism. I don't feel that he was mentally inferior to me. He just didn't have the education. He really wasn't able to write much, or read. It's too bad he didn't realize that he had a wonderful ability with anything mechanical. But his temper, his disagreeable personality got in the way. Even simple things would upset him.

In order to get our daughter's teeth straightened, I took a job in a doctor's office when she was about twelve. I did it to help the family, but it was an affront to him. It made him feel that I was better than he. To him an office job was a big thing. It had status.

He didn't like my going to college at all. I started going when things were really bad at home, and it was what kept me on an even keel, more or less, and it enabled me eventually to become a teacher. He didn't like my aspirations for the children, either. I started them early in dance lessons, music lessons. I took lessons along with them in whatever it was. I can remember sitting at the dinner table—I was always trying to interest the children in something—and we'd get to talking and he'd pick up his plate and go in another room. So the children talked easily to me, and they couldn't talk to him. He was never interested. Even if we wanted to go on a picnic, he didn't want to go. If I had known he would be this way, of course I wouldn't have married him.

I started marriage counseling because our son was having trouble in school. The school psychologist felt the problem wasn't with the boy but with us, so he sent us to the mental health clinic. My husband went three times, and then he refused to go. I continued for a year and somewhere along the line I realized that since my husband wasn't going to go for help, he wasn't going to change. So I had to learn to stand it. The psychologist helped me do that. After the children were grown, though, I knew it was a dead end. Why should I stay with someone who is just so unpleasant? He didn't believe I would do it but we got divorced. I've been single now for over ten years.

My husband wasn't the type of man who talked, so I never had any idea about my body from him. In the beginning my sexual feelings were mixed up with love. I thought sex was a duty of marriage, but it was also something I wanted. It seemed perfectly natural. I had discovered masturbation when I was a very young child. I remember trying to teach my sister, and she didn't know what I was talking about. I never had any of the problems I read about now of women not having orgasms. But later when my husband and I were like an armed camp, I tried to bury my sexual feeling because I was so angry with him that I didn't want to enjoy it. I even tried to hold back my orgasm because I felt there was something wrong with having enjoyment, feeling as we did about each other.

Shortly after my divorce I joined a singles group, but it didn't work out for me. It seemed that the men were all wolves and the women all sex-starved. Although I have sexual feelings I just can't get involved without having known the person for a while. One gentleman, I shouldn't say gentleman, took me out to dinner, and then, driving home, he pulled off the road and wanted to kiss me. Now most people would think kissing was a fairly simple thing. But I said, "Why do you want to do that? I hardly know you. I don't go around kissing people unless I have some feeling for them." I still feel that it's unladylike to go into a bar alone. It's my family training, so I can't do that. In fact, until I was in this singles group, I had never been in a bar. I don't really drink, and if it's to meet men, I think it's not very wise. How do you know, just talking to a man for a while, what he's really like? He might be some kind of nut. And they all seem to want you to come to their apartment.

I had one fairly happy affair after my divorce, but it didn't turn out well. The man was a courtly, hand-kissing, old-world type, really out of date, but sexually we were very, very good. Maybe it was because he was gentle and pleasant, unlike my husband, or maybe it was my age. But I tell you, the amount of sexual feeling I had from about forty-two to forty-eight was really tremendous. I was really surprised at my capacity. Sometimes when we were together, we would have intercourse three or four times in a twenty-four-hour period, day after day. This is something that never happened with my husband. Unfortunately, I lost my feeling for this man because he said he couldn't divorce his wife. In his view, the separation was causing her to lose face, and he didn't want to cause her any more hurt.

Maybe I was wrong to break off with him. I sometimes wonder. He was good for me, good for my ego. For a long time it bothered me that I was small-breasted. I think our culture conditions you to think that the bigger your breasts are, the more feminine you are. As I said, my husband never said much about me, but this man was very complimentary. He said he liked women with small breasts. His wife was really udder-like. There's another compensation that I've thought of now: A woman who is not too heavily breasted in middle age doesn't look so matronly. I know I haven't sagged as much as some women, even though I've nursed two children.

Interestingly enough, I don't think I would have gotten involved with that man I mentioned if it hadn't been for the psychiatrist I was seeing at the time of my divorce. He thought I should get out and get a man and I sort of followed his advice. One time he said something that made me sort of angry. He said, "You know, it's hard for a woman your age to get involved with a man, because there are a lot of homosexuals around and not so many men who want women your age." My psychiatrist said, "I have a patient who is thirty years old and she is a beautiful woman, and she can't find a man." And you know, that made me feel, maybe I got the wrong impression, that maybe I wasn't worth much. If this thirty-year-old woman couldn't get a man, well, what could I expect? I don't think he realized what he was saying. I do owe him a great deal, though.

If he hadn't opened my eyes to my situation, I would have gone along with what I was supposed to do—be a wife, and so forth. At that time in my life, I was becoming a vegetable. I wasn't caring about myself. I was taking care of my responsibilities as a mother, but I didn't have much feeling about myself. I didn't buy myself nice clothes or care what I looked like. I remember it was winter and my psychiatrist held my coat for me when I got up to leave. No one had done that since my father died. I remember being embarrassed because the lining was worn out, and I was very caught up in the throat that someone was giving me this kind of attention. My husband certainly never did that. In fact, at that point, there were days on end when he didn't speak to me. I think that after you've gone through a period without any warm affection, there's a need for it. I remember going to one of those Beauty-for-a-Day places. For thirty-five dollars they do the whole routine—hair, nails, face. And they give you this warm, herbal bath. They treat you like a queen, with all these handmaidens. They lower you into the bath and then when you get up, someone wraps a big towel around you. I felt like crying when I was in that bath.

Frankly, now I'm very discriminating about men. Just because somebody wears pants, I'm not that interested. Our culture seems to say there's something lacking in a woman if she doesn't have a man. I think women are more and more willing to live alone, rather than marry just anybody, at least, women who are independent and can do what they want. They're not willing to be tied up in this kind of relationship where they have to give so much, they have to do what somebody else wants, or take care of another person. Even in the relationship I had that was so good sexually—when I lived with this man—I found I was waiting on him. There was no darn reason why I should be picking up his socks and taking care of him. He wasn't even supporting me. I was supporting myself.

So I really don't mind right now, not having a man in my life. If I were looking for a man to live with or marry I would want someone who was very involved in something like archeology, or birds, or something I could care about, too. I could contribute a lot to a companionship with a man. I don't think that I'm a dull person. I think I've accomplished more than some women my age. I persevered. I went to college with a lot of young kids, and I'm pleased that I'm not rigid and shut off. I keep my mind open and I'm interested in a lot of things.

It's hard to know whether I'll be able to manage in the future. Since I'm self-supporting and don't have a husband to fall back on, I'd better keep working. I've had the experience of living through the Depression, and I know how to be very careful with my money. I want to remain independent of my children, so I'm planning the future very carefully. It's lucky that I managed to get a good job that seems to be secure. I particularly like working with children. I need to work with people. Unfortunately I'm a little frustrated now because I have more contact with paperwork than with the children. And most of this administrative stuff is really unnecessary.

I have one sadness in my life now that I can't handle. My daughter is happily married but is not going to have children. She and her husband have decided that. He's had a vasectomy. My son was briefly married at nineteen, was divorced, left the country, and left me with the problem. He had a daughter. His ex-wife has gone from one man to another and another but last year she got married, and her new husband has decided that I can't be a part of his family. I've been a part of this child's life since the beginning—she's nine now—and he won't allow me to see her. I've been very close to her, and I'm very upset about it. I think she's frightened and wants to please her mother. I tried to see her one day at her bus stop. She was always wonderful to me and is such an interesting personality, but she was completely changed. She was almost afraid to speak to me. I talked to a psychologist about it because I'm so terribly upset. I just can't seem to accept the fact that she's there and I can't see her. I can't even give her a Christmas present. The thing that I feel the worst about is not so much the hurt that I feel but what it's doing to the child. Evidently she told her mother that she had seen me at the bus stop, because then her stepfather called me up and threatened to take me to court for doing that. I spoke to a lawyer, and he said that a grandparent doesn't have any rights.

CHAPTER 4

Josette–A Narcissist

I was always fighting to feel like something, fighting to keep from feeling like nothing.

Josette is a stunning woman. She has a beautiful figure, shining, black hair, and delicate features. She dresses as stylishly as her moderate income allows, and she moves with the cool assurance of a woman who knows the power of her beauty. She is, as she describes herself, aggressive and outgoing.

Josette has had two unhappy marriages. The first, which interrupted her college education, lasted six years. She had two children. The second marriage came after ten years of being single, and she regrets having spent too much energy during that time on lovers. Her second marriage ended in divorce after four years and one child.

Now, at fifty, with a much younger lover to appreciate her, Josette is planning to leave her life as a part-time model and become a business executive. She is anxious to flesh out a life that she considers unfulfilled.

* * *

JOSETTE

I'M ASHAMED of the fact that I've made such a mess of my life, considering the fact that I have intelligence. I'm not proud of my intelligence. I haven't used it. I've created a lot of problems. I hope to change all that now. I'm not only considering cosmetic surgery, I'm planning on it. Once I finish my education, and I'm armed with my degree, I can't go searching for a job as a female executive and say I'm fifty-five years old, or whatever I'll be. People just do judge you by appearances. One must face the facts of life, and the facts are that middle-aged women don't get hired in those good jobs. Secretaries, yes, any day. But I'm capable of doing better things.

I finally decided what I want to do when I grow up and, dammit, I'm going to do it. If I have to lie and have my face lifted, I'm going to do it. Actually I look and feel at least ten years younger than I am. I find it hard to realize that I'm over fifty. Other women my age often don't have their own teeth, their original hair color, they have varicose veins, they're fat and flabby. I take good care of myself. I'm a serious health nut. Of course, age is a mental attitude for a lot of people. I know a very energetic seventy-year-old woman who said that she hopes the good Lord will take her before she becomes a doddering ancient. So you see, she doesn't equate the seventies with old age.

I'm proud that I've taken good care of myself and my body so that I don't look the way Mrs. Housewife looks at fifty. I'll take credit for that. When you're twenty you have to give Mother Nature the credit. When you're fifty, you can take the credit.

I have had no signs of menopause. I'm waiting for something to happen because I'm getting pretty sick of menstruation. For practical purposes I would just as soon it ended, but I do have mixed emotions. If it's going to put wrinkles in my face and cause my breasts to sag, and all the other attending evils we've heard of, then I'll keep it.

I've been married and divorced twice. The main thing I felt after both my divorces was great relief. I had waged and won the battle for my self-respect long before the divorces came about. I had fought for myself all the time I was growing up. I don't know why I did. Sheer stubbornness is all I can think of. I guess that sounds pretty frivolous and flip.

I remember very little of my childhood but what I do remember is all negative. My mother died when I was seven. She was quite ill from the time I was born, and I hardly saw her. As far as I'm concerned, I never had a mother. There wasn't anyone who took her place, just a series of housekeepers. My mother had TB, and I was boarded out in the country with strangers from the age of four to eight. I don't remember much of those four years, but in general it seems unpleasant to me.

My father was a very strict disciplinarian who was not around a great deal of the time, and when he was, it was to tell me all the things I should not do. His goal was that I should be ladylike. Our relationship was pretty bad. I remember being told, quote, that my heart was as black as my hair. This was at the age of nine, ten, eleven, because I had told some little inconsequential fib. I don't see how that could *not* hurt me. Who knows how a child reacts? It must have hurt or I wouldn't remember it to this day, forty years later.

If my father was angry, he would take his belt off, and I would get strapped. I feel that my mother probably would not have allowed that. My father was totally unreasonable. Children today don't know what it's like to have that kind of discipline. I can remember coming home late from school one time. I was frittering away an hour or two with a friend. I had talked her into coming with me and spending my money. My father gave me a licking. The housekeeper we had at the time talked me into apologizing to him. It took a lot of guts and a lot of her persuading to put my arms around him and tell him I was sorry. And when I attempted to do it, he pushed me away.

My friends always seemed luckier and better and superior to me. I was never allowed to do the things they did or go to the places they went. I was very restricted, and I was sensitive to this because I was a fairly intelligent child—an IQ of 135 is not stupid—and my school marks were always in the nineties. I did get recognition for that, yes. A box of Schrafft's candy for a good report card.

One night an exception was made, and I went to a high school basketball game. There was a dance afterwards, and I was persuaded to stay. Well, when I got home, there was my father waiting for me, and before I could open my mouth with an explanation, I had it slapped. It was that kind of thing. I don't think he treated my sister as harshly. She had a more passive personality. I was aggressive and independent and strong-minded, and she was just the opposite. People like my sister have a knack of getting their own way, I've noticed. Plus the fact that I paved the way for her.

My father never made me feel loved. No, never. I can remember him saying that you should love your children in your heart because if you show them you love them, you'll spoil them. Maybe that's why it's taken me so long to learn to love someone. I never loved my father actually. I had been sent to live with an aunt during my fifteenth year when he was ill. I don't really remember the details. I know I was upset when he was laid out in the living room. But I don't remember what I felt after that. I don't think he affected my life in any positive way. I never wanted for material things, there was always plenty of money—I had more, I think, than most of my friends. But I never had love or understanding or guidance or any of those things that are really important. I never had anybody at all to nurture me, so to speak. The reason I survived is that I had to.

I can remember when my father would be strapping me, I'd say to myself, "You can hit me but you can't make me cry." And I'd sit there, and not a tear would fall. I would cry later, after he closed the door. It seems to be something I was born with, and experience just strengthened it. I was always fighting to feel like something, fighting to keep from feeling like nothing. I was very critical of myself because my father was so critical of me, but I didn't let my feelings of inferiority show. I masked them, and probably no one knew. Maybe that's why I went into acting and was so good at it. I never thought about it before but I'm sure I needed the applause and the appreciation I got from an audience.

It seems that I've always been put in my place by some man. Just last week one of the men I work with told me that the trouble with me is that I'm too uppity. It occurred to me that you don't have to be black to be considered uppity. He also said that I would never make an executive. I flippantly told him that I had already made two. I just couldn't let that lie.

Both my marriages were absolute zeros. The first time, I was in college and I wanted to belong to somebody and have a place to call my own. And here was somebody who claimed to love me. I gave up college and did the wife-and-mother bit for six years. My husband and I were incompatible sexually and in other ways too. Who knows which was more important? One incompatibility was reflected in the other. My theory is that it's easier to overcome everyday problems if you have a good sex life. We didn't. He was a complete ignoramus as well as having religious problems—a man who was brought up to believe that sex was nasty and dirty. And he wouldn't learn anything. I think he was almost embarrassed to learn. There I was. Ready. And nothing came. I used to take books home from the library—and in those days you had to take them from a locked cabinet—and practically beg him to read them. I knew something was wrong, but I didn't know what. But his mind and his morals wouldn't let him learn.

I don't think he ever appreciated me as anything, not as a person with ideas, certainly. He was shy and very introverted, a typical accountant actually. A very anal personality, I've heard it said. Also, a very weak man, who didn't want to go anywhere, do anything, learn anything new, have fun, nothing. But he was attracted, as such men often are, to an aggressive, outgoing woman. He gravitated to his opposite. I've always had this fatal attraction for that kind of man.

I had ten years of freedom after that first divorce. I had lots of dates, a big social life. I never let my children hold me back. My life came first. I realize now that I wasn't a very good mother to the older children. I acted with my father's strictness toward my first two girls. I probably felt that because I had to suffer as a child, they also should suffer. I shouldn't have let my life come first as much as I did. I'm a much better mother to my youngest. Really, I never wanted to be a mother. If abortion had been available to me, I might not have any now, because I never planned any of them.

My second husband was just something that passed by, just someone who wouldn't count at all except for the fact that I had a child. At that point in my life I was at an emotional nadir. I had had an unhappy love affair, I was out of a job, I had time on my hands, my daughters were unhappy because I had not remarried and given them what they called a normal home. I felt a lot of guilt about that. At the time I'm talking about, one was fifteen and the other was twelve. And along came this man who was crazy about us. He thought I was a glamorous female—I was a lot younger in those days you know. He seemed to be crazy about the children. There was just nothing he wouldn't do for us. He couldn't do enough. I knew I didn't love this man. But I had waited ten years for the perfect man, and I figured I'd never find him, so I might just as well settle for companionship. The girls would be happy, they'd have a father figure, a normal life, etcetera. So I compromised. I married this guy six weeks after I met him, that's how foolish I was. I had thrown in the emotional towel. I realized three months later that I had made a mistake; in fact I pretty much realized on the way back from the honeymoon when he insisted on stopping to call his mother and let her know that he was on his way home and everything was all right, this thirty-three-year-old bachelor who until then had been living with his mother. I had a sneaking suspicion that something was going to be wrong with this marriage. Of course, he was a baby. He now lives in our apartment. I got the divorce; he got the apartment with his new wife. I really don't want to talk about him. He's still a thorn in my side, this one.

As I said, that marriage wouldn't have lasted six months except that I found myself pregnant. So I stayed four years. Pregnancy has always been my downfall. I always felt that if I had been born a male, with the same makeup and intellectual abilities, that I would have been very successful.

I was forty-two when I got divorced the second time. Both times

I was the one who was dissatisfied and unhappy and wanted out. During this last period of singlehood, I have had a few affairs and sex has improved.

I don't think a woman can ever completely blame a man. I know I had a lot of sexual hang-ups that I had to get rid of and work out. And I did eventually. I found that the older I got, the easier it was. When I was twenty-one, sex was a Great Big Thing. My problem was that I always thought that I had to feel something for a man, emotionally, before I could go to bed with him. Then I realized that that was nonsense. Now I know that it's very nice if you can love the man that you're sleeping with, but you can also have a good sexual experience without loving him. You can just like it. When I finally allowed my body to function without any interference from my mind, that's when things started to happen. I've had these feelings all my life and had to keep them under cover.

In my first marriage I didn't masturbate but, of course, that was often my only recourse later. My husband, as I say, was so sexually ignorant he had no idea how to help me have an orgasm. And my second husband . . . didn't care. The man I'm with now, by the way, has known only one other woman. He's forty years old, and I firmly believe that a man should be younger than a woman. I find that the men I have met who are my age or older are too old for me. People are so brainwashed by society that they don't believe it's right for the man to be younger. But if they'd examine the sexual facts, they'd have to agree with me. Anyway, this man is the best lover I've ever had. I don't really know if it's because he's so much better, or because I'm so much better, or because I think I love him, or what it is.

I never felt close emotionally to either of my husbands, but I do now, to my lover. We like each other. That's probably the key to the whole relationship. He is a man who likes and respects women and treats me with respect as well as love. He has been living with me for only a matter of a few months. He's not legally divorced. We talk about our future together, but we can't really plan, because his life is so complicated. His youngest child is only three, and my oldest is twenty-nine. Think of that! His wife keeps stalling the legal process, keeps trying to get him back. This upsets me terribly. It's enough of a concession for me to be living with a man I'm not married to, without living with one who is still legally married to somebody else.

It's been very hard to find decent, intelligent men. Some women will just go out with anybody, but I refused to do that. Most of the divorced men want women young enough to be their daughters. Something happens to men at this age. They think they're going to lose their masculinity unless they can prove themselves with a younger woman. These are intelligent men I'm talking about. Where their emotions are concerned, they're awfully dumb. A friend of mine will say to a man, "I want you to meet a woman I know, I'm sure you'll like her." And he will say, "How old is she? Fifty? Forget it." They have a stereotyped idea of what a fifty-year-old woman is, and they want nothing to do with her. And so I took to lying. Fortunately, I can get away with it, but I can't fix up some of my friends with dates, because they look their age. And men aren't interested in their great personalities or their souls; they just want young bodies.

I find it more enjoyable to be older. I find that I'm more comfortable with people, the world, myself, and my values have changed. I've learned to like people a lot more, especially women. I'm a little wiser, I think, than I was twenty years ago. The things that were so dreadfully important when I was younger, I can now take in my stride. I can relax and enjoy life more.

I wouldn't mind being a young woman today. There are so many more opportunities. I was so stifled, always fighting the regulations people put on me. I hope nothing stops me now. I'm determined to make up for the wasted years.

CHAPTER 5

Julie–Larger than Life: Black

I'm a character. . . . My being a provider was a major problem in all my four marriages. . . . Don't count me out until I'm buried.

Julie is a handsome, forty-nine-year-old black woman from Chicago. She has one daughter. Julie has survived rape, a husband who beat her, seven miscarriages, and four divorces. Inured to her ghetto life, she has developed a hard-boiled exterior, and a case of chronic hypertension. She has been flooded with more sensations and experiences than any person could reasonably handle.

Julie has fierce pride in herself. Her father said, "Be the most," and she is. Her husky tone of voice and aggressive manner softened when she spoke of her high school days. She is proud of having mixed blood—white, Indian, black—and of having worked in the cause of Martin Luther King. The interview was more important to Julie as a black–white exchange than as one between women.

Julie is a high school graduate who has been a waitress, a saleswoman, and an office worker. Although her family was poor, she has worked hard to support herself and has managed to purchase both a car and a house.

Many black women have managed to combine the traditional roles of men and women—breadwinner, wife, mother, and lover—with a strong sense of identity and self-esteem. These women, black or white, refute the stereotype of women as passive, dependent, or masochistic.

* * *

JULIE

I'M A forty-nine-year-old character, a typical bossy black woman, and I'm a hustler, too. If I make up my mind I'm gonna sell you a Bible, I'm gonna do it. I've had seven miscarriages, one child, a hysterectomy, four husbands, and one rape. The only sign of aging that I'm aware of is that I don't let things bug me anymore. I've worked all my life but right now I'm enjoying being a housewife without a husband. I love talking on the phone and I'll go without food if I have to, in order to pay the phone bill.

If I bother to go out at night, I have to completely dress up; put on the whole bit, all the way from the hairpiece on top of the head to silver shoes and stockings.

I have less sexual desire right now because I don't have a husband. But if I had a husband with me, he could "break" regular. I never did have the problem of "No, I don't want to be bothered" with any of my husbands. To me, with a man that I care for, sex has a beauty like seeing the whole world from a mountain you've just climbed. I've got a sister who don't know what I'm talking about. She's ashamed and thinks the only woman who ever reversed positions with a man was a whore.

When I was little I found out where babies come from. I was a bad girl. I'd get up and sit outside my mother and father's bedroom at night trying to catch them at sex, but even though they had fifteen children, I never did. Today, sex is like alcohol to me; I can leave it alone anytime I feel like it and I don't go nuts. I do know about female masturbation.

I was a virgin, reading Captain Marvel at the beach, when I was knocked out and raped by a boy who had escaped from a mental institution. When I came to, I was black and blue and I couldn't stop crying. The crazy boy's mother took care of me with a lot of kindness and understanding. I never could tell my own mother about it.

About six months later, I had sex willingly. I had the best time, and then I fainted. I nearly scared the boy to death. Since then I have fainted several times in very intense situations.

My mother always said that I was the one who broke away from traditions, because I did. I read an awful lot and I was curious all my life, and I still am. And I'm the noisiest thing on my block.

Before Martin Luther King's "sit-ins" at lunch counters in the South, I sat by myself in Stouffer's Restaurant in Chicago, while the waitresses kept walking around me. I said to one of them, "Come here, honey. You know the longer you leave me sit here, the longer you're going to have to walk around me because I'm not going anyplace. So, if I were you, I'd hurry up and serve me so I'd hurry up and get me out of here." After she turned ninety shades and served me, I left her a ten percent tip for "ordinary service" and when I got up I said, "Be careful not to throw it on the floor, it's green money."

I've paved the way for lots of blacks. There's one employment agency that used to move me from job to job. I'd be the first black to be hired and I'd try to set an example for those who came after me.

I didn't grow up knowing about color. It was the Depression; we were all poor. There were only two kinds of people in the world—the "haves" and the "have-nots." We all ate together, we played together, and we cried together, and, when one of the kids had to move, we had a fit.

I went to an integrated elementary school, but when I went to high school, I didn't see anyone but black kids and I went to see the dean. I said, "I have a problem. I want to know why I have to come to school and the other children haven't?" The dean said, "What other children?" And I said, "The other children, you know, the *other* children." Finally I said, "The white children and the Chinese and the Mexican. Don't they go to school here?" And the dean leaned back in her chair and she said, "I think you had better learn a fact of life. You are colored, and because of our society you go to a colored school, and your friends went to a white school, and I'm sorry you couldn't go with them but this is a fact of life." Until then, I didn't know I was colored.

There was a great big football player in high school that I did not like. He's a policeman now. He grabbed me one day when we were dancing at a school "jam session." I used to wear my father's pullover sweater, a big, long "sloppy Joe" sweater that I had put a hatpin in. That was to stick boys who bothered me. It deliberately was. I told the football hero, "Turn me loose. I don't do that." And he said, "You will today." I said, "I meant that. You turn me loose. I don't dance like that." And he said, "Not on your life!" So I said, "Oh, you'll wish you had!" And I stuck him. He's bleeding all over because this hatpin had scratched his leg. Some kids got the dean, and she said, "That's a dangerous weapon. You go home and come back with your mother." And I said, "OK, but I bet he'll never try to 'juice' with another girl on the dance floor." Then I started to cry and I told the dean, "You know, I have a reputation, and I don't let no boys mess over me. I told that big ape not to use me for a mattress and he kept pulling me into him." When the dean had both the mothers in, she asked Dewey's mother, "Do you teach your son to do vulgar dances with girls?" The dean stood up for me and Dewey admitted that he had been "juicing," and his mother slapped him. That white woman, the dean, was sixty years old and she understood, but she did confiscate the hatpin.

My father and I were not close, but we were friendly. He always told me I was pretty. He told that to all the children, and, in fact, there are no "uglies" in our family, including my retarded sister.

I've tried to live by one of my father's mottoes: "Be the best of whatever you are. If you gonna be a tramp, be the biggest tramp out. If you gonna be a lady, be the highest lady out and recognize success when you get it whether anyone else does or not."

My father was the figurehead. My father was there, but my mother bossed everybody, including him, poor little fella. I used to tell him all the time, "Why don't you grab Momma in the mouth?" Cause she was a nag. God, I can't stand a nagging woman.

My mother is selfish and not loving with anybody. I'll never forget being angry with her when I was five years old. I got a set of jacks for my birthday, and I couldn't wait to start playing with them by myself. It rained, so my sisters had to quit playing ball and they wanted to play with my jacks. I said, "No, they're mine. I got 'em for my birthday and I'm gonna play with them." My mother said, "You're not gonna share 'em, then you're not gonna play with 'em," and she threw them away. She flung them far and wide. And I cried over it, and she made me go and sit in a room all by myself. "Because," she said, "you're being a big, bad girl." I remember thinking, "She's just a mean old thing and there's nothing I can do about it." So I stopped crying. I stopped crying just about for all time where that lady was concerned. That was my fifth birthday.

My mother is seventy-three now and she went back to work last year. You better believe she's tough. She's gonna make sure she has hers and she doesn't care whether you have yours or not. First and foremost, she's gonna look out for number one.

I prayed constantly when I was raising my only child, and I still do. I think more than anything, deep down in my heart, I had a determination that I would *not* be like my mother. I know this to be a fact. It was there. And I had caught myself up in it many times. Something would come up that would remind me of my mother. I would turn myself completely around, and shut my mouth and sit down and think it out.

The husbands came and the husbands went, but the baby was always there to be provided for. I am so grateful that the good Lord gave me the job of being a mother to my special kid, because it has kept my life on an even keel. She's turned out to be a beautiful young lady and I'm still enjoying her.

I didn't marry my daughter's father. When he offered me an abortion, I nearly killed him. When he did offer to marry me, I told him, "You don't kill your own. I don't need the likes of you." And, I didn't. I raised my own child. I always knew she'd be a daughter, because I didn't buy no boy's clothes. I didn't want a boy and thank the Lord I didn't have a boy. What I wanted was the image of what I would have liked to be as a young lady with the freedom to think and make decisions.

If I had it to do over again, I would never have married my first husband. Not because he isn't a nice person, he was very good with my daughter, and even today is still good to her. That's why I married him: to give her a father. It was his educational background that was so far removed from mine. That sounds dumb, because I only went through high school, but he didn't even finish grammar school. When I tried to get him to go back to school, I even told him I'd go back with him to night school. His mother told him I was trying to make a fool out of him, that I just wanted to show him up.

My husband slapped me often. It was the same old jive that everybody thinks is great "macho"—that is, slap, slap on the side of the face. It was a way he could assert his manliness. And occasionally he beat me up pretty bad.

I had orgasms frequently, but he never knew when I didn't because I'm good at fakin' it when necessary. I never believed in regulated sex. I would say, "Saturday night might never come, tonight's Monday, let's get it on." Also I would ask to go to a motel once in a while to play around. I made all my husbands go to the motel.

My first husband cheated and naturally he got caught. When I told him he had to make a choice he said, "I can't quit her." I said, "That's OK, but when you get the divorce papers, I don't want you to object."

I left, got my own apartment, and went back to work. I had to quit that job because I'd sit there and think about that idiot I'd been married to for five years and start crying. But tears in the typewriter ain't the answer!

We became better friends after the divorce. No sexual alliance, just friends. He came to me ten years later. He's been with other women but he's never been happy since I divorced him. He actually cried and said, "Right now, I'm listening to you talk, and I'm listening to me talk, and if you don't explain the words to me, I don't even know half the time what you're talking about; I could have bettered myself, and I let my mother talk me out of it."

My second marriage was a mistake that lasted less than two years. I let my mother talk me into marrying him. I became turned off to him, and when I divorced him, he was living with my sister.

My third husband, Jerry, is the one husband I married strictly for love, and we lasted almost ten years. Jerry and I had gone to the same high school. He loved reading. I love reading. I got into the crossword puzzle habit, and he jumped right into it. We went bowling. We went dancing.

The main problem, the two main problems were money and women. I made more money than Jerry did even when I just took care of kids in my home. I'm a hustling-type woman; I sold jewelry, I sold Bibles. I was always selling something and Jerry never got over my making more money than he did.

I'm tired of working. I started working in high school so that I could buy material for a dress. Later, when I wanted a new car I bought me a new car. It might have taken me longer than someone else, but I always wanted my own house, and without financial help from any of my four husbands, I bought me one.

As for women, Jerry came from a background where it's all right to have outside women. Knowing how his people were, I went along with a lot of his foolishness and he had "outside women" the whole ten years we were married. He was not oversexed; the women were there, always available.

When Jerry got tired of one of his women, he'd let me find out about her so that I would stop it for him. Extramarital sex was part of Jerry's "macho." Tall women should never marry short men. They've always gotta prove they're taller than you. Sex was the way Jerry tried to prove he was a bigger man than I was a woman. The only other explanation I can think of is that Jerry's mother was a "loose woman" and maybe he wanted to pay back all women.

That last woman of his, I refused to intervene. He kept saying, "I wish I could get rid of her." I said, "Well, tell her." I didn't like her calling him on my phone. The phone was in my name and I didn't like being disturbed. And she did call, and I subsequently did go over there, and I subsequently knocked the hell out of her. She didn't call anymore. And when he came home raising hell about it, I slapped myself in the face and went and called the police and had him put in jail, and I said, "That's just a taste of what you gonna get messing with me." I told him to walk out on me, that if we stayed together one of us was gonna end up hurting the other.

My last marriage, made on the rebound, maybe, was going to be an intellectual romance to an impotent man. I made my last mistake ten years ago and the marriage came apart before the year was out, because when he regained his lost potency, he became violent.

None of my four husbands shared in the housekeeping, did the washing, the ironing, the cooking, the sewing, the scrubbing—you name it, I did it! The last husband used to want to cook, but I ran him out of the kitchen because he made a big mess.

All of my men appreciated me as a lover and I have a high regard for myself in that role in spite of all the infidelities I've experienced. They all enjoyed my good eating too.

The reasons I like myself are: Number 1, I'm not ugly. Number 2, I'm not dumb. Number 3, when I work, I make good money. And number 4, I can take care of a husband, a child, and a home. I started waking up to all of this after that first divorce.

I have all the survival skills. I have done without sex. I have done without companionship. I've always worked on my personality and I know that although my personality is a strong one, I like it. I just like being me, who I am and what I am.

I have sung in choirs, I have worked with children, I have done dramatic readings for church groups. By George, when I was young I wanted to be a great dramatic actress, I wanted to write poetry, to go to art school. I didn't do any of those things except that I still write poetry. For example, here's the end of a poem I wrote called "Be a Giant":

> Chant me no chants.
> Sing me no songs.
> Be black, be beautiful,
> But be a giant!

I went to work and I gave up the dreams. I think I have accomplished some of the things that I wanted, but don't count me out until I'm buried! There's always the chance that an outside opportunity will arise that I could fulfill!

CHAPTER 6

Brenda–Portrait of the Artist as Survivor

My writing is a way of dealing with my anger and frustration. I used to deal with it by playing the risky game of having affairs.

Brenda is an attractive fifty-one-year-old writer who has been married for twenty-seven years. She dropped out of college after two years. Her four children range in age from seventeen to twenty-six. She is financially comfortable, but in her early childhood she was confronted with poverty, foster homes, and her father's alcoholism.

Brenda cried twice during the interview while discussing the maltreatment of her brother in childhood. Basically, however, she spoke with laughter and portrayed a much more forceful woman than her petite appearance would have suggested. She told her story as a dramatic monologue.

Brenda's earliest coping mechanism was a hard-eyed recognition of her victim position and a determination to survive in spite of it. Any acceptance of her inferior position as a child was only on the surface; inwardly she raged against injustice.

Brenda is not depressed by her menopause or aging because she has a high energy level and, even more significant, because she was "reborn at thirty-eight" when she discovered that she could write. Writing turned out to be a therapeutic way to express herself and to take some positive meaning from her childhood.

* * *

BRENDA

YEAH, I drink quite a lot. I enjoy beer. I love it. I would say that alcoholism is something I should be attuned to at all times. There's a great deal of it in my family. My father died of acute alcoholism, my brother, who is four years older, is a total alcoholic, and my oldest son has joined AA. On an average day I consume from four to eight beers. I stay away from mixed drinks and I find that the hard stuff is too strong for me. I can't handle it. Once in a while there's a day when I don't drink.

Incidentally, I come from a screwed-up background. My brother was a battered child. You can read my novel about that. I'm working on it now. My mother died when I was three years old, and the family was split up. We were all sent to different relatives. I was sent to a farm where they had twenty-five state children. I was there for about three years, and it was probably more good than bad. My sister was sent to relatives in another state, where she was to replace a daughter who had drowned the year before. She was very badly treated.

My brother was sent to Aunt Bertha's, where I subsequently joined him. Aunt Bertha was a real tyrant. My brother was a bed wetter, and Aunt Bertha would have him go down in the cellar and wash the sheets, and he would have to hang up the sheets without any mittens, and sometimes the sheets would freeze before he could even get them over the lines. When I could, I would sneak his mittens to him. The ritual was that after he hung up the sheets, he would go down to the cellar and strip to the waist, and she would beat him with a razor strap. He still has the scars that he will carry for the rest of his life.

Last week in Ann Landers' column there was a letter from a woman in her sixties who had been a battered child, saying, "How can I get rid of this agony?" When you are a witness as a child to the kinds of things I saw, particularly with my brother, the agony is always there. Well, you can see how it upsets me, even now.

One thing that's really interesting to me is that even though my brother, my sister, and I lived in separate families, living here and there, when we get together now, which is not often, we're very close and our humor is almost identical. Even though my sister is politically to the right of center and I'm to the left of center, philosophically we're very much the same.

Most of my father's anger was discharged on my brother. He beat him as well. Billy was the kind of kid that everybody hit. Consequently I learned to just disappear. Actually I lucked out. I was the youngest child and I really worked on being sort of cute and adorable so that I would not get beaten the way my brother was. I was as obedient as I could be, and I was sneaky when I was bad so that I wouldn't be caught.

My feeling about my father was mixed with overtones of great fear when he was drunk. One incident stands out in my mind. I'll have it in my novel. I was about eight. My father was a hired man on a farm in the East, and he returned from a six-week binge, thirty pounds thinner, with missing teeth, and two big shiners. He was sitting in the kitchen crying, but I didn't feel pity. I was terrified. When I went to bed, I took a butcher knife from the kitchen drawer and put it under my pillow, and I put throw pillows by the door. Years later I thought I must have feared that he might molest me.

My father was in and out of our lives. He was likable when he was sober, but he had what they call "itching feet." We sort of drifted and moved from town to town, and sometimes we moved with him. Usually it would be drunkenness that made him lose his job.

My father had a tragic life and died of acute alcoholism at forty-five. I didn't really know him that well. Maybe I have some blocks about him, but I know I didn't identify with him because he was a loser.

As a teenager I worked my way through high school, living with different families as a mother's helper. When I was a senior I was a kitchen girl living on a farm, and Mrs. Parker, the woman for whom I worked, was very demanding. She was working my ass off. My father was one of six farmhands who lived there. He used to go off on these drunks, you know, and maybe disappear for a couple of months. One day, when he was off, God knows where, Mrs. Parker became very sarcastic about me and my father. At that time I had never heard of Gandhi or anything like that, but I went on a hunger strike. I told her that I would never touch any food in her house again. I began to lose weight—I lost about eight pounds—and this was very difficult for her because she could see me starving to death and casting aspersions on her as one of the prominent members in the town. I sort of enjoyed the whole bit.

I talked with one of my teachers—told her what the whole situation was—and she was so enraged about the way I was treated that she said, "You're going to live with us. We'll go and get all your things." Mrs. Parker tried to stop us, and she just said, "Woman, step aside." It was great, really. I lived with her family until I finished high school.

My sister paid part of my college tuition, but it was mostly a free ride. I was considered an indigent case with some potential. The college took a chance on me. At that time my father was living in a Salvation Army rest home, and he wanted me to quit college, go

West with him, and set up a hot dog stand. I said, "No way. College is the first home I've really had." I was quite cruel, but I had to do it.

I never finished college, because I really wasn't a student, and I had too many emotional problems to be able to concentrate.

The women in my father's family were much stronger psychologically than the men. Even Bertha, the aunt who used to beat my brother, is a survivor. What she did was unforgivable, but I have to admire her in her old age, and I hope to show this in my novel. She had her own problems. I think she was dealing with sexual frustrations; I think if she were young and in this society, she might have made a very good dyke lesbian.

The strongest and nicest woman of my father's family was my grandmother with whom I lived off and on for nine years. She was a great woman. She took care of her health as well as she could. She had friends from the church, and she had a great deal of pride. I remember one time when my father had left us. We were really in a poverty situation, eating dandelion greens. The farmer was giving us eggs and milk to be paid for when my father returned, and the church made up a Thanksgiving basket for us. My grandmother refused it when they delivered it to the house. She just very proudly said, "Thank you, but we are well taken care of. Give it to someone who needs it." Maybe that was a false pride, but it is something I admire. I was very affectionate to my grandmother, but she wasn't a hugger—there were no huggers. She was not well when she took care of us. I think she was mostly busy, and somewhat tired from having raised a pretty stormy family of her own.

Those years were Depression times and my grandmother's goal for me was to survive. She figured that being a woman is an unlucky accident of birth, a tough row to hoe, but women are the ones who can do it. She was the strength in the family but I think she felt you were luckier if you were a man.

I did not adopt her religious values but I tried to copy her honesty and perseverance. I admire her lack of bitterness. I'm not bitter either, but I sure am cynical.

I got married at twenty-four after working as a waitress for a couple of years. I married Tom, whom I had met at college.

In those first years of marriage my total self-esteem was very low. For example, when we were first married Tom decided that I had a very poor vocabulary, and he gave me five new words a day to learn.

I didn't care for the idea of his being my teacher, and I sloughed off on them. When the end of a week came, and it was time to have a little fun, he said, "Let's have a quiz first." We had a dictionary that was a collector's item, and I just ripped out a handful of the center pages, saying, "That's what I think of little quizzes." Tom tried to spank me. He felt that was his role. The only thing I had going for me was my anger. I didn't feel particularly bright. I didn't feel particularly sharp. I didn't feel particularly attractive.

Here's another example of our relationship: I was pregnant with our first child. We had a restaurant that was going broke, and Tom was playing poker as usual in the back room. I went back there to get change for the cash register. I felt that I had intruded into a completely male world. When I asked Tom for the change, he said, "Don't bother me." I said, "OK. Just give me five dollars and the key to the car," and I left him. Before I took off, I took his clean and dirty clothes and dumped them all in the middle of the apartment. I let one friend know where I was going so that it wasn't a complete disappearing act. Tom found out where I had gone and followed me. He gave up poker immediately, ripped all the cards up—"forever." In reality, no.

This has been the pattern of our marriage. When people have terrible fights, usually it's the husband who leaves, but in our case, I'm the one who leaves. I've even left him with all four children. I'm willing to give up everything for the salvation of my "voice"— whatever it is within me that is screaming.

I think I was looking for sort of a daddy image. Tom feels that what I was looking for, expecting, and totally disappointed in not getting, was a knight in shining armor.

Tom was the only man I had intercourse with premaritally. I had a great deal of pleasure during the twenty or so occasions that we screwed, even though I had no orgasms. I think we only had the foreplay before we were married. Afterwards it was "Right on, let's do it, let's get it over with." We were both puritanical in a way. We had never performed oral sex or anything like that. It was strictly the Presbyterian minister's approach with the man spread on top of the woman. It was Tom's choice that I was passive. He thought it was unfeminine for me to be aggressive.

I didn't know what an orgasm felt like until eight years after I was married. It was after the birth of my second child. We had seen one of those porno movies and there was about five minutes of this girl masturbating, and I could see her vagina contracting. I tried it, achieved orgasm, and knew what I could expect.

About this time, seven years after we were married, Tom again became obsessively involved in poker. I took out my anger at him by having affairs. My sex life improved, and so did my disposition. The first time that anything extramarital occurred, Tom and I were playing strip poker with another couple. I went upstairs with the husband and Tom was downstairs with the wife. I thought it was fun, but Tom didn't like the fact that I had had a better time than he did. He said that the other woman's vagina was like walking around in an empty museum. I sort of liked the idea of extramarital sex, and I saw the husband several times after that. I wasn't in love. I just felt more attractive and glad that a man thought I was fun.

The second man I had an affair with was unhappily married. We met at a community function. I liked the idea that I could drive somebody out of his mind with love for me and the experience did increase my self-esteem, but he was really sort of a sickie. He wanted me to get a divorce, leave my children. I was horrified. He thought I was very bright and that I didn't have any confidence because of my husband's superior airs and ways of putting me down. I was very angry with my husband at that time. I was in constant anger.

There was one incredibly handsome man during those years that I was in love with, infatuated with I should say. He really turned me on. The only thing is, he knew how incredibly good-looking he was, and I was only one of about a stable of twenty women who were throwing themselves at him. But still I enjoyed my infatuation with him. I did have some bad feelings about doing something behind my husband's back. I didn't care for the dishonesty involved. I felt guilty about that. But my affairs made me feel more of a woman, and gave me the beginning of self-confidence. I was also getting psychotherapy at that time, and I sort of enjoyed sharing stories of my affairs with my analyst. She showed me that the risky game of having affairs was a way of dealing with my anger and frustration. She also helped me to understand that my being a person without roots explained part of my determination to stay in the marriage.

Several years later we had a discussion of affairs with my husband and my best friend. We were talking about jealousies, and my husband felt that I was unreasonably jealous about a brilliant female he admired who he said "had a mind like a steel trap and thought like a man." My girl friend, whom I haven't talked to since, had too much wine and asked, "Brenda, how can you justify your jealousy when you've had five or six affairs?"

I had decided that I would never institute a discussion of my affairs, but that if my husband ever found out, I would not deny them, because to deny them would be to deny part of myself. After my ex-friend left, Tom almost went insane.

We had a very bad fight, and he felt totally betrayed. Maybe he was justified, but I felt that I had been betrayed, too, by his total involvement with poker. I really feel that if he had done his "homework," I would not have had affairs.

Tom might have had affairs, too. I don't know. I felt he might have had one with that bright female he admired. He probably did. Tom feels if you're confronted with the truth, lie about it. I have the double standard in reverse. Extramarital affairs are fine for me, but I like to think that he is pure.

If "open marriage" had been OK when we were young, I think it would have helped our marriage. I think what happened, and the reason my husband took my affairs so traumatically when he learned about them, was because he felt that I had one-upped him, a competitive thing. Sex should be about as important as your digestive system. I don't put it way up there. What you do with your own potential, which includes sex, is the most important. Sex has been important in my marriage. There would be no marriage without it.

When our sexual relations are nonexistent, I masturbate occasionally. For instance, I was writing a really sexy scene a few days ago and it was so stimulating to me that I went to my bedroom and masturbated. I couldn't stand the tension. Recently Tom and I went through a period of seven or eight months where we had no sex at all. Then, I said, "OK, this has gone on long enough." Even though he didn't used to care for me being the aggressor, I sort of got him off the hook by insisting that intercourse would be good for us. It worked.

In some ways, our sexual relations are better because it takes my husband longer to achieve a climax, which gives me more time to psych out for the orgasm myself. Old age has its assets because now we do have a closer physical relationship than we used to. It's because he finally realizes how valuable I am to him . . . and I mean that sincerely. He needs me more than I need him.

In spite of not having derived a lot of pleasure or pride in being my husband's wife and in spite of all our difficulties over the years, I haven't found another man who would attract me to marriage more than my husband.

Although he used to take me for granted, Tom has changed. He's for what I'm doing, he's for what I've grown into. We share almost no activities. We never did, and we still fight about money. He claims that I married him because I could see dollar signs. Subconsciously I probably was looking for somebody who could provide for me better than my father did. Tom actually does have a very good business sense. He's made a lot of money, and he's tight with a dollar. God is he tight! My frequent complaint to him is, "For people that are supposed to be rich, I'm tired of being poor, and I want some goddamn money."

I tell people that the reason I got into writing is that one time my husband and I got into a big fight. We were at a party, and were drinking, and I kept trying to put my two cents worth into the conversation. Tom likes to have complete control over what's being discussed. He hogs the conversation. So he turned to me and said, "I wish you wouldn't talk unless you have something to say." That's when I started writing because I thought, "Well, I *do* have something to say. It's just that I can't express myself very well, and I need to be encouraged if I'm in a group."

I'm a late bloomer. Eighteen years ago I went back to school and took a lit course. The instructor would assign a lot of short stories. He started reading my stuff to the class, and then he took me aside and said, "You're wasting your time in my class. If I had your talent I'd be at the University of Chicago and really checking out the top writers in the area." He said, "You've got a fantastic voice. Good luck."

I was writing poetry too then, and in the beginning I'd show it to my husband and he'd tell me what was wrong with it and what I should change. He didn't like it when I wouldn't accept his suggestions. We had a big fight over one poem. He thought it was great except for the last line and he insisted I change it. I said, "Look. This is my poem. I want the line the way it is. If you want a different line, go write your own goddamn poem." Now I don't show him anything until it's published. At this point in my life I don't need to measure my worth by his yardstick.

Eight years ago a poem of mine was accepted by a literary magazine, and last year my first short story was published. I spend at least three hours a day working on my craft, and I love it, even though I've published very little.

If I drink just a little while I'm writing, it's like being on a high, having some grass or Dexedrine or something like that. If I just have enough to loosen the inhibitions and not so much that I can't see the keys, I think it frees me, gets into my subconscious more. If I've had a lot to drink, I can pull out of that drunken writing some really damn fine ideas, though the writing is terrible. For a while I was getting up at 4:30 in the morning and doing what they call "automatic writing," done almost like dreaming, but without benefit of alcohol. I've gotten some very strong writing out of that. It's probably more valuable than the "drunken writing."

I think I finally found a way to express myself in an acceptable way. I have a very high degree of imagination. I think of how that was used as a child in the form of lying and pretending, and now I can pretend and it's OK. I can make up fiction. I can lie. I can do anything I want to. I love that feeling of freedom and power. And also a lot of my writing is a kind of message writing. I am writing a story on a battered child, for example. It's a kind of therapy.

If I had life to live over I'd have to think long and hard about whether I wanted to be a married woman with children. I think a lot of the dissatisfactions that I felt in my thirties were from feeling tied down. I wasn't controlling my own destiny, and now I am.

My oldest child, now twenty-six, was a head-banger as a kid. That's what sent me into psychotherapy for two years. He has been an alcoholic, but things are a little better now and he will find himself in his thirties.

My twenty-year-old daughter has been into the Jesus Freak movement for the last four years. She's a beautiful child, a wonderful kid, but I see her as avoiding all one-to-one relationships. She's afraid to become involved. It's easy to become involved with somebody like Jesus. You don't get pregnant, you don't get syphilis, you don't have fights. You give it all one way.

My youngest son is seventeen, living with me, and wants more of a family life. He feels gypped that I've said to him, but not the older children, "Why don't you call me Brenda and forget the

Mommy bit?" You can use "Don't Call Me Mommy Anymore" as a title of your study. I still feel more needed by my children than I would like to be.

My middle son is totally well-adjusted. You figure one out of four, that's not too good odds. Still, I'm proud of my children. They are a lot better than my friends' children.

My current goals for myself are to be published, to be interviewed, literally to finish my novel, and to have a collection of short stories come out in the next two years. My novel has been jelling for fifty-one years, but I've only been working on it seriously for four months.

Mentally I feel I haven't reached my peak yet. I didn't know I was intelligent before I was thirty years old. As yet I haven't tuned into all that I am and all that I have. I haven't tapped my full potential.

CHAPTER 7

Ingrid–A Depressed Woman

It wasn't that I was cold. It was just that I was disillusioned with everything. . . . We spent so many wasted hours talking about nothing. . . . I'm so afraid. I'm wondering, am I going to make it?

Ingrid is a heavy woman with classically beautiful features. She is fifty-three, blond, sad-eyed, and soft-spoken.

Ingrid was married at eighteen and had a child by that marriage. Her husband divorced her on the ground that the marriage was not consummated. Seven years later she married again and had another child. She was widowed after twenty-eight years.

At the time of the interview her husband had been dead only four weeks. She was depressed and worried about making ends meet. During the interview there were long pauses while she held her head in her hands and sighed.

Ingrid's small, rented house sparkles with cleanliness and with her pretty, handmade crafts: flower arrangements and decorated boxes. She was a bookkeeper for a short time after finishing high school. Now, thirty years later, her skills are rusty and she faces an uncertain future—in debt and without work, funds, or hope.

* * *

INGRID

I JUST LOST my husband four weeks ago so I'm really nowhere at the moment; I'm just suspended. My husband left us with nothing. The only insurance he had was two thousand dollars and, considering the debts, you might as well say he left us nothing. My daughter and I have to move, the landlord is evicting us, and I have to have a yard sale, and I have to go to court, and I have to find a place to live, and, until I get settled, I can't look for work. My daughter and I are trying to manage in the meantime. It's dreadful.

My husband and I had terrible financial problems and the stress and strain of it probably helped kill him. His only relaxation was drinking, and I could never talk things over with him. From the time my children were small up to the present day there were so many things that gave me problems, so many things that weren't right, but my husband just couldn't talk to me. Whether it was religion, personal problems, or financial matters, he never wanted to discuss anything.

It could have been a successful, loving marriage, but it didn't turn out that way. And it was all unnecessary, it was all preventable; his drinking, his financial troubles. . . . And I say to myself after twenty-eight years with him, what does it mean? What was it all about? What is it for?

My mother was also a person who never discussed personal matters. She left my father when I was little, and I only saw him once or twice after that. I only remember him vaguely. My mother left me on a farm with my grandmother and two uncles while she stayed in the city working as a secretary. She was a cold, distant person who used to say, "Children go with the wedding ring." She had me because it was expected, but she never wanted another child.

My mother was the type of woman who told me what to do. She never asked me what I thought, or what I wanted, or what I was qualified to do. Once I dared to make a decision on my own. I was actually trembling when I told Mother I had signed up for modeling school. She exploded, "Are you crazy? I won't hear of it. Go and get your money back." That was the end of that.

I was afraid of my mother. She was more generous with gifts and money than she was with feelings, and she often handed money to my son and my husband. I never got a cent. I couldn't even ask her to sew anything for me and she was an expert seamstress. I can remember whenever there was a holiday and we were going to see her, eat out or something, I would be all nervous, afraid I wouldn't be ready, afraid she'd be critical of me. I'd get all upset. In short, I was scared to death of my mother.

And yet I miss her. How do you explain it? When she died nothing had any meaning any more. I go through the motions, especially during the holidays, and there's nothing there. Whatever was there is gone. I think I miss what we didn't have; I miss what should have been.

My mother was a little mellower her last few years, yet we spent so many wasted hours, talking about nothing, meaningless chatter. I would sit there and think we should be deciding things, we should be getting closer, not chatting about all these unimportant, silly things. There were so many things left unsaid and so many things unsolved. And it's the same with my husband's death. There are so many things I didn't ask, and so much I don't understand.

Mine was a strange family. From the time I was five years old the two uncles that I lived with didn't have what I would call a normal uncle and niece relationship. One would take me to the movies and put his arm around me and let me steer the car with his arms around me. Things like that. I just didn't feel it was right at all. I never could understand their behavior, and yet I loved both of them. Then, when I was in fourth or fifth grade there were a couple of men who lived upstairs, and they would wait for me to come home from school. They would get me down on the bed, and I would be struggling and struggling, and I would get up, and they would be fooling around and fooling around, and I would get them out and lock the door. And walking to school, a mile each way, there was an old man in the woods, deranged, I guess, exposing himself.

Before I got married, the man who was courting my mother—he became her third husband—was always after me. He tried to get me when my mother wasn't around. It wasn't just flirty. I was scared to death, but I felt I just had to stand there and take it. That's why I had to get out. I think I would have married the milkman to get away.

Anyway, these strange experiences, that I can clearly remember, must have made me very confused about men, don't you think? Probably that's why I was afraid to have sexual relations with my first husband. It was all those unpleasant memories. And no one to talk to about it. My mother and grandmother never told me anything, not even about menstruation. I had to find out by accident. I started menstruating one day in school. God, I was mortified. And I had to walk that mile home, holding my books behind me.

I was married the first time when I was eighteen. The marriage lasted about four years. It was a mistake from the beginning. My husband was a glamorous football hero in my high school. I thought that was all that mattered, but then I realized that I didn't like him as I thought I did. The whole problem was sexual. I had never been prepared for it. My mother had never been able to talk about anything like that. I was ignorant. I had a vague idea of what to expect and no idea what was expected of me.

I was my husband's first girl friend, I think, but the thing is, he wanted to and I didn't. I couldn't get myself to. It was terrible. My God, we just fought over that constantly. I just couldn't. I was so green.

My pregnancy wasn't the customary procedure. It was a freak thing, because my husband and I never had any sexual intercourse. The doctor said it was very unusual, but that the—what do you call it?—semen, just worked its way in. There was never any penetration. People don't believe this or understand it, but it's the truth. Because of my refusals, my husband went with other girls. After we were divorced, I had dates, and I gradually learned what it was all about.

Like so many foolish girls, when I married my second husband I thought I could change him. He had a drinking problem all his life. I thought it was because of his hard surroundings; he came from a very poor family. His father had left the family stranded when he was young, and went off with someone else. My husband really had no home life. His family lived in a terribly dumpy place with no bathroom. I couldn't picture living like that, and I thought that as soon as he had a nice home and family everything would be OK—that a loving wife would make him a different person.

But my husband never changed. Drink was his way of life. He couldn't stop a lifelong pattern. He always said he never needed to change. He didn't even consider giving up alcohol. I went to AA by myself, but they couldn't help me. I couldn't air my troubles in front of fifteen strangers, so I quit going.

My husband's drinking interfered with everything as far back as I can remember. He was smart in high school, and some teacher helped him get an athletic scholarship to a university. But he lost that by breaking training and drinking. Also in the service, he could have come out with a better rating, except he got into trouble drinking. He always worked hard and long, but then he got in with a bad bunch and gambled, and we lost our home and everything. We had to pay off loans. It snowballs. It took everything I had, everything we had, and now there's nothing.

In the beginning I began to enjoy sex with my husband because I loved him. He didn't talk about sex, just as he didn't talk about anything. I would suggest different things occasionally to keep it from being the same all the time. He wasn't one for novelty. I don't think sex was ever completely satisfying. There's always something that happens that's disappointing. I couldn't help my change of feelings. I got cooler and cooler I guess, and he didn't like it.

I can't evaluate myself as a sexual person. My husband always accused me of being cold, and I'm not. I don't think I'm a cold person at all. It takes very little to make me happy. All I need is a little encouragement or a few kind words or something like that. It's so little, and then when you think that people can't even give you that much. . . . It wasn't that I was cold. It was just that I was disillusioned and discouraged with everything.

My husband thought that no matter what he did, I was still supposed to feel the same, be the same loving wife, want to be with him. But I couldn't. I couldn't. He turned me against him, and I lost my feeling for him. The last seven years we had absolutely no relationship at all, and I know that hurt him terribly. I just couldn't love him. I said, "Every time you drink too much something goes out of me, and each time I can feel it taking longer and longer to come back." And finally, my feelings wouldn't come back anymore. Now that my husband is dead, I feel terrible guilt. I blame myself for lots of things, but I don't really know if I'm right or wrong. I know how he suffered, especially the last few days before he died; the things he said, it was pitiful. That was the only time he would talk, if he drank.

My husband would say to me, especially in the last year, "Don't depend on anyone. You have to do your own thing." He knew that I depended on him, and I felt he was more or less preparing me for his death. He said several times that he didn't care if he lived or died, that our relationship had deteriorated to nothing, that our daughter was mentally sick, that he lost jobs, our house, our money.

He tried to kill himself two days before he had his stroke. I'll never know exactly what happened, but it will haunt me for years. I'll never get it out of my mind. He had come home very late, five o'clock in the morning. He had been drinking. I always listened to him lie down and then I had peace. That morning I didn't hear him lie down. I thought, "What is he doing?" I went downstairs, and he was writing letters to everybody, which I didn't know then; I thought he was working on his financial matters. I went back upstairs again to bed. After a while he came up and stood over me, and he said to me, "I love you. I've always loved you." He hadn't said that in a long time. And, "You'll never see me again." And he walked away.

I just dismissed it as the liquor talking and thought, "Oh, he's feeling low, he's depressed." When I got up at eight o'clock in the morning, I thought my husband had left for work, which he often did after a night of drinking and no sleep, but I saw his glasses on the table, and I was frightened, thinking, "How in the world can he drive without his glasses? God, he'll have an accident." Then it occurred to me that he didn't go to work, that he must be around somewhere. I found him in the car in the garage with the door closed. He was asleep.

I don't know if he changed his mind about suicide or fell asleep, but he had left all these notes on the table, good-bye notes to everybody. They were barely legible. He came inside after that, and he was like a different person, playing with the dog and making silly remarks. He said to me, "You'll never know how close I came." But that's all he said. And he went to work. Then two days later, after raking leaves, he had a stroke. He was in a coma six days and then died. I still can't accept it, but I'm glad he didn't have the courage to kill himself.

I think, "Where do I go from here?" Even though we had our hard times, it was my life and I was used to it. I haven't worked in a long while, and I haven't exactly been in wonderful spirits for years. I feel I need time to pull myself together and figure out what to do, and I don't have that time.

My husband was not a good father. He wanted nothing to do with that. Being a parent was my job. My children feel this. He couldn't face any kind of difficult situation or confrontation. He would say, "Your son said that to you, so you take care of it."

I brought my son up to feel that my second husband was his father, but they were never close. My son has been married twice and has a child by each wife, but he never sees his first child. He couldn't meet the support payments so he hasn't been allowed to visit. And that child loved him so much. Oh, how she loved him! If I were he, I would find ways to see her. It makes me wonder if there is something wrong with him. He has another little girl. Whenever I go over there it's "Grandma this" and "Grandma that." I hate that name. It makes me feel old. I feel eighty when I hear all this Grandma talk. At this point in my life I need encouragement and hope. I tell my son, "Please don't let her call me Grandma," and he gets highly insulted.

Motherhood was thrust on me. I liked the children best when they were small, before they started giving me trouble, but I didn't enjoy caring for them very much. My daughter and I have been alone so much. It was always she and I, she and I. We did so many things together. We like the same things. She enjoys it and she resents it. She'll be nice and friendly one evening, and the next day she'll act as if she doesn't know me, ice cold. If I ask her about it, I get no response. My doctor suggested therapy for her, but we could never afford it. My husband said our daughter needed help years ago, but I refused to recognize it.

Since my daughter was twelve years old, she became strange. I don't know what could have happened, but before that she was a loving, adorable little girl. She changed overnight. I've tried to talk to her. I would give anything to be able to talk to my daughter; I want to be close to her, but she doesn't want it.

My daughter lives with me; she's never been married. She has never had dates; she has never had friends. She is my sole source of financial support. Whatever she makes, that's it.

My son says she should get out more, as if I'm to blame. Why is it everybody blames the mother? Nobody knows how hard you try, and what you've done to help. She's built a wall around herself, and she's become so cold, so distant. If I try to hug her or anything like that, she'll say, "What's the matter with you?" and push me away. Many and many a time I can hardly take it, but of course I'm used to it. She never confides. For instance, now when we're in terrible straits, when we don't know what to do or what will become of me, she wants to go into the Air Force. She got high marks on the test. Maybe the Air Force would change her. I said to her, "How can you go at a time like this? I'm going to be all alone. I can't face up to living alone yet." And my daughter doesn't say a word. I must admit though that if that's the only relationship I have, I must be in pretty bad shape, right?

I have no friends or relatives left. It's funny how you cannot be close to people and yet you miss them. I guess you miss the way of life that you had, the era that is passed. I'm out in the cold. I'm by myself. I always had my mother, my husband, my family. It's a totally strange thing for me to be alone. I know my daughter won't stay with me.

I'm not the type of person who could go out alone and look for a man; someone would have to knock on my door. I don't rank sex very high in my life. Being happy is more important, getting along is more important, security is more important. If I ever met anybody now, the first thing I would want to know is what he had in his bank book. I haven't given sex a thought for ages. I wonder if anybody could possibly be interested in me. About six years ago my mother gave me the incentive to lose weight and I lost thirty-five pounds. Then she died. I didn't care any more and gained it all back. Now where in the world will I get the incentive to lose again? I need a health farm where they could make a new person out of me; then I'd be ready for a new start.

I had bookkeeper's training, but I never liked it. I've enjoyed making these flower arrangements and boxes, and I'd like to find an outlet for the things I make, but that's hard, and to be a partner in a gift shop probably involves putting money in. I'd really like to work with animals because they're the only things in the world that I love. I'd like to work with a vet, but I don't have transportation. I'm sorry to say this but the more I see of people, the more I love animals. The more experiences I have with people the more disenchanted I am. I never seem to have nice relationships. Even with my husband I can't say that we did. I don't know why I stayed with him, I just did. It's easy to say, "Why didn't you move out?" But where was I going to go? At least I knew what I had. Who knows what I might have gotten into?

I don't think I've been useful; I couldn't help my husband or children. If I had helped my husband, he would be alive today. I tried many ways, but I didn't succeed.

I can't look ahead now—I'm just worried to death. Am I going to survive? Where do I go from here? Will I be able to get a job? There's nothing I can count on, nothing to rely on. I can't live alone indefinitely. I'd go bananas. If I had one person, the support of one person, one person to talk to. I'm so afraid. What should I do? Am I going to make it?

CHAPTER 8

Karen–Survivors Don't Have to Be Poor

Most people are rank amateurs in the survival game when you compare them to me.

Karen's expensive, tailored clothes cover a trim figure that belies her forty-eight years. Her face and hair are both natural but styled with thought and care. She is attractive, cheerful, and outgoing. She has two grown children whom she enjoys.

She was married at twenty to a husband who had physical and emotional problems. She took care of him for thirteen years until he died. She was a widow for five years and then married a man who was twenty years older than she. Her second marriage ended in divorce three years later and almost ended in her breakdown. She has been living alone for the last seven years and looking for another husband. In spite of two impossible husbands, Karen retains a fierce, romantic desire to try for the brass ring a third time.

Karen told her story authoritatively. She wanted other women to know what a woman can go through and still survive.

* * *

KAREN

MY PRIMARY RECOLLECTION about my childhood is of the bad feeling that existed between my parents. My family relationships were so "hairy" that I never dwelled on my youth or thought about it. My mother was a widow with two children when she married her ex-brother-in-law. My mother was almost a broken lady. She was grateful to her husband for having married her. They were both in their forties when I was born.

I don't remember much. My mother had to travel a lot to keep up with her husband, so I was brought up primarily by a housekeeper. I loved going to church with her. I became enamoured of the Catholic Church, and I prayed to "belong." I had a tremendous sense of not really belonging anywhere. I didn't know my place between my parents. My half brothers and sisters were many years older. I felt close only to the housekeeper, a warm and lovely woman whom I still see every week.

My mother knew that my father was too strict. I felt that she would have liked to play with me, but she had to satisfy my father. I remember that at dinner there was no conversation. The radio was played. And I remember after dinner waiting for my aunt and uncle to come over so that I would be off the hook. I always wished for a lot of children to play with and have fun with. I don't remember ever having fun with my parents. There was always strain. In later years I learned that my mother had a sense of humor, but it wasn't noticeable until after my father died—a little late, because by then she was old and sick.

My mother never had any career ambitions for me. I liked my mother, but when I was young I felt she was weak. Actually, she was a strong woman who kept her senses when someone else might have gone crazy.

Anything that I did wrong, according to my father, was my mother's fault. He didn't like the way she dressed or the way she acted in public, and he never gave her credit for all her efforts at entertaining and so forth. There's a pattern in my family going way back. My grandfather was a domineering man who kept his wife in the kitchen and made her miserable. My father was a tyrant in his business as well as at home.

Mother never stood up to him and said, "Basta!" I certainly never talked back to him. I don't know what would have happened if I had. Probably he would have taken it out on my mother. I never talked back to my husbands either.

I never felt that I lived up to my father's expectations. I felt that he would have liked to have a son, that he would have liked me to be brighter. He always criticized my mother because she wasn't as bright as he was.

I felt that my father had a somewhat unhealthy love for me. He idolized me and overprotected me terribly. I felt that he was emotionally unhealthy. I couldn't be too close to my mother, or my father would be jealous. He didn't play with me much except for telling me stories on Sunday mornings. I loved that.

My mother had a way of fooling herself. She thought that she heard my father say "I love you" on his death bed, but I was there and I know she made that up. I don't think my feelings for my father ever changed much, and I didn't feel much when he died. I mourned my mother much more.

I can understand how I made my first marital mistake: I wanted desperately to get away from home. My first husband, Eric, was nine years older than I was. His mother brought him to Albany to meet me, and he proposed on the first weekend he met me. The second time he proposed with honeymoon tickets, and the third time I saw him, we were engaged.

I had sexual pleasure without intercourse, but no intercourse before I got married at the age of twenty. Even though I had been a very heavy, miserable, unattractive teenager, I always got dates. I always got to parties at the last minute. I was fun and, I guess, sexy. I did plenty of necking, but I was taught to say no.

From the start Eric and I had terrible sexual problems, terrible. In fact, both of our kids were practically immaculate conceptions. Eric had premature ejaculations. I was "the virgin," and he was supposed to be a "man about town," the instigator of going to the whorehouse and laying all the gals. On our first night I was perfectly at ease and waiting, but we had no success. We had a miserable honeymoon, and when we came back, I went to the doctor and said, "There must be something wrong with me." He took some pliers and broke my hymen. I passed out.

Nevertheless, Eric and I continued to have great sexual difficulties. I then went to another doctor. He examined me and told me again that I was small and gave me all sorts of penises to insert. That didn't do any good. The semen, though not the penis of my husband, must have penetrated me because I got pregnant. Eric would get so nervous that it was almost like an epileptic fit.

I learned on our honeymoon that Eric had seen psychiatrists and every other kind of doctor for his nervous condition, but he had failed to mention it to me. At the time we were first married he was going to some quack in the city. I went with him. There were meetings at night where people would get up and tell about their nervous disorders, and then the quack doctor would shoot the patients full of hot oil to make them feel better. And if Eric was nervous during the day, he would go to that doctor for a shot.

Later, in discussions with Eric, he admitted that he had never really had successful intercourse with any gal; he had always had this problem. So I knew the problem was not me. In all the thirteen years that I was married, I was never attracted to another man. I never had any sexual desire, although that worried me because I never got any satisfaction at home.

Our relationship was very close. Eric became dependent on me and I was very emotionally involved with him in a motherly way. He would go to work in the morning and then he would be so nervous that he would be home in an hour and a half. I'd almost have to treat him like a baby. He was a hypochondriac. When he had these terrible attacks, he'd think he was going to die. If he sneezed good, he'd take a thermometer and work it up to 100°. Every time he'd pass a mirror, he'd look at himself and stick his tongue out. There was so much going on with him that I just didn't have time to think of anything else.

We moved into an apartment in New York and had his mother to contend with. He was an only child. He visited his mother every day. I never liked her but she was actually glad that I was taking care of Eric, and she said to me, "I'll stand by you. Do anything you want."

For six or seven years Eric went to a psychiatrist five times a week. The doctor wouldn't talk to me individually, and Eric didn't want me coming with him, so I finally went to see a Viennese psychiatrist who told me on the first visit to lie down on the couch and talk about my dreams. It just turned me off. I walked out and never got psychiatric help.

Eric would come home during the day, and although he was not a drinker, he would use alcohol as a tranquilizer. He'd almost need rocking and holding. After a drink and a hot bath maybe he'd be able to go back to work.

I remember standing with the baby in my arms, watching Eric leave for the office. I was shaking because he was driving a car. Then in a couple of hours he'd be home. Or, when I'd take the baby out for a walk, I'd wonder if I should be back in the apartment waiting for Eric.

Much, much later, well after I had the children and at the time when Eric got so involved with the stock market, I got fed up. I laid down an ultimatum that either he get out of the stock market or I was going to leave. He was neglecting his real estate business and spending all day at the stockbroker's office. He would trade "big" and then come home a nervous wreck about the market. Mentally he couldn't take it.

I never said a word to my parents about any of the difficulties with Eric. But finally I told my stepsister all my problems, sexual and emotional. She felt that I should get a divorce, and I remember saying, after long deliberation, "I can't, I can't. I have two babies and a sick husband. I can't do it."

That was the only time in my marriage when I seriously considered giving up the struggle. There were so many things in my life; my parents didn't get along and I didn't want to go back to them and I had no place to go. And I did understand my husband. I knew that his behavior was not directed against me. We'd go to a party and he'd give the high sign that he was getting nervous, and I'd leave with him. I'd go through marital anguish when someone else would drive with us to a party, but no one ever knew. He hid his trembling as best he could. One time my husband's boss asked to talk to me and told me he was going to have to fire Eric for absenteeism. I told him that Eric was a sick man and that I was having difficult problems, but other than the boss and my sister, I never confided in anyone.

It was as though I had three children. During the last five years Eric began to resent the children and hate me. He developed multiple sclerosis. At first he found it difficult to walk and write. I remember crawling on my knees on the sidewalk to help him into the barbershop, and then going to get a wheelchair.

During most of this time I was sleeping in the bed next to Eric and many times he wanted to try intercourse. There was a terrible odor to him, and he shook with a terrible palsy. I used to lie there in bed praying that he wouldn't ask me to get in bed with him, and I would stay miserable all night. Eventually I moved into another room. That's when my husband became physically violent. He came to hate me and took all his frustrations about his illness out on me. I'd be helping him up the stairs, and he'd push me down. I had to get a male nurse in the house. I was doing everything I could to take advantage of what little functioning remained to Eric. He would be carried down to dinner by the male nurse and then at the table nobody could understand his garbled speech. The kids were frustrated, and I was frustrated. My doctor came over one night to see just how bad things were, and then he told me, "You've got to get your husband out of the house. Neither you nor the kids are going to survive this."

Eric lived for six months in the nursing home. I went to see him every day. I never missed one. During Eric's last five years, I almost never went to a social function. I felt that I should always be "on deck" at home. Eric stopped seeing people because he couldn't make himself understood to anyone but me.

I lived with lots of hate to the point where Eric had the nurses in the home write me terrible letters. I didn't handle that very well. But I know that before he got multiple sclerosis he loved me and appreciated me to the extent that he could. I came first after his mother. Eric's death was a blessing. I wished that he could have died sooner because of his suffering.

I feel that most people are rank amateurs in the survival game when you compare them to me. I felt deeply that my role in life was to be a good wife. I had seen my mother play it. I felt that working on her marriage was a woman's lot.

I was a widow for five years before I made my second and even more disastrous marital mistake. Before I went out with Jerry, I didn't go out much. I wasn't that popular. I felt very close to my kids. I loved being a mother even when I had a sick husband and was homebound. I'm sure I had my depressed moments, but I look back on it as a happy time. During my widowhood I enjoyed the kids, I had a big house to take care of, I didn't have time to worry much about men, and I didn't like dating.

I enjoyed a very glamorous affair with Jerry. Our premarital sex was super. It was romantic. It was everything I ever dreamed of and hoped to enjoy with Eric. I heard that Jerry had been a poor husband and father in his first marriage, but I rationalized that either the trouble was caused by his wife or else that he had changed. While Jerry was courting me, he idolized me, put me on a pedestal, was super to my children, and he was very exciting to be with.

The year that I fell in love with Jerry and married him I told the children honestly that I was not primarily providing them with a father, but rather that I was providing myself with a husband. It was probably healthy for them that I stopped concentrating on them. They were both teenagers.

After we were married the shit hit the fan. Jerry was a schizo. He changed the night we were married. He was lousy to his own kids and he was mean to mine. I didn't recognize the picture immediately. I thought Jerry was behaving badly just because we no longer had our romantic privacy.

I quickly decided that to make this marriage go I had to be available at all times to do whatever Jerry wanted. After working at the office half a day, he'd come home to play golf. He played very well, and I was always made to feel inferior. He'd say, "You're ruining my game because your golf is so lousy."

Jerry took over every detail of managing the house and the meals, and again when anything wasn't right, it was my fault. There were a lot of similarities in the way Jerry treated me and the way my father treated my mother.

Jerry became obsessed with getting old. He was handsome, but he was twenty years older than I. First he had a face lift, and then he worried about his sexual prowess. He began reading all the books on sex that he could find. Then, not only was he reading the books, he was referring to them before, during, and after intercourse. Then he criticized my performance. He said that I wasn't performing sexually the way I did before we were married, so we were reading the books together to find out what I was doing wrong.

Jerry decided to start collecting erotic art. He already had a fabulous art collection. Jerry was exciting to travel with, he was brilliant, and he had good taste. However, collecting erotic art turned into a nightmare. He wanted me in all these erotic positions like the ones in the pictures. He'd have me on an Indian swing, and even though I tried, it became unbearable. Eventually I became unable to operate sexually with him at all. I began to realize that I would end up mentally ill if I didn't get out of the marriage.

The period before my divorce was the most unhappy one that I ever experienced. The marriage had lasted three years, and I was utterly miserable. It was so bad that, for a long time after Jerry left, I couldn't get dinner on the table because mealtimes reminded me of him. I was humiliated telling the lawyer my marital history. Besides, I was not occupied productively in any way. I was overwhelmed by a sense of failure. My second marriage was more traumatic than the sickness and death of my first husband. Divorce was a horror, but I am over it. I know now that I can survive anything.

I enjoy being alone. I decorated my apartment, it's pretty, and I enjoy hibernating there. Sometimes I force myself to call someone and go out to dinner. I enjoy my kids. Occasionally we go to offbeat theater together or go to ethnic restaurants. I don't want to volunteer, and I have inherited enough money to live on. I've thought of being a decorator, but that takes four years of school, and I was a lousy student.

Any woman who says she would not like to get married again is a liar. I am not an aggressive woman, and I don't know where to look for another husband. If somebody finds me my only worry will be making a third mistake. Basically I'm domestic. I like men and share their interests. I've had a few affairs since my divorce, and I've regained my sexual self-esteem, but when all is said and done, I'm the marrying kind looking for romance. I've never wanted anything, really, other than to be married and have children. I feel that I would make someone a good wife, and I think it's a dirty shame that I can't find somebody.

CHAPTER 9

Virginia—"Gaslight"

Howard needed a woman to tell him he was marvelous forty-eight hours
out of every twenty-four. No one woman could do it. He had several.

*Virginia is a big, attractive woman of fifty-four with green eyes and ash-blond
hair. She laughed nervously during the interview and told her horror story with
difficulty. Her twenty-eight-year-long marriage ended in divorce two years ago.*

*In spite of having been trained for a career, motherhood and domesticity were to
be Virginia's fulfillment. Virginia entered marriage as though it were a maximum
security prison: The marriage was hard work, the husband was demanding and
cold, and the sentence was "life." For a few years after college she was a rising
young industrial designer in New York. But she abandoned her career to raise six
children, all now in their twenties, and to maintain a lovely home for a brilliant,
perfectionist husband. However, this formerly competitive, assertive woman became
a doormat for her increasingly sadistic husband. She came close to losing her sanity.
Now, phoenixlike, she is reborn.*

* * *

VIRGINIA

I'VE LIVED ALONE now for four years. I love being alone. When I
left my husband I felt, all of a sudden, as though I were let out of
prison. I said, "I'll never marry again! I'll just be by myself!" I had
never thought before about how to please myself. I had always tried
to please other people. Now, for four years, I have been standing on
my own two feet, supporting myself, doing the work I love, doing
what *I* want to do, and feeling like a human being. I have a lot of
children—six—and I love them, but I've told them I don't want
any of them coming home to live with mother. I spent a good many
years raising children. I'll visit them, of course, and they can come
to visit me. But I really feel that I'm entitled to my own life now.

I've been engaged for a year, and I'm in no rush to set a date. I
love Stan. He's good for me, and we'll be great for each other, but I
like it the way it is. There's a problem with my job, too, which he
doesn't like. I design industrial products and do decorating of office
buildings, and I have to travel quite a bit for some of my clients.

Stan trusts me away alone. It's just that he can't work while I'm gone. He says he misses me too much. But I don't want to give up the job. It means too much to me. If I hadn't had it to hang onto, I'm sure I would have gone to pieces years ago. Sometimes I'm torn because I could actually go much further with my work if I sacrificed Stan's feelings. I feel sad about it. Stan has even encouraged me to go ahead, but he doesn't realize that it would mean committing myself twenty-four hours a day. He's such a great person. I know it would hurt him. And I want him to be happy, so I think I've given up any thoughts of being more successful.

I think I've come a very long way from the person I was. I think I'm quite a woman. Isn't there a song, "I'm a Helluva Woman"? I heard it on the radio one time, and I said, "Gee, I feel that way about myself." Not five years ago, but now. I went back to see the marriage counselor I had talked to during my marriage, and I said to her, "I thought I was going to be one of your successes." And she said, "What makes you think you're not?" The people I work with say I'm a different woman. I'm more open, more relaxed, more giving. Some people who haven't seen me for a long time don't even recognize me. I must have looked terrible during the last year of my marriage. I hurt all the time.

I didn't have any sexual desire at all for years. It's coming back now, which is very nice. Stan has a lot to do with it, of course. He thinks I'm attractive even though I am overweight. I had a mastectomy—also during that last awful year—and that doesn't matter either.

My husband, Howard, and I had no sexual relations for seven years. I enjoyed sex with Howard at the beginning, but I wouldn't say that I felt free. I had the old feeling that it was my job to please my husband, and I didn't worry about whether I had orgasm or not. It was part of marriage, and maybe you didn't feel like it, but it was your job. To him, love is sex. He didn't express any affection after a while. I didn't feel he loved *me*. It was just physical with him. That's too bad. As I look back I think sex is kind of dirty to him. I don't feel that way. I really don't.

He couldn't stand to be touched. We were never physically close. You accept it. You figure you're married for life, and this is it. You adjust to it. Of course, I don't feel that way anymore. Emotionally, Howard seemed to be afraid to let go. He seemed very open with other people because he talked a lot, but I think there was so much buried deep inside him. It didn't have just to do with sex. There was probably some cruelty in Howard that I was never conscious of that affected everything. Something very cruel, very cold about him.

In the beginning I had all these little complaints, felt these slights. But I had to hold them in. I almost left once, when I had just the one baby. I felt a total lack of consideration. We made a ten-hour car trip when the baby was tiny, and I had been very ill with anemia. Well, he would not let me out of the car that whole time. So you do what your husband says. So you stay in the car.

We had no social life then at all. Howard would leave me at home with the baby while he went off to visit friends. I complained about that, but it didn't do me any good. He was a very rigid man. I think it might be that he was unsure of himself, and if you put up a rigid front and keep somebody else down, you feel stronger. I don't know though.

Howard appreciated me as long as I was the perfect wife and mother. I had a reputation of floors so clean you could eat off them. Even with six kids, there was not a thing out of place, not a speck of dust, nothing around. I used to can and make jelly. We had an enormous kitchen, and once the table was covered with jams and jellies. They stayed there for three days while I was doing it, and Howard was furious because the kitchen was a mess. He wanted to be able to bring people in and show them the house and open the closet doors and have everything fine, and have the children perfectly dressed, and, of course, have the perfect wife, too. He did compliment me a lot for having the house and the kids look right. He did appreciate that. In the beginning he was all right about most things. Isn't that funny?

He and I shared religious values, but he resented my working as a volunteer for the church. I remember one time I had been working at a bazaar and we were all sitting around at the end of the day having a hamburger before cleaning up. A man came in and told me that my husband just drove by and said, "Tell my wife to get home!" I got in my car, threw the hamburger out the window, and raced home. He definitely resented it.

Howard never shared in any of the household things. He was around the kids, but he didn't play with them. If he was watching television, they would be there with him, but I was the one to take them to games and to travel with them. He wouldn't take vacations. He *would not go.* Just once we went on an overnight trip with the kids. When we came back, he was livid! You know how it is with kids in the car. He said, "This togetherness bit isn't for me." Remember when that was very big? He stopped going to graduations, school things. He just didn't go. Mother went. Mother was the bad guy in everything. When things went wrong, I had to straighten them out. I was at home all the time and I thought I should do these things, so I did. I didn't feel that Howard was unfair. It was a long drive to and from his work, and you have only a certain amount of energy. I did have words with him about not going to the children's confirmations. He was like a stone wall. He said, "I did my part by having them baptized. I don't have to be there."

Howard felt that women's place was in the home. Things really started to go bad when I went back to my designer work. I never dreamed that I wouldn't. What happened was that as I was coming up in recognition as a designer–decorator, he was going down in *his* work. The counselor I went to told me that we had been competing all our lives. In high school he got the biggest scholarship and I got the next one, just for example. Our marriage was fine as long as I was at home and was a wife and mother. But sometimes instead of his coming home and being greeted at the door he would find I was still at the office. I can see that he started to resent it as competition. My mother had been saying to me that I should resume my work because I would never feel fulfilled as a person if I didn't. Previously she had thought that art, even designing, was too impractical, and that I would be a failure like my father. But I took a course, and there were all those doors again, waiting to be opened. I think Howard was kind of proud of me at first. I remember him telling people about an award I had won.

But he didn't like the people I began to have as friends. He wouldn't allow them in the house. He said they were all crooks or homosexuals. Prior to the time I went back to work our friends were his friends. For a while that was all right, but then I noticed that he made a play for the wives. He would pay a great deal of attention to other women, charm the daylights out of them. It made me feel neglected, and then I just didn't like to go to parties anymore.

We had one couple as close friends, but Howard antagonized

them. He had a way of making people I liked feel unwelcome. My aunt said the same thing, and even my sister said she didn't feel welcome in our house. They stopped coming. He would sit and read, leave the room, watch television. He never fought with them, nothing like that.

I was very proud of him and his work. He's very bright. A genius. But he made a lot of enemies at work. Many people really hated him. I think he needed somebody to dominate. It was one of those mutual weakness things. I needed him to lean on. I was willing to be dominated. I thought it was my job. But I didn't enjoy it. It all goes back to that rigid upbringing. You do what is right. Period. No matter what it does to you, you do it. I think I excelled in school because I wanted to please my parents and teachers. I was good for the same reason. I was trained to please people. So I felt forced to stay in this marriage, forced to make the best of things. I behaved in the expected way in order to keep myself together. It was a self-preservation thing. I think I was not such a pleasant person to be with. One of my colleagues said, "You're an easier person now. You used to make people feel uptight and watch their p's and q's." Black was black and white was white. There was no gray. I buried my resentments. It wasn't until I left my husband that I opened up all of a sudden and became a different person.

I really loved the kids. That was good. There was enough satisfaction in that for many years. I know I couldn't have raised my children by myself if I had left earlier. I'm glad I was able to hold out as long as I did. The only thing I wish is that I hadn't gotten married. I wish it hadn't all started. But it's done. I did think about the possibilities plenty of times, and I knew I had to stay.

Howard needed a woman to tell him he was marvelous forty-eight hours out of every twenty-four. No one woman could do it. He had several. I think a lot of our friends and acquaintances knew it long before I did. I was very upset when I found out that everybody knew but me. I was in a store one time when a friend came towards me, looked at me, and turned around and walked out. She knew she couldn't face me. I was really upset.

My pastor said to me that I probably only knew the tip of the iceberg. And the husband of one of the women he was involved with said to me that Howard was going after this guy's wife when I was pregnant with my youngest child, twenty-one years ago. But I wasn't aware of anything at that time. I just knew I wasn't very happy.

Howard always refused to talk to me about our troubles. That's one of the things about him. He didn't talk to me for two years, never said hello, never said goodbye. And it was the last years that he really cut me off. We didn't have intercourse and he ignored me. I hid it from the children. I never talked to them about their father. We lived in a very big house and people were all spread out and it's amazing how you can keep out of each other's way. When we moved to a much smaller house, the whole thing came apart. I couldn't get away from it. It closed in on me. My oldest daughter said the only thing the kids noticed was that I didn't laugh as much. We were acting parts, putting on a good show. Howard would leave in the morning before the children got up and would come home after dinner when they were out or doing homework. On the weekends I would go for a walk or sometimes to a client's. And the TV was always there. Howard had said to me, "I neither like you nor dislike you. I won't discuss it. I just want a minimum of contact with you." And that was it. I think he got very sick, because he used to sit in the television room with his undershirt up over his head, all curled up, watching television. And he didn't change his clothes. He wore the same jacket every day for a whole year. He wouldn't let me touch his clothes. I think he went off the deep end mentally. He went down and down and down in his work, and while that was happening, he was involved with women who could boost his ego. He was involved with his secretary, and with a much older woman, and with my cleaning woman. They would all be flattered, right? I suspected some of these things, but I figured you love somebody and they're having troubles and you're willing to put up with it. But you can put up with things for only so long.

He said we had to sell the big house. He said, "No matter what you say, this house is being sold." So I thought what he needed was a smaller house. Well, he stole every penny of the profit from that big house, over eighty thousand dollars. Then he put the new house in his name, and he changed all the beneficiary insurance policies, all the stocks and bonds. All of a sudden I realized I had nothing. I never had emotional security with him and now I had no financial security either. I was facing the future with nothing. That's when I confided in my sister. Her husband told me that Howard had been seeing a lawyer. We had never discussed divorce. Then he took out an accidental death policy on me. That was the last straw. I really got scared. He never talked to me about that or about anything. There was no contact, but I felt this withheld violence.

I was cracking up. I lost a tremendous amount of weight. I stuttered. I couldn't sleep. I would get in the car and close the windows and scream, and drive along screaming. I almost committed suicide once, I was so depressed. I had it all planned. You could cut your wrists, you could be in bed, you could be in a plastic bag, there wouldn't be any mess. I was really serious. Howard had been involved with these women, and then I said to myself, "Why should I destroy myself and give him a clear field?" And that's what stopped me.

One day my sister and her husband forced me into their car and took me to a lawyer. Then to a psychiatrist. Later I heard the psychiatrist tell my lawyer that if I hadn't left when I did, I would have been in a mental institution for the rest of my life, unable to cope with anything.

My lawyer felt that Howard had had a plan to divorce me in a few years, after the kids were grown up and after he had all the money in his name, and that I had made him really furious by beating him out of his plan. The law says that if a wife doesn't object when her husband puts everything in his name, it's assumed that she agrees. If you don't object within a few years, five, I think, you've lost all rights.

The judge was very good. He split everything right down the line. The judge said I could have the divorce on the grounds of sexual abandonment, but I didn't want to stir up a lot of scandal. It was just as easy to do it the regular way. I was in no hurry, because I had recently undergone a mastectomy and then a hysterectomy, and I didn't have the energy to get a divorce. Then my lawyer called and said I should make my move before too much time had passed after Howard had changed things to his name.

When I served him with the divorce papers, it was a complete shock to him, and he went off the deep end. He refused to leave the house for the next six weeks. I was afraid to be in the house alone with him. I used to drive around until I was sure one of the children was there. I was very much afraid of him. That accidental death policy scared me.

Howard never talked to me during the separation. He tried to give me a hard time about the money, but he didn't succeed. The judge was fantastic.

I think it was a marriage that should never have taken place. We were both too young, still at school. He was the apple of his mother's eye, and he never learned to appreciate women as women. He was always catered to by his mother and his sisters. There was never the consideration that I now see in Stan and in some of the young men I know. And besides I had wanted a career. It was just a mistake. Then it was done, and after the war any woman who worked was thought to be neglecting her children. We were supposed to devote ourselves to our families. I do think I would be more successful and even famous if I hadn't become a wife and mother. But I had to make a choice.

The fourth child became a problem after the split-up. I had to lay down the law. But he's OK now. And I had a real battle with the youngest. She had been in a private school, and when she went to high school, it was like the gates of hell had opened. We had our times. But we're very close now. These problems and rebellions were with me, not with my husband. He wasn't there. He wasn't around. That's probably why they like him all right. Also, he's changed since the divorce. I think he's afraid of losing them now, so he gives them money and whatever they want. I'm not like that. If they borrow money, they have to pay me back.

The children were very angry with me for leaving my husband, but I think they thought I was a good mother. I've learned to enjoy them as adults, and I'm happy that they have left the nest. The wrench came when the oldest went off to college. I had a terrible time then. Howard wouldn't let me go up to school with my son when he went for the first time. Howard went. When he came back he was sneering at all those mothers there, hanging on to their children. He made me feel very weak, that something was wrong with me for being upset. Of course Howard and I were having troubles.

Besides my kids, another reason I stuck it out in my marriage so long was that my parents were divorced when I was fifteen. My father couldn't get work. It was during the Depression, and my mother was working in a store. One day she brought her paycheck home, and my father spent it in a bar instead of buying groceries. By that time he was drinking heavily. So my mother just said, "That's it. Get out." I saw him only once again, when I was in college. My uncle sees him, and I hear about him that way. But my mother was very bitter, and if there had been any contact, it would have upset her terribly. I blamed her for the breakup of the marriage.

After my father left, my relationship with my mother was pretty bad, all during high school. I look back on it and realize that she was tired. She worked all day to support four kids and went to school at night. I took care of the younger kids while she got a teaching degree. She was quite a woman. She just died recently. I think I'm very much like her now, but she didn't want us to be the way she was. She thought women should be in the home, not out working. She felt that she was too independent. Her advice always seemed to be: "Do what your husband says."

She was not a loving person, I would say. I remember my sister sitting on her lap and hugging her, but I couldn't do that. My brother seemed affectionate with her, too. I think I couldn't show my feelings as much. There's a key to something there. People give more attention to the children who seem open and affectionate, but the one who seems to be independent and standoffish needs it more, really.

I was closer to my father. Not physically close. Both my parents were undemonstrative, I felt. But my father was able to give more to me. I didn't feel shut out by him, as I did by my mother. If I wanted to do something, he helped me do it. He gave me attention. I remember him helping me build a crate and skateboard. He was very patient, had tremendous patience with me. He was a very loving father. I hate to say that he encouraged aggressiveness, but in a way he did. I always felt that I could do anything. There was no job that I couldn't do. There was an older boy who lived down the street who took my marbles. My father gave me boxing lessons, and I went back and beat that boy up and got my marbles back. I wasn't brought up to feel inferior to boys. If anything, I felt superior. I was always head of my class, and I expected to be. But in high school—it was after my father left—I began to feel that I shouldn't be, that I should let the boy feel superior.

I don't know why I've made it. I don't know why I didn't give up. My mother, my grandmother, and my favorite aunt were all accomplished women. They all had to fight for success and survival. I think my attitudes were affected by them. My father did give up, but his are the words I remembered: "Get out there and get your marbles back!"

CHAPTER 10

Marion—God's Gift to Middle-aged Men

I don't think I've ever said no. When I get to the point where intercourse is inevitable, I feel sorry for the fellow. I know that's dumb.

At fifty-one Marion is vivacious, good-looking, an excellent office manager and a flirt who has to be one of God's gifts to middle-aged men. She has two grown children. She lost a severely brain-damaged child when he was fifteen. Marion cried when she spoke of him.

In twenty years Marion has divorced four husbands. Two of her marriages lasted less than a year, one of them eight years, and her most recent and best marriage lasted five years. Three years have passed since her divorce. Even though Marion works full time, her last husband left her financially secure. She shares her small home with her youngest son and his girl friend.

Marion has experienced more events than she can digest, but despite bouts of depression she remains primarily joyful, lives for the moment, and is perpetually romantic about men. She is comfortable with the new, freer life style of today and wishes it had always existed. She has enjoyed nature, traveling, cooking, and working. She has some independence, but does not like to be alone for any length of time.

* * *

MARION

I HAD NO LOVE from my father. He was forty-three when I was born. He came to the United States from Norway, a child of poor parents, and spent all of his life working. He made a tremendous success of himself financially.

There were never any arguments between my parents. If my mother was late, my father might clear his throat, but that seemed to be the extent of his emotional range. Our house was a very silent one. My father discouraged any conversation. He had most of his upbringing in lumber camps since he was seven, and silence was the law when he ate.

My father valued his privacy, his aloofness, and the success of his dairy farm. I felt that if I distinguished myself in school, my father would like it. The truth was he never seemed to notice.

The only time I got any notice from him, I wasn't trying. When I was fourteen he saw me in shorts, and he got angry. He said, "I do not want to see your body exposed. Go put on a dress." His outburst made me feel physically unattractive. I never gave up trying to please my father, but I did become devious. If I wanted to go out with a bunch of kids, I would lie about where I was going.

It was my mother who held all of us together, with the aid of my oldest brother, who was fourteen years older than I. My brother was the disciplinarian whom I hated. Once when I was sneaking out at night he said, "It's better to raise pigs than girls." I don't like him to this day. My brothers and sisters are all very straight and hardworking. All my relatives are. I'm the maverick.

My mother was distant, and she was terribly busy. She worked from dawn to dusk. She was forty-one when I was born, and she lived to be eighty-nine. She was glad that I was a girl. She occasionally went to bat for me, and she did give me a lot of freedom within the house while I was growing up. Her motto was, "Put steel up your spine and never show your weaknesses to anybody." She was not at all social. She had come from an isolated farm in Norway, and she never had any friends. It was a typical life of Scandinavians in the North Woods.

I opened up a lot more with my mother in recent years. I think I became her favorite even though I had been away from home for years. She confided in me that she had had quite a few abortions since there was no birth control in those days. I think she liked my father, but she didn't care about sex. She remained pretty active in her old age, but she would have been awfully lonely without my younger sister and myself.

I never had an orgasm until my fourth marriage at forty-two, but I have been sexually active since I was sixteen. I have always wanted to please men; I need to be liked and accepted by men—I don't think I've ever said no. I probably "had" about twenty-five different fellows between the time I was sixteen and twenty-one. I felt dirty as far as society went, but not as far as my relationship with the fellows. I was faithful to the boys that I went steady with, and I was always faithful when I was married.

I was going to college during wartime, and I met this pilot who was sweet and fine. We got married because I got pregnant. He was tender with me, but unfortunately he just couldn't cope with marriage, much less fatherhood. I probably was with him about four months out of the two years we were married, and we were separated before our second, brain-damaged son was born. My husband was extremely proud and happy about his firstborn. But he couldn't find a job or figure out what to do with his life. He was overwhelmed. He went out of my life totally.

I was a divorcée in a small town with my two small children, and I met a bright, compulsive fellow who was a geneticist. My sister told me to jump at the chance. I had only seen him about eight times when he married me, and we all thought he was very magnanimous to take me and my two children including the brain-damaged one.

Living with Joe, my second husband, I learned how to cook caribou, bear, and squirrel. Joe was an avid gardener. He raised kohlrabi, okra, you name it. I was on a very limited budget and I learned to be very economical. I also took a few classes and enjoyed university society.

Unfortunately Joe was an "old maid" at heart. He married me when he was thirty-six, and he considered sex as being invented strictly for breeding purposes. Once during intercourse I said something about enjoying it, and he went off into a lecture about an African tribe that cut out the clitoris. That really turned me off.

He made love very infrequently, and near the end of our eight-year marriage I said to him, "You know, we haven't had intercourse for six months," and he said, "Really, is that what's bothering you? We'll do it." Then it was another full year before we did it again. By that time I was so emotionally cowed, I don't know what enabled me to get a divorce.

One time Joe saw a man at a party make a pass at me, and I let it happen because I wanted my husband to get jealous. I asked him, "Didn't it bother you at all?" And Joe said, "No. If nobody else wanted you, why would I?" I was so deflated by that. What I wanted was a close relationship with him, but I was just window-dressing to the public for his marriage.

Six weeks after our baby was born, Joe had me give a big party. He announced to the assembled guests that he had a parturition present for his wife—a pair of diamond earrings that he showed to everyone before he showed them to me. They were for pierced ears that I didn't have. I thought, "What an ostentatious and unloving gift."

It was Joe, Jr., our mutual child, that really contributed to the breakup of our marriage. My husband had to be totally involved in his care, and it got to the point where he was sleeping with his son, and I was sleeping in another room.

By the time we were divorced little Joey was a wreck. He had been the victim of his father's desire for exclusive attention. Father and son were constantly picking on each other. Joe had often taken the child to work with him and had overstimulated him in a dozen ways. Joey has improved over the years, and he and his father are friends now. Joe just became more of an old maid and never married again. He has not forgiven me for divorcing him.

For fifteen years I had the twenty-four-hour-a-day job of caring for my brain-damaged son. My sister used to "spell" me. The postman did too. He would take Timmy with him for an hour and a half while he made his rounds. My sister took him for a week at a time, and twice she took him for the winter. In fact, my sister at one time wanted to adopt my children. She loved them and she had only one of her own.

There were emergencies all the time with Timmy because his seizures wouldn't stop. Sometimes he got bad side effects from all the drugs the doctors tried on him. I could see the look of terror on his face when he knew a seizure was coming. I took him to every doctor and clinic.

Timmy was not always trouble. He brought a lot of joy too. He was a nature lover and he got all of us involved in seashells. And even though he could barely read, he knew every leaf and tree. Because of Timmy I put too heavy a burden on my oldest son, and always expected him to be helpful. We've talked about it now that he is grown, and he said, "I never dared to be naughty. You laid too big a burden on me." I have put Timmy out of my mind now and I rarely think of him.

I was always convinced that I was a good mother. I was criticized for giving my kids too much freedom, but I was pretty close to my kids and felt I had a lot to do with their becoming fearless, nonsuperstitious, open, and curious. They liked learning for its own sake.

I lived for about two years with my three children, and all the time I was starved for the company of a man. I fell in love with a big, rugged geologist. It seemed that the day I married him the sky fell in. Now I was thirty-seven years old and had four children. My husband was my fourth child. He would hide the cookie jar so he could have cookies. We lived together only four months. His mother would come over and lie with her head in his lap. There was a real love affair between them, and she constantly cooked and brought over food. She thought I wasn't taking good enough care of her little boy. Also, he had lied to me about having finished school. I got another divorce, and then I knew I had screwed my life up just terribly, and I saw a psychiatrist.

As for what I learned from psychiatry, it wasn't much, and I've continued to make plenty of mistakes. I know that I was brought up to be seen and not heard, to be a good wife, an obedient wife, and a good mother. I come from a large family, and I am the only one who's been divorced, and I've done it four times. One of the reasons for my bad choices was the bad situations I was in: The first time I was pregnant and frightened; the second time I had two children, one of whom was handicapped and needed care, and that influenced me in my third bad choice too. . . . He had been wonderful with the kids.

My son Timmy died, and I went to work. After two years of secretarial work I changed jobs, and it was "love at first sight" between the boss and myself. We had a torrid romance, and two years later we got married. Until this marriage when I was forty-two, I was really ignorant about love and sex. I knew nothing about masturbation. I was really inhibited and afraid of pregnancy. I knew I was good-looking, I knew I could run a home, but I missed being appreciated just for being me. Our sex life was wild. We had intercourse almost daily, and I began to have orgasms. I think it was because Alan was much more involved with me than the other men in my life had been.

My marriage lasted only five years, but it did more for my self-esteem than any job or anything else that I have done. My husband opened up the world to me. I became more comfortable in more situations than I had ever been before. The husband, the marriage, the life style made me feel less like I was on the outside looking in. My kids grew up, and it was a better environment for all of us. I have enough money thanks to my last husband to work or not for the next few years.

Unfortunately, Alan had even more emotional problems than I did. He had a lousy image of himself, and at times he couldn't believe that I loved him. As soon as we were married, there were problems over the children. His children were deeply troubled, and he expected me to save them overnight. He was jealous of my two sons. He was guilty in relation to his kids, and we were never more than four days without them. He played Santa Claus with his own kids, and towards the end he wanted me to go camping with them and exclude my own.

Then when I took off on a vacation, Alan committed himself to another woman. We were divorced, and he married again immediately. I was never so hurt, and I never expect to be so hurt again.

Part of my problem is that Alan has consistently reentered my life, and I have always been putty in his hands. He says, "I'll always love you. You opened nature to me. You opened the world to me. But I can't leave my dying wife. You're so much stronger." He broke up our marriage after it had gotten better and better, and last week I began to hate him because I think he enjoys being a martyr and feeling guilty.

I finally realized that our hanging on to each other in this futile fashion isn't good for either of us, and I told him not to come back. He is the only man I've ever loved and still he rejected me. He once returned to me for three months after he remarried, so I have been like a Ping-Pong ball in relation to him. I have been unable to bounce back from his leaving me, even after three years.

When we first separated I couldn't sleep for a month. I was in an extreme state of anxiety. It was the first time I had been rejected in my whole life by a man, and all I could do was drink. Finally I went into a state of numbness. The doctor gave me sleeping pills, but it seemed I couldn't face nights after that. Alcohol is my crutch at night. Probably I am consuming two tumblers of wine or three or four highballs—I really don't measure. What I need it for is just to go to bed. I guess that it's my aloneness that I am trying to cope with. I hate myself that I am not stronger. I went to an Alcoholics Anonymous meeting a few weeks ago, and I heard some of their stories, and I thought, "My God, that's not me yet." But it could be.

Maybe I could use a five-year lover with whom I could be warm; someone I could laugh and fight with and not be too predictable. I was involved with an ex-priest some time ago who was younger than I, and his stamina was too much for me. We did canoeing, horseback riding, rock and rolling, bicycling, camping. I had to rest in the afternoon to keep up with him. He was just growing up and when I started working there was no way I could keep up with him. When I wanted to stay home, he got impatient, and I'd tell him, "Go get yourself six other women and then come back to me when you're worn out." I was quite relieved when he married someone else.

I have gone through dozens of men since my husband left me. Today I'm not too comfortable about going out with younger men. I still find it hard to say no to a man, but I can do it occasionally. I recall very recently when I "did it" on our first date. I was thoroughly repelled at myself and him. But usually when I get to the point where intercourse is inevitable, I feel sorry for the fellow. I know that's dumb, and I should learn to keep a little more distance.

I will never give up men. Even without love I prefer them to women. I would like to find a man who wouldn't totally dominate me. We could explore each other and still lead separate lives.

I like the job of office manager that I have right now. It has a lot of variety, and it calls on all the social and secretarial skills that I have. The office is filled with younger people and they seem to appreciate me. Sometimes, however, I feel overwhelmed that there is so much for me to do and the bookkeeping really staggers me.

My female friends compliment me on my appearance. They envy me, but they are not a vital part of my life. I am not as honest with them as I am being right now.

Even though life has played dirty tricks, it's been terrific. My life has never been worthless to me. I am proud of my sons; they are productive and not money-oriented, and they think well of me. I wouldn't want to be young, because the hurts are not as sharp now or such a surprise as they used to be. But I do admire the new life style. I think it's more honest than what I had, and the responsibilities are more shared. I have no goals for myself right now but I have a number of strong interests. I have activities that are a pleasure just for myself. I know my life would be a desert if I lived only for human relationships.

CHAPTER 11

Lynn—A Mature Woman

I wouldn't want to be anybody other than who I am—a woman, and middle-aged, and all the rest.

Lynn is fifty-one years old, has been married for twenty-nine years, and has three grown children. A central fact in Lynn's life is the loss of a son when he was a teenager. That fact has made her family unusually close.

Lynn is tall, thin, natural, dynamic, and sure of herself. She speaks rapidly. She was both surprised at and good-natured about the many intimate questions she was asked.

Throughout her life Lynn gave her time generously to volunteer work. Then, at forty-six, she graduated from law school and embarked on a professional career that three years ago culminated in her election to the legislature. She expects to be reelected. The interview took place in her office in the state capitol building.

In Lynn's life there was a felicitous meeting of parental expectation and her ability to fulfill it. Her watchwords have been those of traditional American society: "Work hard, do good, and make a better world."

* * *

LYNN

THE PACE of life that I lead as a legislator makes me quite aware that I am aging. I don't have the energy I used to, but there are certain compensations. I have more tolerance. I don't think I could have been in the legislature when I was twenty-five or thirty. My expectations of myself would have been too high. Now I am able to close the door on disappointment. Compared to my colleagues, it's an advantage to be a middle-aged woman who doesn't expect to run for higher office. I can enjoy doing what I'm doing where I am. I have a sense of humor, and I can say, "OK, we've lost this one, but tomorrow is another day." A bill gets defeated, and it's not the end of the world. It can always be changed or reintroduced.

It's not just age that has changed me. Our family has had our share of worries and problems. I had a radical mastectomy five years ago in the middle of my second political campaign and I had to deal with it openly and publicly. Otherwise I'm in excellent health.

That experience makes you think a lot about your body. You have to get used to being deformed, in a sense. I *am* quite used to it now. Our twenty-five-year-old daughter was in a serious accident, and she's going to have a permanent leg disability. Accepting what has happened and watching my daughter's tenacious bounce back has helped me to feel that my invisible deformity is minor.

My husband had a terrible heart attack three years ago and almost died. He had open-heart surgery. I went through a period of regarding him as an invalid, but I don't anymore. He's doing extremely well.

If I sound philosophical about these grim events, it's because real tragedy struck our family when our oldest son, Steve, aged fourteen, was drowned in an accident. Although this loss occurred ten years ago, it is the most central fact about our family. My husband and I had some of our most serious arguments about Steve in our early married days. Our expectations of him and of each other had been too great. This had taken its toll on Steve, but mercifully by the time he died we had worked through many of our conflicts and Steve was feeling better about himself and about us. My husband and I had a special intensity of feeling about Steve, and I don't think we will ever get over his death.

Our other children have been marked by this experience. They have greater maturity and are very attached to each other. We had always been a very close family, but I think that experience made us even closer and more open and sharing with each other. It led to some deepening of my personality.

Looking back on that year when I lost Steve I realize that I was very seriously depressed. I had moved from a community that I had lived in for ten years, a cooperative community with all kinds of relationships that were sustaining. It was just after moving that our son was drowned. It was a ghastly year, but I gradually began to find my way back to life.

Now if I meet someone who has experienced a loss, I have no reservations about asking about the circumstances. What I realize is that most people hesitate to ask. People who are suffering begin to have a sense of unreality because nobody is dealing directly with the most important thing that is happening to them. Some friends recently lost a child in an accident, and I spent three evenings in a row with them. I couldn't have done that a year after my own son died, but I can do it ten years afterwards. I shared a lot of my own feelings. I spoke at the service. I was able to give to others because others have given so much to me. There is a community of people who reach out to you in tragedy who would not reach out to you in other circumstances.

I've thought about my own death a lot especially because of having lost a child. I will fight to live every day, but I do think of death as a friend I must learn to accept. Right after Steve's death I found out that a very dear, older friend was dying. I spent a lot of time with her because I was in need of her. She had lost two children herself many years before. This woman made new friends even in her seventy-fourth year. Her secret of staying young was to stay outwardly tuned. That's what my effort has to be. That's why I want to stay in the legislature. At the same time, I have to rehearse aging. There are all sorts of ways to rehearse. I can do it with friends who are aging, and each time I am dealing with my own mortality.

My husband and I have had a lot of ups and downs in our relationship. We are both very forceful personalities, rather strong-willed, and we fight, too. There's a lot of pride involved. We are both very much "first children." What happened over a matter of time was that our ability to know one another and understand how the other one was feeling was greatly enlarged. That is reflected in our sex life, too, as sexual pleasure has greatly increased over the twenty-nine years of our marriage.

My husband and I are tremendously respectful of each other as individuals. He encouraged me to run for political office right from the start. I think it's been very difficult for him because he's given up part of me. I didn't realize how much of a sacrifice it would be in terms of our private life. I make a major effort to protect our family life together. My husband doesn't like to accompany me to political affairs, and I have accepted this. When I think of the number of things I did for him and his work when we were younger, occasionally I get resentful and feel that he should go to a banquet with me. But largely I know that it's hard to learn new ways at our age, and I only ask him to go when I know it will be fun for him, or when I'm desperate.

That adjustment of our private life for my political life was so difficult for both of us initially that we couldn't talk about it explicitly or easily as we do now. We deal with it a great deal better.

I had a very loving relationship with my father. I don't think there's much question that the reason I have the intellectual self-confidence that I do is because of all the encouragement he gave me.

It wasn't so easy for me to get along with my mother when I was young, and I'm glad that I have had my mature years to grow to appreciate her. Only in recent years has she opened up about the strong feelings she had that she had suffered job discrimination as a woman when she was young. As a top graduate student in chemistry she was completely unprepared to find that she couldn't get a job in a laboratory.

She married my father while they were both working for a large corporation. Then she quit working. In retrospect I realize that the combination of baby care with a great deal of social life in a company town was very frustrating for her. She was a very intellectual woman out of a Victorian background and with no experience with small children. She worried about my clothes and manners and things that seemed superficial to me. In a sad way, her feelings of inadequacy as a parent led to feelings of inadequacy as a child in me. What I didn't see until later was how much I took from my mother's intellectual quickness and her demanding standards for herself.

I remember that in high school I began to fight with my father a lot. One part of my father was a southern gentleman who wanted me to play more conventional, feminine roles, but the real message from him had been his enjoyment of my intellectuality. The real praise came in this area.

I pulled back from the intensity of our earlier relationship by disagreeing with him. I was a very strong interventionist just before World War II and I remember saying to him in a perfect fury, "I'll come visit you in a concentration camp," and I stalked out of the room. I suspected that being allowed to do that was unusual.

Partially due to my father's democratic ways and partially due to my own intensity, I became an "interrupter." I was amazed and amused to read that one of the things they teach you in "assertiveness training" is how to interrupt. It was also one of the things that bothered my husband. When I discovered that, I thought, "Oh, my God, I have to learn not to interrupt." I have learned to moderate my manners, but my very intensity still causes me to slip.

I've had a number of jobs, but I learned more from my volunteer work than from any paid job. It's where my ability in the legislature comes from. Being on boards and committees has stood me in good stead for the endless meetings. My work in politics and civil rights helped me to understand how to organize a campaign. I didn't mean to, but pretty soon in most organizations I found that I was playing a key role because I knew what was going on and because I have a fair amount of energy and ideas. I got a lot of satisfaction from my volunteer work, even though I found it competitive with the demands of home. I always worried about getting too involved with life outside my home. I've always needed both quite badly.

I never had any professional expectations about my life. It seems to me that women in general don't look ahead and ask, "What will I be doing in ten years?" For example, even though I had talent in graduate school and worked for my master's, it never occurred to me to go ahead to a Ph.D. Once I married I looked forward to having a family. In some ways I'm glad that I didn't have the pressure of a career while my family was young. I loved that period, and I made the most of it.

When my youngest child was five I went back to work as a part-time economist. I was still feeling my way, wondering whether to become a professional, when we had to move. After our son's death I decided to retool myself and raise my status. I began law school when I was forty-six years old. Law represents the analytical side of my nature, and politics represents the gregarious side.

What I love about the legislature is the interplay of people and issues. It takes both consensus-building with people and attention to the nitty-gritty in legislation. I am drawn primarily to human-service issues, an area that I have always enjoyed and gotten recognition for. I think "doing good" is very much a part of me, that is, the Puritan ethic. That was my parents' value too. They always participated in community affairs. Not that I'm compulsive about working; I don't feel a bit guilty about lying in bed on a Saturday morning and reading a book. I feel that my own personal pleasure is deserved.

There is very little that I do now that I don't enjoy. I don't have as much time to cook or do things around the house, so when I do, I value my domestic tasks more than I used to.

Even though I know I could manage my life financially and professionally, I think I would be just terrible at living without my husband. I don't think I would be able to bear the loneliness.

I wouldn't want to be anybody other than who I am—a woman, and middle-aged, and all the rest.

CHAPTER 12

Mary—Penis Envy, American Style

I had eight children in the space of eleven years. And I never wanted to conceive. . . . When I passed my Ph.D. exams, I shouted at the top of my lungs, "I did it! I did it! And I did it without any fucking man!"

Although Mary is forty-one and has eight children, she looks like a teenager with her petite, blue-jeaned figure and her long, blond pageboy. Her voice is soft and childlike.

While Mary was at home with her children, playing the traditional role to the hilt, she was only minimally fulfilled. She would have preferred playing her husband's role—that of a brainy scientist. As a child Mary was cast in the role of princess while her brother was king. Her lifelong envy is of a man's position, not of his penis.

Mary has been married for twenty-one years. She lives in a pretty suburban neighborhood. Her home is spacious, comfortable, and decorated with art prints. Mary is a solitary woman who often spends her time with books when her husband and children are absent.

* * *

MARY

I NEVER WANTED to have children. I was pregnant when I got married. I thought I would do more with my life, but I had eight children in the space of eleven years. And I never wanted to conceive.

I believed that birth control was wrong and that if children came, you must take care of them. That was the principle on which my husband and I were both raised, and we never once questioned or discussed it. I don't believe it anymore, but it's too late.

I did not enjoy bringing up babies. I found it frustrating. The only part of child-rearing that I consciously enjoyed was reading to my kids when they were little. The rest I did because I felt that I should. There must have been moments that I enjoyed, and I did like my kids better as they got older. I also knew that I *should* love them or they would turn out badly, and I did love them. I felt sorry for them because they were so unlucky to have me for a mother. I overcompensated by cuddling, smiling, and talking to them. If someone had offered to do these things for me, I would have been glad to be relieved of my role.

When I was in Greece, estranged from everyone and having a breakdown, my second son was born. When I thought of suicide, I knew that baby needed a mother. Just loving him helped me stay together, and he is the child that I prefer above the others. My oldest daughter, I have six, has learning disabilities, so I kind of worry about what is going to happen to her. She's only a year behind, but she can't read very well. She has a marvelous father though and some very unselfish teachers. Most of my other kids are relatively bright. I just have so many girls, and the trouble with my girls is that I know what they're thinking.

My relationship with my mother was pretty bad. When I was little, she didn't pick me up when I cried, and I was fed on schedule. I had Dr. Spock to tell me different. My first memory is of my brother biting me and my mother telling me not to make such a fuss. He was eighteen months younger, but my brother was king. There are certain values in my family that make boys more important.

Then, like me, my mother had all these kids that she didn't want. She was a proper Irish woman, and I was kind of wild during my adolescence. I had intercourse with two different boys when I was sixteen. She was pregnant at thirty-eight and again at forty, and I was an unsympathetic, lousy daughter. I have a lot of guilt about it. When she was pregnant, I would say, "Well, it's your fault." That comes back to haunt me. My mother still cannot show love for her children except by buying things for them.

I think my father was probably loving. I have difficulty remembering my early childhood. He encouraged you to be bright and obedient, to read, and to get good marks. Maybe he encouraged excelling a bit too much. You had an obligation to be interested in politics and in the community you lived in. He is himself a politician and a businessman, and he wanted you to be a leader. I pleased him very much by taking an interest in politics.

My father is a very competitive man. I've tried not to encourage competitiveness in my kids, but otherwise I've passed on his message, just not quite so heavy. And I've added concern for people, a value that comes from my mother.

My parents had bad times. My mother was mentally ill in her thirties, and I know that my father had affairs. My mother was not a happy woman. I did my share of contributing to it, too. I was not an easy daughter for my mother to raise. Until I was thirty, I blamed my mother for everything. Now I see that it was a fifty–fifty proposition. My father had faults too. He didn't handle my mother or his problems in the wisest fashion. My parents live a few miles away now, but we see each other only rarely.

Henry, my husband, and I took it for granted that we would be faithful to each other. I think it was easier for us to discuss sex in our early years than in our middle years, because now there is such an overload of other things. At the beginning we were both very interested in sex and very active. We enjoyed very good sexual relations even though I didn't always have orgasm. We thought we were very close, but now I'm not sure. I began to fear pregnancy and then I would be nauseous during pregnancy. We set up destructive patterns because of so many children and the fear of more. We also drifted apart because Henry wasn't home a great deal.

He was working on his Ph.D., and I was totally housebound. He went to school at night and tried to save Sundays for us. That lasted for about five years and then it got worse. I thought about leaving him, but it was impossible with all those kids. I was infuriated, and I still have a lot of anger. I was trapped. Intellectually I saw what he was doing and I approved, because it meant that someday we could have the kind of life we wanted. Besides Henry was very bright, and he should do all these things. By the same token, I was very bright too, and I was stuck home with all these kids. It set up this thing where I was very angry with him, but I shouldn't be, right? And he felt very guilty towards me, and he should have, right? All that has affected the way we treat each other, even today.

Henry would try to handle everything except the children and the house. He would pay all the bills and try to just protect me from life. Maybe it was a good thing. I didn't have any energy, so I was glad for anything he would do for me. But I never grew up, and we really drifted apart in a big way.

Then Henry took a post for one year in Greece. We packed up

seven kids, the oldest being eleven and although I didn't want to go, I went. It was one of the worst years of my life, and I became pregnant with our eighth child. I had an image of myself as this nice girl who would do as she was supposed to do, who was also intelligent and understood why her husband had to get an advanced degree. But I skirted very close to a nervous breakdown. My self-esteem was at an all-time low when we were in Greece. I had all kinds of fears, all kinds of no-nos. Those started before we went to Greece, but they got worse. I didn't learn the language, and that was supposed to be my province. I always help the kids with their English assignments, and my husband helps them with the math and science. We both tried to learn the language, and when Henry surpassed me, I stopped trying. And, oh, that hurt so! Isn't that silly? But it did. I just lost my feelings of self-confidence. Probably the thing that saved me from total depression was that I got angry.

When we came home, I started back to school. Then Henry decided to move to Berkeley. I didn't want to. I was a bitch! I knew how to move to and enter a new community, but I refused to do it for a whole year. What I didn't know at the time was that it was a new and hard experience for him too. We had a real bad time from the time I was twenty-nine to the time I was thirty-six. Our sex life went from normal, but with my being a little apprehensive about pregnancy, to hectic, to no sex.

After I had my hysterectomy I became very loving and my husband became very impotent for a year and a half. He's not anymore. He refused any psychiatric help. At the time I was just beginning to get into the Woman's Movement, and I was beginning to verbalize my anger. At the same time, Henry wasn't sure that he was cut out to be a scientist. To my knowledge he has not been unfaithful to me, but he wasn't talking about all the things that were worrying him.

I was and am and probably always will be in competition with my husband. I would never compete with him in his field, of course. I should be a better writer, and I'm finding out that he's a better writer. I was always the one who made our good friends and I was the one who took our friendships seriously, but since I've been in graduate school, he's the one who's social and I'm not.

I was raised in a real competitive family. Sometimes I feel it with the kids when they seem to prefer Henry. My girls go through a period of thinking their father is the best man in the world. I'll hear one of them say to her girl friend, after her father has said no, "Well, my mother won't let me do it." I'm the negative and he's the positive parent. Henry is the visiting good guy, while I'm stuck with all the hard realities.

My husband always knew that I wasn't happy in my role as housekeeper. I don't even like to cook. I have a daughter who is a marvelous cook, and Henry praises her to the skies. That hurts sometimes. He has appreciated me as a mother and as a lover when all was going well. As for sharing, he was and is an excellent father, and he has never been averse to pitching in. Now that I am going to school we share, and, although I have girls old enough to help, my husband cooks one night a week. He does all the grocery shopping. I have not always appreciated him. We have both taken each other for granted too often.

It used to be that if I didn't have sex a certain number of times a week, I felt rejected. Now when our sex is good, all is well. I'm prepared to be even more active as we get older. Right now my sexual image is not as important to me as it used to be, but when we're sexually "together" the little things don't bother me.

Basically, in money matters and life-style matters and raising children, we agree. Our greatest area of conflict has been how much of my life needs to be devoted to the role of mother. There are other things we need to work out. One of my kids said, "I don't know why you two got married. You have nothing in common." That really applies to our free time. When I started back to school, I didn't have the energy to go out much and Henry started going places without me. I got scared. I was afraid he didn't love me any more.

My husband's opinion of me, when it was negative, used to destroy me. I need a lot of positive feedback. If I don't get it, I'm easily shot down. But during the last few years I've been building myself up in my head and deciding that Henry is wrong when he is negative about me. Obviously it still bothers me.

Henry was happy to have me go back to school. School has done more for me than anything. I've proved myself to myself and to other people. At home I always fought being *just* mother and wife. I knew that I had to be, but it was damned hard, and I didn't always succeed. I refused to learn to sew. I had sitters come so that I could escape and read.

I think Henry is in sort of a male menopause. He bought himself a red convertible. He's spending more money than he ever used to. He spends more on his clothes, and he tries out his personality on young women too. If I said anything to him, he would deny it. As long as he doesn't sleep with them, it's OK.

Two years ago I fell in love with somebody else. The man that I fell in love with was my best friend's husband. He found out that his wife had cheated on him, and he came over here for mothering, and the next thing I knew we were going out for drinks. We didn't sleep together. It was adolescent. We were each other's escape. But his wife found out about it. It was a mess. I felt guilty about being a bad friend, but even though I lost a friend, I am not sorry about what happened, because I obviously needed the love and attention so badly. I needed to know that I was a desirable woman and that someone wanted to be with me all the time.

Going to school has left me less time for my friends. That is one unhappy place in my life right now. It is the first time in fifteen years that I haven't had a very close girl friend. I valued friends so highly and now that I have betrayed my friend, I feel friendship is a scary thing. Emotionally I know that I overreact. If I fail in some area I just won't enter that area again. I know that's silly.

My mother always told me that I was lazy, and laziness has always been part of my self-image. It didn't occur to me until I had gone back to school that I worked harder than a lot of people. So I realized that I'm not lazy about things that I like to do. I'm more sedentary than lazy. My husband has a very high energy level, and that contributed to my feeling of being lazy.

I am not too self-conscious about being middle-aged even though most of the people in school are much younger. If I could be young, the only thing I would want would be those love affairs. I wouldn't want to go through my ignorance of what goes on between people or relive any of the pain. I think I know how to love, but I have my hang-ups, and there have been times when I was amazed that anybody could like me.

I am worried about my survival skills. Having lived among so many people for the last twenty-two years has diminished my ability to live alone. I may have to go to England and live by myself to finish my Ph.D. dissertation. So far I have put off taking professional trips that I could have taken, because I was afraid. I have many survival skills to develop.

In my twenties and thirties I wasn't glad to be a woman because it was so obvious that if I had been a man and I had reversed roles with Henry, I would have been doing what I wanted to do. Today I'm sort of glad to be a woman because I am now doing what I want to do while most people my age or a little older don't have a whole bunch of well-defined goals and I do; I want to write my dissertation, do research, and get a job. I'm lucky that while many of my men friends have already achieved whatever it was they wanted to achieve, they're in a rut, or in some cases they're in a male menopause and want to change their family situation, while I am at the beginning of my career.

The biggest moment of my life was when I learned I had passed my Ph.D. exams. I was alone in the house and I poured myself a drink and shouted at the top of my lungs, "I did it! I did it! And I did it without any fucking man!"

CHAPTER 13

Phyl–Let Me Lean

A lot of my own image was built up from the image I thought Pete had of me, his acceptance of me and my talents. So when he took them away I was crushed, really crushed.

Phyl is a young-looking, forty-five-year-old woman with white hair and a trim, athletic body. She touches people a great deal. She pats a cheek, squeezes an arm, and is friendly and extroverted. She threw herself and her feelings into the interview. Nevertheless, she was thoughtful and paused frequently to consider her answers to questions.

A gifted child of humble parents, she moved easily into the middle class, as her mother was anxious for her to do. She has a master's degree in library science. She was married for nineteen years and is the mother of four children. When her husband asked for a divorce six years ago, Phyl was surprised, hurt, and confused. She still is. Now on her own, divorced for two years, she feels lucky to have a job as a librarian. Greater independence is her goal.

* * *

PHYL

I THINK I've grown up an awful lot in the last six years. Crises have a way of doing that for you. Six years ago was the beginning of the end of my marriage. Pete was so attractive, intelligent, talented, and we had all these memories we shared. I thought, "What does this man want? What makes him want to leave? I just don't understand." Even now, I don't know what went into this upheaval.

It started when I contradicted him in front of the children at the supper table. Pete went upstairs and packed his bags. This was his reason! He said, "Phyl, I'm finished. I've had enough. I'm leaving." It was a complete shock. I became hysterical! I couldn't believe it!

But he didn't go then. He changed his mind. He didn't actually leave for four years. He said later that he stayed because I needed him all that time, that I would have fallen apart without him. I think it was really harder having him stay. I had to live with his lack of loving me. There it was, day after day, and I couldn't change it. He had cut off any kind of intimate relation. I was a nun for five years. When he cut off our sex life I said, "Well, all right. If this is what you want, I'll do it." I never complained, but I was irritable and I was taking it out on my children.

I tried everything. Pete said that I'd better go see a psychiatrist because it was my problem. I did go for two years, always waiting for him to come, too, but he never did. My psychiatrist said, "No man will leave without a reason." It's true that at that time Pete hired an assistant and he married her two weeks after our divorce.

Besides my marriage troubles, I had to get another job. I had just finished being a temporary replacement for another librarian. Pete said I had to get a full-time job. It turns out he was making my future secure.

I did get a new job but it just added to my anxieties. A lot of my own image was built up from the image I thought Pete had of me, his acceptance of me and my talents. So when he took it away I was crushed, really crushed. The doctor put me on Valium. I was allergic to it. I started itching. I had to take oatmeal baths twice a day. I was having trouble with diarrhea, my periods went haywire, I was getting boils, I had infections in my nose, my back gave me trouble. I was a walking psychosomatic case and I resented being so unhealthy. I kept thinking, "Is this going to get worse and worse, and I'm going to end up a cripple or something?" I can remember going to the store and standing in front of the dairy counter and I couldn't make up my mind whether to buy American or Swiss cheese. It got to that.

I had thought Pete and I shared the same values, humor, ideas, but, looking back, maybe I was wrong. I thought we got along very well our first years. But maybe I've blocked things. When he left, I talked to my matron of honor, and she said, "Do you remember that first year you were married you told me it was very frustrating to be married to a man who was always right?" You know, I had forgotten.

After the first year I never had any close woman friends. Pete was everything. I dumped everything on him. He had said that he always wanted to have a younger sister, so I thought he enjoyed my being dependent on him. I enjoyed having him like a big brother to me. I don't know when or why I became less important to him.

I see now that the same thing happened with the children. He was a very good father when the children were little. He liked them a lot then. They were eager to please, you know. He couldn't understand why, as they got older, there were disagreements and dissension. To him, arguments meant anger, and he could not handle anger. Not in himself, and not in his children. I learned that. And I played the role. I was acquiescent. I was brought up to please everyone but myself. Pleasing myself was considered selfish.

But as the children got older I would joke a lot with them and we'd argue and throw ideas around. I always liked discourse. I like ideas. But Pete felt we should all agree. He isn't the type to say, "My ideas are better than yours." Really, he comes across as a very quiet, considerate, reserved person. Maybe we overwhelmed him with our constant bantering. It got so he was not there for me to bounce off my ideas. I'd come home from a meeting all fired up and he wasn't that interested. He had his opinions and he didn't want to discuss it. He'd say, "You can't change things in the world, so why are you knocking your head against a wall?" I never got feedback when I told him my feelings about things.

I know everything wasn't always perfect early in the marriage. I was discontented to some extent. I resented the fact that these children were so close and all I seemed to be doing was being mother. For years I was very, very tired. Exhausted. I didn't even have the time or energy to pursue my most satisfying hobby, which is music. All during high school and college I played the violin in one orchestra or another. It meant a great deal to me and I missed it during those years, maybe more than I realized.

And I had this trouble with my back. That bothered me. I'd tell all my troubles, physical and otherwise, to Pete. I considered him my friend. Maybe he didn't like to hear? And when I went back to being a librarian, I was anxious about it. I got bogged down in the nitty-gritty and put in too much extra time, instead of making simple decisions. I brought too much work home. I had wanted to have a year of rest and freedom after all four kids were in school all day. But my mother and husband thought I should get right to work. I didn't argue with them.

When Pete left he said, "You were becoming too much like my mother, with all your little illnesses and things." If there is one woman I am not like in this world, it's his mother. No way am I like his mother. I want to give her credit where credit is due. She had a hard life and she certainly brought up the man I fell in love with, but we had nothing in common, intellectually or otherwise.

So why did he say that? I do cry easily. I cry at B movies on the TV. I think he associated that sort of thing with his mother. Sort of maybe being helpless and sentimental.

Another comment he made was that he felt like he was doing all the giving. I said, "That's very strange, because that's the way I have felt." I *was* very dependent. He took care of all the money. He put my paycheck in the bank and I always asked him when I needed money. One time I had a lot for Christmas shopping and I lost my wallet. I felt just terrible about it. Of course, Pete was disgusted and never gave me that much money again.

Pete and I never could talk about it, but another big problem was our sex life. We had been engaged for four years and during most of that time our petting was pretty heavy. A couple of times we decided we ought to cut down on the petting because we were getting so emotionally involved and there was no place to go. No privacy anywhere. We brought each other to orgasm but no intercourse until much later. When we did finally have intercourse, it was nothing. As far as I was concerned, nothing! I thought, "What is this? It's supposed to be so great. What happened? This is nothing!" I had all kinds of sex manuals out of the library, and there was the written word: Technique was all, and it would bring us to simultaneous orgasm. Really, if I had a hang-up, that was it. I always enjoyed everything, all of it, and I was normally orgasmic. I mean, I would have orgasms, but there was this thing about it was supposed to be together or something was wrong. It had to be like the book. Now I know that's ridiculous. There are wide variations.

So, there was always this anxiety about performance, for both of us. Sometimes he would have trouble keeping his erection, or he couldn't control his ejaculation, and I would think it was my fault that I was not responding quickly enough. To have him whispering "No, no, no" in my ear was not the most romantic thing in the world. "There have got to be other ways of doing this, Pete!" But I never said that. I've read that there are some techniques to improve control, but I never had the opportunity to try them with my husband.

Still, in spite of these sex worries, I thought I was attractive to Pete. If our sex life hadn't been as important as it was, maybe we would have broken up sooner. It was one of the good things in our marriage. It was one place where we were close and affectionate and sometimes very successful. I have a lot of good memories.

I was always the more affectionate one. I'd hug him and kiss him. I think maybe what he liked about me at first was that I was more open, bubbly. His family was not demonstrative at all. Looking back, I had thought that our backgrounds were similar, but they really weren't. Ethnically and economically they were, but the upbringing was different, much different. If I were to use one word to describe his family it would be "dead." When we went to visit, he would end up sitting behind a newspaper while I carried on a conversation with his mother, which was really very difficult. His was a family that had no fun.

By contrast my grandparents and parents were always having a good time. They went to ethnic dances and weddings and the kids would always come. My mother and I played the violin and my father played the accordion and everybody would sing. And people would get very excited about politics and religion. I used to stay awake nights listening to all these stories and arguments. They were great storytellers. But my husband's life was nothing like that.

My father was a baker, a jolly, happy-go-lucky type. He'd take us to the zoo and the parks and the ball games. He wasn't involved much in bringing up his children, but he loved me and I feel he did the very best he could. He was always proud of me, proud of my accomplishments. I was the first girl in either family who went to college. My parents were both proud of that.

My mother was the dominant one in the family. She would say to my father, "Why don't you better yourself?" This always bothered me. He had an accent all his life and he got pretty heavy and sometimes he'd drink a little too much at parties. He'd sing these risqué songs and my mother would just die. He was just having a good time and so was everybody, but she made me feel uncomfortable about it. I wasn't sure which side to be on.

My mother is a perfectionist. Her philosophy was like, "If you practice a little more on the violin you can be a concert violinist." That is not true! You also need ambition and a certain kind of confidence. Underneath I was not a confident person. I'm much more confident today, but I will never get rid of that little person inside me who has diarrhea fifty-eight times if she has to make a certain kind of phone call.

Mom always wanted me to be popular, to be happier than she was, to move into a better class. She thought that with education I could do anything. She herself is a wonderful cook and she sews beautifully but she has never taken pride in her own abilities. She wanted me to be brilliant and accomplished and yet she said that a woman's husband should be her whole life. I could never quite please her. The house wasn't neat enough. I didn't work hard enough. The children should do this and that.

When Pete left she was sure it was my fault. She wasn't supportive at all. It had to be something wrong with me, my housekeeping or my cooking. She came to the therapist with me because we'd see each other and it would just lead to crying and screaming. "You're always picking on me, Mother. I'm not a child anymore." The therapy helped some. She laid off me and I backed away too. She's seventy years old and she's not going to change just because I want her to. I know I've been overreactive the last few years. Very thin-skinned. The two people I loved most in my life were the two people who put me down. Of course all this was upsetting her too. I'm still not close to her the way she wants, though, as friends. The few times I have opened up I felt she wasn't supportive so I just can't let myself.

The children aren't very close to Pete. I must say I've been angry with him and I've laid a lot on my kids. But I'm better now than I was. The youngest is the most torn. I wouldn't say that the kids were uncritical but they've stayed with me. They say, "We don't want to get in the middle, Mom." And, "You've really got to find someone else and forget Daddy." How can you forget twenty years of your life? Their attitude is, it's over, so forget. "He's not worth it," they'd say. Maybe I want their sympathy more than anything else. Lately, they said something that surprised me. They said I was the strong one, not him. Yet I was always sure it was the opposite. I guess I was mistaken about myself. I don't think I realized the strengths I do have.

If I had a wish it would be that we could have lived more in the "now." Somehow, we did not take time to enjoy the present; we were always involved in the cleaning and the cooking and doing things, and before we knew it the children were grown up. We rarely took the time to just relax and enjoy the kids and each other.

There would be a lot less bitterness on my part if Pete and I could have talked through some of these things. We probably would have split anyway but, at least, I'd feel better about the whole thing. It was part of me not to be angry or to argue with him. Pete would say, "You don't love if you're angry." If I told him my feelings I never got feedback. It was like trying to reach a ghost.

I've had supportive friends. That's meant a lot to me. There are divorced women who find that their friends absolutely disappear. You need something like Parents Without Partners, no matter what you think of it. They keep your spirits up during this crisis. It amazes me how many women come through in one piece because they're practically falling apart all over the place. I know how it is. I've been down in the depths and I'm never going there again.

I've thought about marrying again. It doesn't have to be marriage. It doesn't have to mean living together. I'm kind of game for anything. But I would like someone I could count on. Someone on whose preservation list I would be high, to quote a book I read recently. I think I have a lot to offer. I mean, I'm fairly bright, I'm warm, I'm friendly. I can be a good listener but I also would like someone to listen to me. A person who is sensitive to others' feelings. I am, I think. Most of the time. I really try to be.

It's very hard to meet men, at least intellectually stimulating men. I've joined a couple of groups and maybe some will turn up. I've recently gone to a few of the bars. I was very uncomfortable at first. I'm still not comfortable with the whole thing, actually. One friend says to me, "Come on now. We have to make a concerted effort, every Friday." That gets to me. I just can't do that kind of thing easily.

Music has always been my major hobby. It's a great source of satisfaction and some pride to me. I recently went back to playing the violin. The orchestra I play in is a challenging one. I might even meet a man through the group.

I haven't really grappled with the thought of still being alone in a few years when my kids are really gone. I have the skills, now, to do it; that's no problem. But there is part of me that would like to be taken care of, even now. I couldn't live as someone else's chattel. I've become too independent for that. But it would be nice to have someone to curl around in the night.

CHAPTER 14

Debbie–Hollywood Revisited

I have often wished I had less sex drive. I might have accomplished something in this world. Actually sex is one of the things I'm pretty good at. I'm proud of that, but I think it's nothing to be proud of, if you understand what I mean.

Fifty-year-old Debbie is petite and cute. She has a boyish figure, curly red-brown hair, and several thousand freckles. She is ebullient and a marathon, nonstop talker.

A product of a comfortable, small-town family, Debbie aspired to the position of the happy, financially comfortable, American housewife that she had read about in women's magazines. She was partially rewarded: Motherhood satisfied her, and for thirty years she pleased her well-to-do, easily pleased husband. But after her two sons left home and married, Debbie felt incomplete. Like many housewives, she dreamed of being a successful, brilliant Mrs. America while simultaneously enjoying a lover who would cross the moat, scale the walls, and take her to another land where they could live happily ever after. She acted out part of her dream which was followed by a period of depression. Now, five years after the affair, Debbie is realistically trying to explore another part of the dream.

* * *

DEBBIE

I HAVE HARDLY any gray hair, hardly any wrinkles, and frankly I think I look a lot younger than I am. I know it's just my particular physical type; auburn, freckly types seem to age well, don't you think? Anyway, I'm pleased to look younger because I feel young, except that my stomach is getting a little flabby, and my exercises don't seem to be tightening it up. I just never really felt grown up, whatever that means.

When I was little, I didn't see much of my father because he was so busy pursuing his career. I think he expected to be President of the U.S. He was politicking all the time, running for things, glad-handing people, doing favors, giving speeches. He was very popular, and I'm surprised he didn't go as far as we all thought he would. My mother seemed to worship him, and so did his parents, and my aunts and uncles, and in fact everybody I ever had anything to do with. He was the most important person in town, even if it was a no-account, nowhere town. I was pretty sure my dad was the smartest, best-looking, most important man in the world. I wanted to be just like him, and I wanted him to pay attention to me. When he occasionally did, I was thrilled. I think my father loved me very much although he wasn't at all demonstrative. He would take me with him to meetings, to political picnics or to celebrations of one kind or another. I was bored and ignored most of the time but I felt useful and proud to be my daddy's daughter. People were nice to me because of him. I wanted to make him proud of me, so I was very good. I guess this continued until my puberty began.

I was more interested in my father's attention when I was little than I was in my mother's, and anyway Mother was always out at a meeting or leading a discussion or planning a fund-raiser. Besides the domestic arts of cooking and sewing, our maids taught me what clothes were stylish, how to put on makeup, how to catch a man, how to make my breasts bigger, and what movie stars were immoral. I heard *True Story* out loud, heard what Hedy Lamarr did in *Ecstasy,* and got help in learning to smoke when I was fourteen from the downstairs maid of our "Upstairs, Downstairs" home. I often lived in a world my parents didn't tell me about, one they ignored just as they ignored me.

From the moment I have a memory I was very interested in sex. I was removed from a sex romp of some kind when I was around three. I was whisked off and scolded for my curiosity. My curiosity was not killed, however. My childhood was replete with running naked, playing doctor, examining bodies, and even group masturbation.

Subsequently in high school I necked my head off as much as I could. At the same time I began getting poor report cards, playing hookey, and staying out late drinking with fast boys. My adolescence was bubbling over. An attempt to lose my virginity ended in pain and failure, or I might have disgraced my parents with a baby.

Coinciding with the beginning of adolescence I began feeling neglected by my daddy. He didn't take me anywhere anymore, and it seems to me that all I got from him was a pat on the head in the evening, if he was at home. My older brother and sister got his attention by "talk." The three of them discussed things: the latest political moves by Dad's opponents, the Depression, Roosevelt—oh, how they all hated Roosevelt—Europe, the world. I felt left out and stupid. I tried over the next few years to get into this act and to regain some place in my father's life, but all I got was put-downs, and playful references to my being cute, bouncy, and brainless.

My mother wasn't part of that triumvirate; she was left out too. The difference between my mother and myself is that she had a perfectly good opinion of herself, never mind what her family might have thought. She only wanted everyone to be happy and successful, and not take up too much of her time.

The emphasis on "success" is part of our family pattern, and scared me personally. I have always wanted to reject the whole idea, but I know I haven't. I know I want it for myself, and I admire successful people out of proportion to their desserts. It's jealousy of course. But success would mean approval, too. I have tried to avoid my parents' snobbery, and I have gone to the extreme in my lifetime of so rejecting snobbery that I have found myself with impossible bores and nitwits as friends. It's still a dilemma for me, but I'm trying to give that up and not make friends with people who are flattered to have my friendship because they are so limited and dull that they think anybody who cracks a joke or uses polysyllabic words must be a genius.

I always thought of my mother as dumb until I was thirty years old. I was going to an analyst and talking about my childhood, and I came to realize that my mother was much more admirable than I had thought—she managed to keep independently self-sufficient and was admired and liked by intelligent people—and my father was much less admirable, less smart, less everything. That was a very liberating experience, that reassessment of my parents. And yet, I still resent what happened to me, resent my parents' neglect, and resent my brother and sister.

Once about ten years ago I tried to tell my family what it was like when I was growing up, but they all laughed and said, "Don't be silly dear. We all loved you. You were our cute little mascot. And now why don't you sing a song for us with your pretty little voice?" My brother and sister are very successful professionals, by the way, and I'm nothing. I'm not even determined to make a success of my latest venture, a coffeehouse for young people. I want to like mad. I'd love to prove to the world that I'm not incapable of success. But I think I'll fail. My parents are dead so it doesn't matter to them. I can't impress them. The fact is, I suppose my brother and sister would be perfectly happy to see me successful. They don't really think that much about me; they don't have these patterns ingrained in them that make success or failure important. I know I have to do things for myself now. Just for me. Not for them.

You may wonder how I went to college, and how I managed to graduate if I was so stupid. Well, everything is relative. I'm really not dumb at all as it turns out. It's just that I think I am. I'm not sure how I can hold these two ideas in my mind at the same time, but I do. It's like the other contradictory ideas I seem to have, such as that I should be a good, loving wife and at the same time I should have all the lovers and all the freedom I want. Can you believe that I resist stealing from stores?

I think I eventually ignored and rejected my parents, but I'm confused because I don't think I ever became a real person. I didn't reject them enough to be able to create a new personality. I stayed tied into their view somehow. I've never quite integrated my little-girl self with my wild-sexual self, my wish-for-fame self, and my decent self. Now that I'm, ugh, middle-aged, I feel that I should be more grown-up. I should be resigned to being that decent person. I think I am resigned actually, but it's only possible by allowing myself to pretend otherwise some of the time. I mean I fantasize that I'm starting a wonderful, thrilling new affair, or that I become a great success in something or other. Everybody would be jealous of me and think I'm super.

I have been married for thirty years and for the first fifteen, I was an "ideal" wife. I loved being a mother, and people do compliment me on my grown children. Would these people blame me if they were rotten? Are children really the creation of their parents? I often wish I had a daughter. I imagine the relationship being very close and loving. I love to see mothers and daughters being chums. I realize that it might not have turned out like that for me, but in my secret heart I envision a lovely young woman, a bit like me, who loves me and understands me and thinks I'm a wonderful mother, and who would be happy to let me live vicariously through her life, enjoying her triumphs which would, of course, be numerous, and crying over her sorrows, which would be only enough to build character, not enough to scar or embitter her.

Being a mother was my main occupation for most of my married life. I learned to do a lot of things as a spin-off from motherhood, and this coffeehouse project that I'm in now results from my feeling that I can relate to young people.

I've never had a real job, a paid job, and this is something I'm ashamed of. I know that I've been useful as a volunteer, but I hate being asked, "What do you do?" and then getting that "Oh" of dismissal when I say, "I'm a volunteer this or that." Now that my project has business aspects, my stock has risen.

I've known for decades that the American woman was given a big, phony myth about how she was supposed to be wooed by a handsome Robert Taylor type who was dying to make mad sexual love to her, but was too pure of heart to corrupt a decent all-American, freckle-faced sweetie who was saving herself for marriage to the right guy, even though almost swept off her platform shoes by some cad, a daring adventurer. She'd come to her senses and see that that suave, sexy cad would have turned her into a tigress, for he was a man who didn't know the "finer things of life." But he would have left her weeping with five kids in a cold-water flat, after he had spent all their money. The women's magazines promised that women were tempted by a "bad guy" and saved for a "good guy" by some fluke of fate or by another woman's sad experience. The "good guy" would give her five adorable kids, a lot of sweet kisses, and her very own bank account. She would smile on her Christmas card surrounded by her grateful and adoring family. She would take courses in macrame, or maybe painting on velvet. She couldn't think of a nicer cookbook than *Joy of*.

I'm saying that we were sold a bill of goods, and half the women my age don't know it yet. I don't pity them, heavens no! If they still believe it, they're lucky. Hubby swats her behind as he dissolves into his chair to watch TV and congratulates himself on having a wife who loves him enough to keep the lint out of his underwear and the cat hairs out of his dinner. He doesn't run out of toilet paper or cheese or beer or golf balls. He has someone who cares.

I was going to be one of those *Ladies' Home Journal* wives, and I tried hard. I think I was good at it. Jason, my husband, was happy.

I really think so. You might call it ignorant bliss, but I thought he was happy enough. I guess I'll tell you about him now. He was a good husband and a good father, and there is no reason for me to complain about him. He loved me and still does and he's even encouraging me to make a success out of a small complex I've bought into in order to change it into a coffeehouse. I have done my job as wife and mother so well that Jason has never known that a ferment was going on in my brain. I never complained about anything.

Jason is good-looking, smart, successful, everything *Redbook* talks about as the perfect man. But he's a little remote and not exactly fun-loving, and can you imagine, I was more interested in sex than he was? He just wanted a few minutes in bed and then he was satisfied. But I taught him how to satisfy me. Then that became a routine. He's great for routine. I had thought that all men were passionate brutes who had to be tamed, whose desire couldn't be stopped. Well, Jason was one of those guys who have such quiet, quick orgasms that you aren't sure anything has happened. And once in a while was enough for him. Strange, I thought, but what did I know? I took to masturbation because I didn't want to upset him and seem to be overdemanding.

After fifteen years of performing the roles of good mother and ideal wife I became active in community politics, but Jason was busy and in some ways we began to live separate lives.

I was becoming more and more dissatisfied with our sex life. I wanted to have another experience. I was meeting lots of men and some of them seemed available. There were a few abortive attempts and a few short infatuations but nothing ever really happened. I was embarrassed to get involved with these brainy, important people. I thought I'd be rejected when they found out I wasn't so smart and wasn't so beautiful with my clothes off. I hate to admit this but I wore padded bras in those days. No more! I'm free to be me!

I found Jim, an ordinary, unhappily married man, whose only passion was football. I knew him from the PTA, and the truth is that I felt superior to him. He was going nowhere in his life, and we flirted at a meeting one night.

I went to talk to him the next day and said, "Hey, what was that? Do you want to forget it or shall we go on from there?" We went on. I told him I was ripe for picking, and if he didn't want me

I was going to find someone else. He said, "I'll be damned, my exact sentiments!"

It was a surprise to him that I would throw myself at him. He had thought of me as off-limits, and the novelty of my assault took him by the balls, you could say, and we made love like two suddenly uncaged tigers. It was sensational! An affair! He had tried to have an affair for ages—gotten his hands in the bras and pants of half the town. But for some reason or other—we liked to think he was waiting for me—he could never enjoy these experiences. Mostly, he couldn't even get his prick up for them. Something turned him off. Well, I turned him on. I think I figured it out after a while. I think he couldn't stand women who were very demanding or critical, and he couldn't stand them if they were abundantly giving, or smothering. Maybe it doesn't leave too many suitable types in between, but somehow I was exactly in the niche. And he became mad for me. And I returned the madness. And we fed one another's egos and ids for five long years. No, the last year was not the same. But more about that when I come to it.

It started out as a sex affair, and became a love affair. Our sex arrangements were often ridiculous, you might even consider them sordid, but we never did. We made love in the woods, at garbage dumps, in parking lots, in private driveways, in broad daylight, and at 2 A.M. All those public places were terribly risky. I know I must have been crazy but I guess it was a measure of my passion. I was willing to take very big risks, and so was he, don't forget, to feel the thrill of touching and loving one another. It makes me weep to talk about it. We also went to motels but it was too expensive to go more than once a week. We had one favorite with two huge mirrors on two walls. Years ago I couldn't look at my body and now here I was watching it in the mirror. He adored that, so why shouldn't I? The motels were great because we had three or four hours to just love it up. I felt the best I've ever felt in my whole life while I was making love with Jim. He thought I was a super sex-queen and couldn't figure out how I got that way. I don't know. He just somehow brought it out.

I used to be ashamed of my body. I despised it utterly and didn't even look at it. I undressed so that I couldn't see it. I had a few cruel remarks made about my small breasts, and I was absolutely certain that no man would ever find me attractive. For years I imagined how I'd live if I just had beautiful tits. I'd still trade my pair in for a bigger and better model if I could. But slowly I discovered that there are men who actually don't like those enormous jobs. I'm amazed, but now I can actually walk around naked and feel good about it. You can't imagine what a change that is. I think only another "flat lady" would understand.

I thought Jim must be kidding for a long time but he really seemed to mean it when he said that he loved my breasts. I just lucked out with him on that score I guess. Maybe he had something a little peculiar going for him. The fact is, he was turned on by very young girls, nymphets or young teens. He used to pretend that I was his ward, his friend's niece or something like that. We did a lot of funny, sexy scenes where we pretended things. Things we wouldn't ever really do in life. I mean he wouldn't really pick up a nymphet and teach her to screw. And I wouldn't really work in a brothel. But we played games like that and had terrific fun. With him I did just about everything I've ever heard about or read about or seen that was sexually appealing to me. Not everything a person could do, God, no. We weren't turned on by sadomasochism, for example, although we pretended it a few times, without really hurting one another. And we would pretend that there were people watching or others there in bed with us. I don't remember how we got started on this sort of thing, but it was amusing and exciting. Sometimes we'd read porno stuff together, and once we went to a porno shop, but we were too embarrassed to buy anything. I don't mean that we never had plain, ordinary sex. Sure, millions of times. Well, hundreds. We weren't dependent on kinky sex. It was just fun. Sometimes I'd let him tear my clothes off. We always laughed about these kinky things. I suppose the change in attitudes in the last few years made it possible and easy for us to indulge our fantasies.

I'll never forget the time when my feet were sticking out the window of Jim's car, and I could see his white ass pumping away, and I was about to scream with pleasure, when up drove a truck, and two guys started hollering at us, egging us on. It broke the spell. But just for the moment. After those guys left I had the most fantastic orgasm known to women. I damn near flipped out of the car. It took me a half hour to cool down so I could go home and cook dinner and act like a proper, normal, American housewife.

We thought we were very special and that no one else shared the kind of sexual rapport we had. I suppose that's ridiculous. But there was a magic between us. It's something I'll always treasure. I could lie in bed with him for hours and hours and never be tired of him. He made me feel totally accepted, totally sexy, and totally beautiful. And I guess I did the same for him. It was perfect, just perfect. The sexual ecstasy was incredible. I felt as if all my dreams had come true. Jim was a big part of my life for five years, but then he married someone else, and I haven't seen the bastard for three years. It broke my heart, but sometimes I think realistically, and then I know it had to be.

We had always talked lightly about the time in the nebulous future when we would be living together. I already felt more like his wife than my husband's wife. And he still talked that way, but I began to notice that he avoided real, nitty-gritty discussions about what we would do, where we could go, when, how. In short, he didn't ask me to marry him. I think I could have manipulated the situation to make it happen. I could have just left my husband, let the whole thing out. But I wanted him to do it. I felt that he needed to take charge of the situation, be responsible for it, for his actions. He was always the kind of person who just let things happen. Of course he could blame everybody else that way. And I figured he would blame me if things went wrong, if I took over and managed our elopement. I don't know what to call it. Doesn't matter, because it didn't happen. I finally had a confrontation about it and said, "Do something, or it's the end."

Midway in our affair Jim had committed his wife to a mental institution. She was a fat, unattractive crazy, and had been for years. He was broke now and divorced. He said he desperately needed to marry this rich widow or he'd go under. He said that of course he loved me, that of course I was the greatest in bed, that of course he wished that life was different, but he really needed this marriage for financial security. He didn't mention whatever else this "other" woman offered. I felt angry, inferior, rejected, and revengeful all at once. Now I feel that I should be glad that things turned out the way they did because my husband is really a better person.

But during the next year I missed Jim so much I could hardly stand it. In fact I went to him and threw my body at his once. Twice, actually. The sex was still great, but the depression afterwards and the fantasies of revenge were too much for me.

Fortunately he and his new wife moved away, and I don't have to see him or think about him all the time the way I used to. Last year I called him up, and he wasn't wildly enthusiastic about his marriage. That made me feel happy. I don't want him to suffer, but I don't want him to be happy either. I occasionally still wonder how it would have been with us, if he had carried me off on his white horse. I would have had to go to work, and I have no skills, so he probably thought I wouldn't like a life of poverty, compared to what I had had. Really, he's the one who wouldn't like it. I'm the romantic one who wanted to live on love. Romanticism is probably at the root of my trouble. I think I wanted to give up something for love; that's my romanticism. I wanted the *Redbook* story to end differently. The girl should have said "nuts" to the "good guy" and gone off laughing in the night with the "bad guy." They would have proved everybody wrong; they would have loved and loved and loved forever.

I would say that sex has played a very big role in my life, and I'm sorry it has. I wish I were more like my husband who seems to enjoy it but isn't obsessed with it, as I think I am. I don't think I've had a fantastically interesting or unusual sex life, compared to some of the things I've read, but I do feel that sex has been on my mind all the time. I have found myself so often thinking of sex instead of something important, thinking or fantasizing when I ought to be doing something worthwhile. In that respect I resent the power sex has had over me. I have often wished I had less sex drive. I might have accomplished something in this world. Actually sex is one of the things I'm pretty good at. I'm proud of that, but I think it's nothing to be proud of, if you understand what I mean.

It's sort of interesting to me that during the five years that I was having that torrid and superactive affair with Jim, I was also being very productive in outside activities. I was very successful and had a lot of approval from the people I was working with as a volunteer. I was doing a super job, but then when Jim began drifting away from me and I was upset, I couldn't keep my mind on the jobs I was supposed to be doing. My sex drive took over my mind, almost. It was a real obsession. I wanted to have so many orgasms that I would black out. I was really tripping on sex.

I'm glad that phase is past. I can concentrate again. I don't know why my life's energy has gone into sex. I wish it weren't so. I've been trying lately to understand myself better and I've wondered whether sex would have been so much on my mind if I had had a really important career, instead of all those dilettantish and volunteer things. Or did I just need a different kind of man than Jason? I don't feel that it's fair to blame him.

Along came Jim who was the answer to my prayers, but I wasn't the answer to his. I mean, he loved me, I'm sure of that, but not enough to risk anything over, not enough to work hard for, or give up something for.

I suppose it sounds as if I did neglect Jason, giving all that time to Jim and, before that and in addition to my affair, the time I spent with my community meetings, but I just had to get out of what seemed like Dullsville and do something, learn something new. I think what I learned benefited me. I'm more interesting now than I used to be. I'm doing something useful in this town, and I feel good that I had what seemed at the time to be a terrific love affair. Now that I devote my sexual energies to Jason, he seems more lively too. I couldn't be that way without the experience I've had. I still shed a tear over that bastard who didn't want to marry me, but I'll bet he knows he made a stupid mistake, and that's some comfort.

By this time Jason and I have worked out a mutually satisfactory arrangement, although I still masturbate. I do try to save myself for him. We still don't really talk about this. We both know that our appetites have never quite matched, but I think he thinks women are different and can hold back their desires easily. 'Tain't so. I've struggled a lot in my life to keep my sex drive manageable. I could have been much more promiscuous. Gosh, I'm sure I could have had hundreds of partners. But shame and fear of the consequences kept me from it.

By the way, I firmly believe in the ability, mine anyway, to love more than one person at a time. Jason and I are a little closer nowadays. I'm more dependent on him than I used to be. I do need a man to lean on, no matter how independent I start acting. And with old age looming up I'm very grateful that I am living with a man I admire and have pleasure with, and who will take care of me if I decline. I'm no longer looking for adventure. I'm concentrating on this coffeehouse and keeping blinders on about men. I don't need another fling. One is enough.

I'm all for women's lib now. I hate myself for sneering at it once. But total equality is a scary thing. I want to try my wings, and I did to some extent, but I always had that security behind me. I don't think I have the guts to do anything all on my own. I might have been a successful man if I had had to be, and I blame my wasted life on being a woman. But I am scared to go out there and pit myself against a million other people. If I fail at making a "go" of my thing, I can cry or shrug it off or make up excuses, but in any case, I can go home to my husband and say, "I'm through. You do the work of the world. I'll retire to my kitchen, or books, or whatever."

I'm proud of my kids. Proud that I managed to live through that love affair without losing my mind and my husband, as well as my lover. I sing a lot, but I'm not proud of that. It's a gift and I'm not responsible for it. Same with my appearance. I try to keep healthy and attractive; that's all one can do. I do catch myself glancing in mirrors more lately, come to think of it. I'm sure I'm trying to reassure myself that I'm not too bad for a fifty-year-old American female.

CHAPTER 15

Candy—What Every Woman Knows

I was the prize in my family, because I danced and sang and made people laugh. I was the kooky relative who was always leaping around in ballet shoes.

Candy lives in a small, row house in a lower-middle-class neighborhood. Inside, she has created an atmosphere of beauty with her naive and charming wall hangings. She has many other artistic interests as well.

From her early thirties to age forty Candy was pretty but plump. Then for a few years she became dumpy and matronly. Now, at fifty-two, she is svelte, stylish, and attractive. She is very proud of her transformation, which she believes to be more than just physical. She wants to grow up and stop playing the childish roles she has played for fifty years.

She is on stage a good bit of the time, laughing, gesticulating, making faces, and cracking jokes, just like the noisy little girl she describes. She seems more the contemporary of her three young children, barely into their teens, than the contemporary of middle-aged women. She has been married for twenty-four years.

Candy's life is fairly circumscribed. She has never worked outside her home and does not drive a car. Lacking sufficient opportunities elsewhere, she is creating a few small dramas in her home.

* * *

CANDY

I'VE ALWAYS BEEN the artistic type. Romantic. Sentimental. I hate the business world. I hate my husband's work. I love music and dancing and opera and museums and the life of the city. I think the thing I love most in the world is sitting at my loom and watching the colors and designs grow before my eyes. I have to admit that's my true joy. After I've stolen a few hours for myself weaving something, I'm elevated a few feet off the ground. Art makes you different, in a sense. If you're artistic or creative in any way you leave the crowd. I'm certainly not a genius, and my work is not great, but the point is that as an artist I have a whole different mind set. I don't want to be pigeonholed.

I do think that women have always had, in a sense, more freedom than men, because we don't have to go out and support a family. I said to Fred the other day, "I'll never divorce you, because I'd have to go to work, and I'd hate to have to do that." I thank God every day that I'm a woman. Women have more to give. But I think all the publicity with women's liberation has made me braver. I used to feel such guilt that I wasn't the perfect mother like my mother. But now I see that I can be a person and still do the things I love.

How did my mother put up with me? It must have been hard for her. I remember she'd be doing the housework, and I'd be babbling in her ear about the ballet I saw or the marvelous painting at the museum. She was terribly patient. She was an intelligent woman. She went to business school, but she never worked. She was never fully a person. Her idea of herself was always—"the mother."

We were poor when I was little, but we didn't feel poor. I remember being shocked one time that my mother was weeping because we couldn't find two cents in the house to buy a newspaper. I said, "Let's make a game," and we went looking all over, in all the coats and jackets, while she sat there crying. We thought she had lost her reason. We didn't know what it meant really. We were unaware that we were deprived. Some of my mother's relatives would make fun of us. They would say that we ate from one big pot in the middle of the table. But that's all we had. If we had dessert, it was a slice of bread, dipped in cold water, wrung out, and sprinkled with sugar.

I was the product of a marvelous public school in Chicago. It had so much to offer for a child of poverty. We went to the museums every weekend, lectures, and other events. We had a little book for a dollar with coupons in it for all these extra things.

I used to sit and do my homework in front of an old iron kitchen stove, and I remember there were traps behind it for rats, and the rats and roaches would crawl around under that stove. I think that's why I went into art. I was brutalized by ugliness.

My father was uneducated and made twenty dollars a week. His idea of being a good husband was going to work, bringing home the pay, and going to bed after supper. What did that leave my mother spiritually? Nothing. Yet if I voiced that to my mother, she'd be enraged with me for picking on dear old Dad. I would say that my father was a very rigid man, and I regret that he never showed enough emotion to us. Yet he was dependable. My mother was more the one that we ran to and confided in, but both my parents were very, very strong on honesty and truth and love of God, and that's something that I took on. There was no pressure for me to get married. In fact my mother sort of regretted it when I married, because I was her companion.

I used to go to the opera with her and shopping and so forth. She missed me quite a lot. Sometimes I see in her attitude toward Fred, my husband, a jealousy. It's kind of shaky. She's very apt to take offense at things he says. I have to be the intermediary there. I think she loves him, but she feels that he robbed her of me and also that he isn't good enough for me.

I was the prize in my family because I danced and sang and I made people laugh. I was the kooky relative who was always leaping around in ballet shoes. But my mother and sister always reminded me of how good they were to me. I adored being loved by them and indulged and patted on the head. Yet it was all to their own purposes. For example, I remember my sister worked in an office once, and she wanted to give everybody there a beautiful Christmas card, hand painted by me! This was forty cards. I did it, but I kept saying, "Why am I doing something I don't want to do?"

My sister almost seems jealous of any attention other people give me. I *must* do things when she wants, or she gets annoyed. After all, as she says, hasn't she practically given me all my yarns and looms, and hasn't she always brought me gifts, and doesn't she bring us bags of groceries when she knows we're low?

The other day she called and said, "Get over here right away. I want you to look at some dresses and tell me which one to wear to the city." I went, but I said, "We were just sitting down to coffee." And she said, "Well, I've done plenty for *you!* How many times have I brought food over?" I got very upset, and I said, "I was hoping we didn't count." She thinks she owns me, because she gives me things.

She always scared me to death, and, to tell the truth, she still scares me. She's very dominating, and I'm her pet, her little girl. A few years ago I realized that I have been spoiled by love, that I am still a little girl in many ways. I still love my mother and sister, but I want to stop playing their little game.

I think for years I was suppressing all my feelings about my mother and sister. That's why I became so overweight. I felt I *had* to be nice; I had to do things their way. I spent my life always putting other people first. I was always doing things for my friends, making things, trying to please. Why did I do that so much? It was to get a pat on the head. I still want to do things for people, but not in a silly way. There is a new me emerging.

I think I carry on emotionally more now than I ever did before, even though I've always been considered outgoing, noisy, talkative. I'm always accused of being drunk at parties. It's unreal. I like wine, but I don't drink a lot. My mother will say, "You're being very loud. How many drinks have you had?" I'm so annoyed. I decided I'm not going to pay attention to it anymore. I like fun. It's just my nature to be gay and noisy.

I tend to blow up at things; I call Fred names and threaten to throw things. But he laughs. He thinks it's cute. That's how he stops me, by saying that. Luckily he's not the type to be mean. He can break the tension and stop my anger. It's hard for me to stop sometimes. I want the anger to stay a while.

You should have seen me a few years ago when I noticed the fat and the wrinkles. I took a look in the mirror, and I didn't like what I saw, and I didn't like the feeling of martyrdom. The truth is, I was daydreaming about some handsome man falling in love with me, and I realized that it could never in a million years happen. Really, I could never have an affair. My rigid Christian conscience wouldn't allow it. You owe at least loyalty to the person you're married to. But I wanted the luxury of imagination, and it was pretty hard with seventy-five excess pounds holding me down.

Fred used to say that he didn't mind my being fat, but, believe me, it makes a lot of difference. I can tell. He likes introducing me to people now that I've lost those excess pounds. But now Fred says, "I've never known you to be such an egotist. You're so concerned about the way you look!" I said, "Fred, I'm sorry. Chalk it up to my age." But I *am* more conscious of clothes and of my appearance. It's better than what the lady next door is doing. She's such a non-person now. She hides in her house and washes windows every other day. She's a vegetable. But to me right now it's important to like the way I look and like what I'm doing. I think Fred likes the new me in some ways. He thinks I've gotten terribly glamorous, but he doesn't like me in other ways. He keeps telling people that my new glamour is "just a stage." It's a threat to him. He would really prefer me to be fat and housewifely. I don't want to put Fred down entirely, but I would say that he is a typical male chauvinist. For Fred, the wife's place is in the kitchen with her children and she shouldn't think of frivolous things like the "latest styles." I woke up to the fact that that's bunk.

We've never had trouble communicating, but I think Fred's a little shocked that I jump on him for every little thing now, every chauvinist attitude. I won't stand for it anymore. I'm not a moron, and I've had enough guilt about the fact that I'm a lousy housekeeper. Fred's image of what a wife should be is that she shouldn't say bad words. And I love to say "son of a bitch" and "bastard." It's not the end of the world! I'm not really given to bad language. How we treat each other is much more important than what we say. But his idea is that I should be not only soft-spoken and charming and lovely, but a perfect housekeeper, be able to bounce a quarter off the bed (I run and pull the covers up as soon as I hear his car in the driveway), be able to clean beautifully and bake beautifully and entertain beautifully. You know what? That's not me. I used to feel guilt about those things for years, but I don't anymore. For example, Fred spent all night mopping the kitchen floor, because he knew you were coming. "Be my guest!" I said. Then he said to me, "Do you have coffee? We don't have any filters for the basket. What are you going to do?" I said, "I'll strain the coffee through a strainer!" See, those things do bother him. I was vacuuming when you arrived so he wouldn't be ashamed of the living room. I don't want to make it seem like I'm the heroine; I must say he has a right to his stupid ideas.

I was married to Fred for three years when I decided I had married the wrong man. But what could I do about it? My best friend told me to divorce him but I couldn't hurt the man, and there was nothing to complain about except that we don't have the same tastes. He'd make fun of the arty things I liked. Maybe because he felt threatened by my intelligence. He's satisfied with his boring job and those inane TV programs, and yet, he has always told me what to do, always treated me like a baby. I know I used to let him, and now I want to change all that. It had never occurred to me to say, "I'm a person. How dare you treat me like a moron?" Now he can't adjust. He's so touchy. He's used to treating me like a moron.

Fred is good; he doesn't drink, he doesn't swear, he's a good provider, and he loves me a great deal. It's nice to be adored by somebody. I truly wanted the father image and, for better and for worse, Fred is my father in many ways. He's always said, "Do you have enough groceries? Did you do this? Did you do that?" I don't regret the decision years ago to stay with Fred.

I think it's beautiful that my husband says, "Like wine, you've aged in the barrel; you've gotten better." In fact, one morning I came to the table, and I guess I was feeling a bit anxious, or something had gone wrong, and I had been weeping; and my eyes were puffy and no makeup, and I looked in the mirror and thought, "Oh God, are you ugly." I get to the table thinking I really look like a wreck and my husband looks across at me and says, "You know what? You're the kind of woman that any man would want to wake up next to in the morning." I started to weep. It was such a beautiful thing to say. He *is* a nice guy. He's good.

Fred was very understanding when I married him. I thought that sex was going to be all so easy and marvelous, but instead I had a very difficult period of adjustment. I was shocked to find that at the point where he was going to penetrate me I used to get physically sick. I couldn't bear the thought of someone else actually being in my body. I would try not to do it but I would put my head over the edge of the bed and actually retch. Isn't that awful! It took a year of Fred's patience and understanding. It's funny in a way. I tell people that when I first met him I threw up. I actually did. I had eaten a huge meal, and then I went for a car ride with all this heavy food in my stomach. I had to be dashed up the steps, dashed into the bathroom—this is the kind of guy Fred is—he slammed up the toilet seat and held me while I was sick. This was my first date. But he was so gentle and good. And in sex he didn't push me. That could have turned me off forever.

I think I was affected for a while by a bad experience I had when I was little. An uncle, the usual thing, took me to bed when he took his nap. I was about seven, I think, and I didn't know what was happening. He didn't rape me or anything. He just took me to fondle, I guess. I was very confused, and I didn't want to go near that uncle anymore. Years later it came to me what had happened, and I felt guilt. I remember weeping every night when I went to bed, feeling that I was doomed to hell. God was going to punish me. I was a young teen. Then I made a mission. There was value to those old "missions" where the priest would come around giving talks at the church, a Lenten kind of thing, where you sort of did your mental housecleaning. The priest made this marvelous speech one night about children and how careful you must be with their minds and their bodies and he went into this business of sexual abuse, and he said, "You people out there who have had this experience, throw it out of your minds! You were in no way responsible!" I actually felt a load lift off my shoulders and I remember going out of the church feeling renewed. Isn't that marvelous! But I was so naive that I somehow thought it had been my fault, and I think that did affect my sexual thinking. I was very anti-male for a while and didn't go out with boys until I was nineteen or twenty. I used to tease and joke with them and I made a big thing about girls being as good as boys. I think I put them off and they were threatened by my intelligence and my independence. I acted as if I thought men were laughable.

So, I was still a virgin when I got married at twenty-six. I knew that a "nice girl" wouldn't get involved in sex, so I held back. I'd be putting my soul in jeopardy. I wanted to be in what I thought was God's good graces. I really believed in the faith that I practiced, and I still do. I'm sure it saved me from promiscuity.

When I was first married, I didn't question Fred's sexual ability. I was more concerned that I wasn't adequate. In fact Fred told me he thought I was a little frigid years ago but there were times when he would just destroy me mentally. I would be reading him a poem across the table, and he'd say to me, coldly, "Would you pass me the butter?" He couldn't care less. Do you know what that did to me being such an emotional person? He had stepped on my ego, on my joy! This kept repeating itself, and stupid little me, I kept coming back to be socked again. That night, though, he'd want me to respond when I was ready to kick him in the teeth.

I read an article that said a man must also consider a woman's emotions, and I said, "Aha! So I wasn't wrong!" Like I needed that article to really clarify to me that I wasn't cold, that I had every right to be annoyed with my husband when he expected me to perform like a trained seal after he stepped on my emotions. I don't think you can treat a person badly and then jump into bed and say, "Adore me." It would take a great acting ability to be responsive under those conditions. When I'm mad at you, that's it.

I was never the active partner. I've never felt that adoration of my husband that would make me take the initiative. I maybe thought for a while that I was frigid, but I know now that I'm perfectly capable. If I adored him, I would make no bones about being quite the aggressor. But I'd rather have it this way. Let him be the aggressor. I make jokes about preferring a good book to sex but I would say that really, Fred's drive is greater than mine. I was taught that you never refuse your husband, and I always "did my duty." That's kind of a sad way to look at it. But I'm still in that syndrome, because I would never say no. He makes cracks to our friends about my denying him, and it used to upset me when we were younger, but now I just laugh. Fred needs a woman who is much more of a toucher than I am. He would love, sometimes, to have me make a fuss over him. But I can't do it. To me, it's false. I can respond sexually, but, see, that's in the dark. My family always acted as if nice people don't show their feelings. My father never kissed us. He would be enraged at people petting in the parks. My mother upset me terribly—I remember it so clearly—when I kissed her, and she turned to me and said, "What are you looking for?"

Sexually I'm not the greatest thing since Cleopatra, but all I can say is that my husband says he's never been so happy as he is now. I don't say it's because I perform so well. Frankly, I hate to say this, because it might reflect on Fred, but I would say that I've never fully given myself. He doesn't know the difference. I think I'm capable of much more. That mad love is not there, and I think I reserve myself. My mind's not in it. I always feel guilty about my lack of response.

I'm still clinging to my background in many respects. I do feel that being a wife and mother is a job I took on, and I have to do certain things. I don't feel as bound to my children as I once was, but I do have a conscience. I thought I'd be a perfect mother, and I'm shocked to find I'm not. I lose patience, and I can't solve certain problems. I can't figure out why my daughter has problems that the boys didn't have, except that she's my rival. She's very independent, and she won't listen to anyone in authority right now. She's a tough cookie, and I want her to be a little more feminine. Fred thinks I spoil her, but I don't want her to feel that she's always being talked to negatively. I want to show her I love her even though she's being very difficult.

I adored them all when they were little. I like to tell them how I used to kiss every inch of them. I was thrilled to be a mother. I knew that it wouldn't be my whole life. I don't think people should be just parents. I always foresaw the day when I would create, learn another language, be something else. I never felt I wanted to be a total mother. I feel that I give more to my children by having other interests. I can't make them like my music or my books, but it's there, it permeates something. My son listens to the most horrendous rock music and reads nothing but monster books, but at least he sees another atmosphere.

I do feel that I owe my children something. I owe my children to be here when they come home. Some children don't need it, but I know that mine do. I believe in cutting the umbilical cord. I don't want them to be a reflection of me. I can't program their lives. My husband is going to have a terrible time when they all leave home, but I don't expect to. He accuses me already of maybe not being caring enough, but I want to see them become independent. Motherhood is not the most important thing to me anymore. I feel that I do my best, and I'm not going to carry guilt around about whether I fail or if the children turn out a certain way. They're not my creation.

My children are still young teenagers, so they have a long way to go before they are fully formed. I really believe they give me more than I give them.

Maybe you get more sentimental as you get older. I always did love life, but now I adore it. The sky never seemed bluer to me. I feel that part of my personality is to make people laugh. It's kind of a show-off thing I suppose. I know I should tone it down. I love to say what I think without being unkind. I love to tease, and I love to shock people. I guess Fred bears the brunt of it. But I think it's a duty to smile even if you're dropping dead. I really do believe that. Too many people go around trying to share illnesses and troubles with you. Why don't they share their joys?

CHAPTER 16

Pam—Poor Little Rich Girl

The only thing that Mother didn't get me out of was my marriage.

Pam is fifty-five, tall and dark, with chiseled features and sporty good looks. Her accent and manner are clearly upper-class New England. She "belongs" to a certain elite group, and she is proud of that background. Her pride, however, is mixed with shame over her many years of alcoholism.

Unhappily married for nineteen years to an unambitious man who lived off her inheritance, Pam was divorced ten years ago and gave her husband custody of their twin daughters. The twins are now grown and married.

Pam has always cared mainly about sports, club life, and social drinking. She did not go beyond preparatory school and she failed to develop any non-athletic interests or skills. Now on the verge of separating from her female companion of many years, she is reassessing her life.

* * *

PAM

I DON'T KNOW if my problems are mental or physical at the moment. I suppose you'd call it menopause. Anyway I feel inadequate because I don't have anybody dependent on me.

I've been sober for five weeks. I just joined AA. I've been trying to get involved in AA for years. I'd go to meetings but I'd be intellectually proud. I'd say, "That's not me. I haven't been institutionalized." But, hell, you can be on Skid Row in your own kitchen.

It's hard to know if what my body feels lately is withdrawal from alcohol. Maybe my aches and pains are arthritic. I'm pretty religious, and I made a promise to God that someday I'd wake up and I wouldn't smoke or drink again. And that's what happened. I don't really miss the alcohol or the smoking either.

The Demon Rum did me in. If I hadn't been drinking all these years with my country club friends I could have been a hell of a horsewoman and tennis player, a really super athlete! Drinking is part of being "in" at these clubs and I've noticed that some of my drinking friends don't pay as much attention to me now as they used to.

I'm trying to do a lot of reading which I've never done before because I was usually too tight when I went to bed. I would read things over and over again without being able to remember them. I'm just now beginning to regain some memory power.

My worst character defects came out when I drank. If I was depressed over a bad tennis game or too many third-place ribbons, I could get verbally and even physically aggressive. Probably I don't know half the stuff I've done. Sometimes, that is, when I'm sober, I can be perfectly calm and compassionate.

When I was fifteen I fell in love with my cousin, who was twenty-two. My mother took me to a mountain resort for a month, saying, "It's wrong to be in love with your cousin. I brought you here in order to break it up." That upset me terribly. Even now I feel that if I had been left alone that "love" would have run its natural course and turned into a sentimental memory.

Mother then sent me to a girls' boarding school. That was the start of the "crush-on-girls" department, encouraged there by the horsey teachers in their beautiful riding clothes.

My mother was an absolute neurotic. She always overprotected me and never let me do anything on my own. I think the reason I'm an alcoholic is mainly because of the poisonous sex education she gave me. Sex, by the way, is never discussed at AA meetings, at least none I've ever been to. Mother was fanatically anti-sex. She hated bodies. She always said, "Let me know whenever you have the curse so you can rest in bed for three days." Even when I was eighteen years old I had to sit in bed for three days. It was a strange family. I could write a book.

Mother was an amazing person. If there was something my sisters or I didn't want to do, she'd say, "Well, don't worry, I'll think of an excuse," and she'd get us out of it. It was very bad for us, believe me. Very bad. We were terribly spoiled. When I was a kid in school, we had to get up in front of everybody and recite something or give the news. I always made people laugh because I was so nervous, so I refused to do it. My mother went to school and arranged for me to be excused from public speaking.

The only thing I didn't like that Mother didn't get me out of was my marriage. Later, when she knew I wasn't a very good mother to my twins—I was always running off to ride the horses—she still paid for my membership in the hunt club. She seemed to encourage that; she felt I needed the outlet.

She would do other things for me, like, all of a sudden she would pay my oil bill. Money was always forthcoming from her; she was very generous. I never really learned about money. It always just came from somewhere if I was in trouble. We always got large sums on holidays and birthdays—one year, twenty-five thousand dollars for Christmas. She just felt we needed it, I guess. If this hadn't been so, I would have had to go out and take courses and make a living, do something with my life, instead of sit back. It never occurred to me to do anything.

Mother was very ill her last years. She was cared for by servants. I came to have coffee with her every morning and discuss the disposal of her affairs. She gave me power of attorney because, she said, I was the one who would miss her the most. I was amazed at how much money she had been giving away. She was very brave about dying and very orderly. There was nothing left in her bureau drawers when she died except clean paper and sachets.

Both my parents were overprotective. My sisters and I were never allowed to go and play at other people's houses. They had to come to ours. In 1929 my father made a ton of money in Wall Street, and we moved out of a perfectly nice eighteen-room house to a sixty-four-room house, ten miles away. Sixty-four rooms and twelve servants. Then one day my mother got all these threatening letters, "Your child is going to be killed, kidnapped." It was about the time of the Lindbergh situation. So we lived in the house with a lot of detectives for a while.

I think I was one of these people who really and truly needed and wanted discipline as a child. I was badly behaved, at home and at school. I think I was asking for limits, as they say. I remember I was even unkind to animals at one point. When I think about it now, it just horrifies me! I remember playing backgammon when I was about ten and getting mad because the detective beat me, and I threw the dice cup in his face. No one was disciplining me at all, even the governess. I was so rude to her that it was unreal. I was a real shit, if you don't mind me saying so. I was filled with rage and frustration. I craved attention. But there was something wrong. I don't know what. My older sisters were thin and much more attractive than I, and I resented the fact that my friends seemed to like them better than they liked me. I got very heavy, and that was frustration, too, I suppose. My younger sister was a beautiful little gal too. She's been married four times. I think there was a lot of jealousy among these sisters.

I do think I was my father's favorite, but he wasn't there all that much. He wasn't involved. He used to take us out on his boat every Sunday. That's the thing he did. Sometimes twenty kids. Mother never went; she didn't like it. We'd sail down the coast and go out to a nightclub, and my dad would buy us all dinner and drinks. It was nothing but fun and games with him. That's when I learned to drink, when I was fifteen. We had a ball. All the time. When he died, I took over his boat and had my own parties.

I absolutely adored my father, to the point where I tried to imitate him. I wore a polo coat and a yachting cap, had to drive a Cadillac, and tried to be just like him. My father was very strict in many ways, but not in others. He kind of gave up because Mother was the dominant force and he hated an argument. He'd always give in to avoid an argument. He never said an unkind word about anybody, at least when he was sober. He was one of those guys who, even if he was drunk, would always walk down the hall and pat me on the head and kiss me goodnight before he went to bed. Mother used to say he would pass out saying his prayers. She was violently opposed to his drinking. I thought of my parents as being happy, but I know there were things that went on that were not good. Mother claimed, "Your father did something once that was so bad that I will take it to my grave," and as far as I know she did. My father could get violent. Once he was angry at my older sister and pulled a chair out from under her as she started to sit down. He didn't remember a thing about it afterwards. I realized that he had a problem but I didn't understand it.

I know that I thought my father was just the greatest guy that ever came down the pike. I remember being very disappointed when I found out that he was a drinker. At some age I realized that he was cross at the dinner table at night, and I didn't understand it. But it was the cocktails that made him cross. And then it got so that I'd drink with him, especially after I was married. I remember one afternoon he and I decided to invite a bunch of friends up to the house to "tie one on." He wasn't supposed to be drinking because of his health. He was a very sweet person and very quiet and played the piano marvelously by ear. But he was so shy that he drank to give himself social courage. He was a Jekyll and Hyde. He became a different person, more fun, more open and relaxed. I know that I was that way too. I didn't go to anything, a party or anything, without having a drink first. I didn't go to a wedding this Saturday because I knew I didn't want to drink, and I'd be just too nervous at something like that without fortification. If I have a few drinks, I can walk up to a stranger and talk; but if I haven't, I'm timid. I think I was special to my father; I felt that way. He and I were very close. Even later when he was sick, and my mother asked him what he wanted to do that day, he'd say, "Let's just have Pam come out for lunch." He understood me, and I felt safe with him. I know he appreciated my athletic ability and my sense of humor. He enjoyed my company. I don't think he wanted me to get married particularly. Just before the wedding I went into his dressing room and we each had a nip of a martini and I didn't dare say, "Dad, I don't really want to do this." And he didn't dare say, "You shouldn't be doing this." But I know we thought it. When he gave me away, he kissed my hand. It was really traumatic. I felt awful.

My husband and I had fun sailing together, but otherwise we didn't have much in common. I was reasonably ambitious for him. I would have liked him to work. I wanted to respect him. Maybe it would have made a difference if I had respected him. He had everything going for him. He's a bright guy, he had a hell of an education, but he did nothing with it. If he tried something and it failed, somebody always seemed to take care of him.

I had all the money, inherited, and my husband had no dough. He claimed that my family's money killed his incentive. Whether this is true or not, I don't know. I can see where it could be. I used to scream that he never did anything, and I got fed up with it towards the end. I was perfectly open about it. Then he stopped giving anything at all to the household, and yet he ate and slept there. He claimed he stayed because of the children. I'm not so sure they wouldn't have been better off if we had gotten a divorce much earlier. But I was afraid to get a divorce while my mother was alive. She was heartily opposed to divorce. I was separated very soon after she died.

By the way, I took my pregnancy seriously. I didn't drink or smoke during it, and I led a very healthy life. I thought it was a big deal to have a baby. But having the twins didn't bring us any closer.

I was a terrible mother. Some of it was my own damn fault and some of it I blame on the bad marriage and some on the interference of his family. But I felt fulfilled, because at least I had done one normal thing.

The only affairs that went on during our marriage were mine with women. My husband didn't know about it. He just thought they were childish fancies, or something. Because I was a good athlete I seemed to attract these younger women, and my husband just thought they had a crush on me. They were unmarried and much younger. It wouldn't be with every one of them. Just some. I feel embarrassed talking about this, but it's the truth. It was a pretty constant pattern in our marriage. It was just some chemistry, some awareness between us. There was no similarity in the women, except that they might have been looking for an escape. I have very little experience or understanding of all this, but I consider it a mutual masturbation proposition. I'm perfectly good friends with these same women, those that I still see in my life. There's no animosity as there might be in a love affair. Not that we've ever talked about it or laughed about it.

Peggy, the gal I've been living with for ten years now, came along at a time when she needed someone to lean on emotionally. Her mother was dying, and I needed someone too. So there was more than sex. I'm sure there was. She's very self-sufficient, really. I never told my husband any of this, but he guessed what was going on with Peggy. Why else would he hate her? He thinks she broke up our marriage, and he hates her because of that. We went through a really gruesome time, a really bad time. Those last few years it was very uncomfortable. My husband had a terrible temper. It was growl, growl, growl. It was all very peculiar, the whole thing. What I wanted was a home and kids, and yet I wanted a divorce. My husband didn't want it at all. I had to surrender control of my daughters' lives in order to get the divorce. Of course my daughters have always resented that.

Some people lead homosexual lives, and they're perfectly happy. I don't think I could, because I'm not happy about it. It isn't really what I want. I'm not comfortable with it. I don't know what the reason for it was except that it was just a good old healthy desire to have some sort of sex, physical contact with somebody rather than just by yourself all the time. I don't know. It's too complicated for me. There was one time with my husband, after a luncheon cocktail party, when we both had a good time sexually. It was the only time. Usually it wasn't a mutual thing. I just didn't love him, and I didn't feel attracted to him at all. The one time it was really good it could have been anybody instead of him. Yet we could have been perfectly good friends. We played tennis together, we were the undefeated champions in mixed doubles at our club for a long time, and we fished and hunted together. If I had just loved him, we could have had one hell of a good marriage, because he felt sexually attracted to me. But I didn't want any part of him, really. At all. It's hard to explain.

Except for masturbation, I was sexually inhibited. I always had this fear of pregnancy drilled into my head from the time I was tiny, from the time I had the curse especially. "You couldn't be sure about those condoms. Don't trust them." I used to hear that jazz all the time, and that fear spoiled any pleasure I might have had. I tried not to think about being sexually satisfied when I was married. My husband is really a nice guy, no doubt about it, and that's a guilt complex I have.

I don't really know how big a part sex has played in my life. I suppose, now that I'm talking about it, it was much more important than I realized. By keeping it in, I made it more important. The guilt gets me, I have to admit. I feel very guilty because actually the business with girls during my marriage was adultery. Let's be honest about it, I feel ashamed about that lesbian business in my life. I know I shouldn't. There's no real reason to. But I do. The fact of the matter is, I do because I feel that homosexuality is not the normal, natural way of life. A lot of people feel that it's a sickness, and I was brought up to feel that too. I'm definitely concerned about other people's opinion of me.

I've lost all desire to do anything sexual as far as my companion, Peggy, is concerned. Nothing at all. It just disappeared. I just don't feel anything. And she sort of said, "Well, that's that." And I said, "Well, I think it is." It's a stage that's been outgrown.

Togetherness is something I miss, though, even if it's just a pal. I've lived with Peggy for a long time. But now I feel our paths are going in opposite ways. She seems to no longer need me and I wonder if I'm a hang-up for her right now. It's upsetting. On the tennis court she doesn't talk to me if we're alone, but if we play doubles, she talks up a storm. I say to her, "Hey! The name of the game is camaraderie. What's the matter?" I'm confused. I'm not really sure. I don't know if I have the guts to start a new life—just pick up and go someplace else.

I really don't think I'm repelled by the thought of sex with a man. Honestly. But again, how do I know? I haven't had the opportunity to try. I think I might consider geting married if I had the right person, a pretty strong, pretty understanding person. I couldn't do what a friend of mine confided in me about, namely, that she had had several liaisons, affairs with husbands of her friends. I couldn't do that. I'm sort of moral about that. I can't do the bar scene either. One of my younger friends does. She lives the life of a whore without getting paid for it. I couldn't look at myself in the mirror. I would feel unclean. I would have to have sex with someone I could get to know, and who I would at least consider marrying. I don't think the changing sex scene has loosened me up at all, because I know that I have to meet my maker some day. It's all down there in the Ten Commandments. I do believe in resurrection. It's not that much comfort because of the old confession department. I have to think of all my sins and atonement. I don't think you can get away scot-free. Every day, when I wake up, I put my life in God's hands. If I could think of that before every sentence and every deed, I would lead a better life. My faith is very simple. I think it has kept me from going under. It's a support, a crutch. I don't mind saying it. Alcohol was a crutch, but also a terrible escape from myself, from knowing myself.

I'm in debt. I have an income from trusts, but I can't invade the trust, so it's very hard to pay off my debts. But it's my fault. I remember the last month that I had my father's boat, the liquor bill was 360 dollars, not counting the liquor I consumed at the house. Giving up drinking is going to save me a lot of money. I've never thought of working. Perhaps later I will. I can't decide where to settle. This town is fine, but there aren't too many people around here like those I was brought up with. I don't like to sound like a snob. It doesn't really matter to me. I can like anyone. Peggy, for example, is from a different walk of life. She has always had to work. But it mattered to my parents. They had fits because I had friends who weren't the "right kind." I don't understand it, but I seem to be a combination of inferiority and conceit.

I expect to make it. I'm curious about the future. I have a fairly optimistic outlook and it doesn't take much to make me happy. A little goes a long way. To stay alone is the thing that would drive me out of my tree. Real loneliness upsets me. My oldest sister lives alone now, and she loves it; but she works part time, and she has a million hobbies. I'm afraid I'm not that type.

I love being a grandmother. I can remember when my first grandchild climbed into my lap and said, "I love you, Gam," the tears fell. They give me some lovely moments and sometimes make me wish that I had had a big family.

My daughters had all sorts of hang-ups about me for a while. They used to complain that the divorce had ruined their lives. It's true that we all went through a bad time. In AA you're supposed to take an honest personal inventory with someone else and then make reparation for your wrongs, as long as it doesn't hurt anybody. I hope I have repaired some of the damage done to my girls. Time has helped too. They seem much more understanding now.

Memory is kind, I feel. Most of the things I laugh about, the fun part of it. But if I really dig in, it's been a pretty wasted life. If I had been channeled in the right direction, I could have had anything I wanted. Money, in my case, has been very destructive. That's how I really feel about it.

CHAPTER 17

Meg–If I Had a Hammer

I don't like children either, but I had the good taste not to have any.
I'm a homosexual. I could live alone if I had to. As long as I have the
animals, my whole family is around me.

*Meg is a pretty, sun-tanned, gray-haired, fifty-four-year-old computer operator
who has a comfortable income. She is an atheist and a homosexual. She survived a
distant father and a mentally ill mother who hated her. She took her identity and
self-esteem from her Prussian grandfather who respected her and treated her like a
boy. She became a mechanic, a carpenter, and a machine-gun instructor.*

*Meg's need to testify that a homosexual can be a capable and happy person led
her to the interview. Although she does not discuss the pain of being "different," it
is a central fact of her life, of which she is constantly aware. Her awareness is
largely a result of our society's punitive attitude toward homosexuality. She regrets
with her unique, salty humor a misspent youth chasing the girls when she could
have become a veterinarian.*

* * *

MEG

I'VE NEVER BEEN PREGNANT and never practiced birth control. I
had no need to. I'm a homosexual. It used to be that you could
never open your mouth and admit it. People might guess it and
whisper about it, but Jesus, don't ever say so! You and I would have
known exactly what the score was, but never in a million years
would I have simply come right out and said, "I'm a homosexual.
That's the way it is, take it or leave it." You don't know what it
costs some people to admit it. You have this big weight of the
establishment that falls on you. The social pressures are fantastic. If
I say, "I'm not married," people ask, "Oh, you're a widow?" I say,
"No." "Oh, you're divorced?" and the mouth gets a little tighter.
"No, not divorced." "You've never been married?" and the mouth
is a slash, like, "You're a failure!" So, most homosexuals get
married. It's easier than remaining single.

I, however, never had any intention of getting married. I'm not in the least ashamed now. I came out of the closet a long time ago. I finally became mature and intelligent and realized that I was living a very decent, exemplary life, paying taxes and contributing to society, and that the fact that I'm a homosexual was no worse than the fact that I have blue eyes. And I'll discuss it with anybody who wants to discuss it with me openly, even though people today are *not* more accepting of homosexuality. There's more talk about it, that's all.

I had a very strange childhood. My mother, I realize now, was seriously, mentally ill all her life. I was her first child, and she was thirty-six on my birth certificate, but she always lied about her age, and I know she was older than that. As I say, I was her first child. She hated me. Really hated me. She hated children. I don't like children either, but I had the good taste not to have any.

My parents were in the hotel business in Salt Lake City, and here I was, this little kid, and my mother—she was very, very beautiful, considered herself a movie star—and here's this little brat running around, and she hated my guts. Of course, I knew this, I sensed it, children always do. And I insisted on living with my grandparents. I insisted. I mean, can you imagine a little kid three years old? I made them come and get me in the middle of the night, screaming my head off. They took me, and I never went back. Never, that is, until I had to in my teens. Anyhow my grandparents raised me. I considered them my parents.

It was a foreign household, and I learned to speak German before I did English. My grandmother spoke no English. She did not vote, she stayed at home, the *hausfrau*. A lovely, gentle person. My grandfather was every inch the ramrod Prussian. He gave me more respect as a person, you might say, than he gave to my grandmother. He asked my opinions, and he treated me just like a peer, like an adult, always. There was no Santa Claus, none of that crap, nothing. They weren't progressive, now don't misunderstand me, it was far from being progressive. If anything, they were very old-fashioned.

My grandfather never treated me like a child. I was expected to act like an adult. I learned to drive when I was ten years old. I read all the road maps when we went on a trip. It was expected, and I did it. I sat in the front seat, and my grandmother sat in the back. I don't know if it has anything to do with my being a homosexual or not, but my grandfather treated me as if I were a boy. He expected me to do everything a boy could do. I learned to be a mechanic, and I'm still great at it. I can tear down an engine and fix it in a whipstitch. My grandfather thought of women as nothing, chattels. That's how he felt. But I never felt inferior as a female, because, as I say, I was treated like a boy and like an intelligent adult, always.

Of course, I wished I were a boy. Sure. For many reasons in our culture it's far more advantageous to be male. I'm sure you know that. I certainly didn't want to be a woman in the stereotyped role. See, now it's too late for me. Now women are emerging in all the things I wanted to be. I didn't want to type and all that crap. I'm an excellent mechanic, but in the old days unless you had a penis. . . . Did you ever hear of anybody holding a screwdriver with a penis? But sure, women mechanics can make it now.

My relationship with my father was quite distant. He and my mother had no relationship at all, except that he was terrified of her. My father was a very handsome man, but he just buried himself; he was just a presence. I was always sorry after I left home that I didn't get to know him better. I had very few dealings with him.

My mother was a violent woman. Anything would send her off, any mechanical object. I was thinking the other day when someone mentioned window shades—"God, how many shades have I hung!" She'd rip them off and throw them on the floor. She broke everything. If you liked something, she'd break it.

I saw my parents frequently. We lived in the same city. They would come to our house, and we would go down to the hotel and visit, but I never stayed there all night. *Never.* Then, in my mid-teens, came the traumatic shock: I had to go back and live with my parents in the hotel because my grandmother broke her hip, and we had to hire a nurse to care for her. My grandmother died five years later, and so did Grandpa. Anyway, I hated every single moment of living with my mother and dad. I just waited until I could get out.

And Mother got worse. I didn't realize what was wrong with her until I grew up. And that's one reason I'm so open. I hate this covering up. Everybody covered up, pretended she was all right. "There's nothing wrong with her," they'd say. "She just has these temper tantrums. You know how she is."

My mother would do anything she could to make trouble. For instance, in speaking of my brother she would always say, "At least

I have *one* good-looking child." He *is* good-looking, but Mother didn't like him either, and he had nobody. After he left home he would never go back, even when Mother was sick and elderly. It was even harder on him than on me. In spite of what my mother tried to do, my brother and I are very close. I don't see him much because he lives in Los Angeles, but we talk to each other often.

I was the only one who ever rebelled against her. I gave up church. I told her, "I'm never going into that goddamn church again!" and that was a big crisis. She hit the roof. Another reason she despised me is that I would not put up with her foolishness. For instance, she loved to ride in the car. But I was the only one who would say, "All right, you want to go with me? You be ready, or I'll leave without you." And I did.

In a way I'm glad my mother was as vicious as she was, because otherwise compassion might have overcome me in her old age. I would go back every year and paint the house, fix the gutters, and do all this stuff. And there was this poor old woman, out there alone in that house after my father died.

I often considered bringing my mother back to live with Dottie and me, but after I went out to see her, I'd come back in a towering rage with violent migraine headaches.

Eventually I had to place my mother in a nursing home. She didn't last two months. She had had so many operations that, when she died, she had no more moving parts than a Volkswagen.

I certainly consider my mother a good example of survival. Officially my mother was eighty-six when she died, but I think she was older. She outlived my father by a long time, and he was younger than she. She was so completely self-centered that nothing, *nothing* ever interfered with what she wanted. She was completely without tension, and her family protected her from the consequences of her action.

When I was young, I had boyfriends, just like everybody else. One of them was a nice boy I had grown up with, and he wanted to marry me. We were pushed together, and it was getting to the point when I had to get out of it, so I tossed him over. You know what he did? He came to me the day before he was supposed to marry another gal and told me that this was my last chance. The biggest favor I ever did him was not to marry him. I didn't tell him why at the time, but I knew why.

When I was fifteen I visited my cousin for two weeks, and she became my first homosexual experience. She was the aggressor in that situation, and we only slept together a few times. I didn't know any of the street words or the technical words for what we were doing, but I went to the library and learned. My cousin was apparently straight because she got married and had five children. We never spoke of it again.

Subsequently, I found a high school classmate, a girl, and we stayed together for years. At that time I had to get out of my hick town. I thought, "My God, I'm a freak! Nobody in the world is like me, at least, not here in this God-fearing, small town." When I was twenty-one, my girl friend and I enlisted in the Navy together. Well, my friend got married while she was in the Navy. After the war she wanted to come back to me, but I wouldn't; I don't fool around with married women.

After the Navy I came here. It was a woman who led me here. People ask, "What brought you to St. Louis?" And I answer with one word: "Lust." That usually stops them. Eyes drop. You don't know how chicken-livered people can be.

Most people consider themselves good in bed, but I think that I was never really very red-hot as far as sex was concerned. I was with some very active women when I was young, and they all left me eventually. I would talk a great game. The spirit of the sport was more interesting to me than the accomplishment. I'd rather paint a room or fool around. And I could never really separate sex and love. I could never hop into bed with people who turned me on until I got to know them. If I didn't like ya, I couldn't love ya.

My family never mentioned my homosexuality, but they were not fools. I mean, one woman after another. But see, there again, what you don't say doesn't exist. Cover it up.

I have had several experiences, five or six, of varying lengths, two years, three years. Some of them were pretty wild. But I'm basically a homebody. I lost one gal who constantly wanted to go to bars. I hate bars. The bar scene never turned me on. I couldn't take it. Another one drank, and I don't care for that, either.

I've lived with the same woman now for more than a quarter of a century. I met her when she was still married. She and her husband bought a pair of Italian greyhound dogs from me. Her husband subsequently died, and after a while she moved in with me. I'm her first experience, and, also, her last. When she moved in with me, of course, I knew the score. In our active years we had sex often; then later, about once a week, and I'd say that our experiences were satisfactory to both of us. I think she'd say that, too.

My sexual desire now is practically nil. I don't know whether it's psychic or physical. I just lost interest. It began to wane when I was about thirty-five, and that's supposed to be the peak of your sex drive, isn't it? Well, now, for all practical purposes, my sex life is over.

I'll tell you something interesting, though. About six years ago, Dottie and I took a trip together. We went back to my home: She'd never been back there with me. And we did have a sexual experience then. And not again. I don't really know how to explain that. Maybe a different environment or something.

She shares my attitudes, so it's mutual. She's older than I, not that her age makes the difference. She mothers me more than anything else. She was very concerned that I was going out tonight. She said, "Leave the phone number in case you're out late." I mean, I'm a big girl, you know. But it's always been that way.

Sexually she was the passive one, and I the active. And, oh yes, I've had another affair behind her back. She doesn't know about it, but, really, it didn't affect me at all. It was somebody I had known a long time. It happened a few times, and it was just nothing; it didn't affect my life, my relationship with Dottie in any way. I just didn't connect it with her. And it's been years, it was years ago. I never confessed. Listen, I found the best thing to do is keep your mouth shut. As for my sexual future, to tell the truth, it doesn't cross my mind. What comes, comes.

For the same long period of time that I have lived with Dottie, I have been a computer operator in a hospital. It's important work, but it's so routine to me. I'm stultified. My job requires practically none of my talents, so I do other things. I expend my energies elsewhere.

Dottie and I are very active in animal welfare, and we raise dogs. And we're the ones who feed all the abandoned ducks on the pond. I dread Easter. People buy all these ducks and dump them on the pond after Easter. Well, you know, somebody has to feed them. Maybe on Sunday they'll come down with the kids and a loaf of bread, but that doesn't do it. We have to go to the feed store. Do you know what those food pellets cost? Fantastic, and going up all the time.

I *am* an animal lover. We run a little wildlife refuge in our woods. In fact, Dottie found a dead coon today, and we were very broken up. We get possums, coons, a shy red fox, and innumerable birds. We feed them all. We also have a dozen cats that we haven't raised. Every single one is a reject that we're caring for. A lot of people say to me that my love for animals is displaced motherhood. I don't know about that. I'm thrilled to death that I'm NOT a mother.

I'm disappointed in women these days because my experience has been that they do not and will not back each other. We have a large voting block. We could pass anything, elect anybody, but it's women who defeated the Equal Rights Amendment.

I'm now having menopausal symptoms: I have the hot flashes, and I never know when I'm going to menstruate. I may go three months without a period, and I think, "Hot dog! It's all over now, this useless mess is finished." Then I get it again, in fact, just last week. It may last three days, or it may be very heavy for a day, and then, nothing. I'm not really suffering. I don't really think about it much. I would only take estrogen as a last resort. I accept most signs of aging. You can't very well put on a pinafore and go backwards. But I fight. I refuse to acknowledge that I can no longer do the things that I used to do. When I was young, I could stay up all night and paint an entire room and then go to work. So I keep trying. I should consider diet—I'd like to get rid of some flab—but I think I'm just as comfortable with my body as I ever was. I always thought it was a pretty good mechanism. It did what I wanted it to do most of the time. Dottie says my hair's getting thinner.

I guess much of my self-esteem comes from the skills I have developed. I have been a machine-gun instructor, a legal secretary, an excellent mechanic, and an X-ray technician. My grandparents were very proud of me when I was a child, and they expected me to be great. I should have gone to school and become a veterinarian, but I used poor judgment and was too busy fooling around with women.

My self-esteem is also bolstered by my male friends. They are very important to me, and we talk to each other—more or less as men would talk to each other. For example, the janitor came in today and asked me about a fuel-injection problem he's got on his car. I get along better with men than with women, because I share their interests, and there are no sexual overtones.

Dottie and I have a fairly busy social life, both gay and straight.

Most gay people live in a gay world, but this bores me, because I don't know that many interesting gay people. Gay people are just like everybody else; they come in all kinds and flavors. They can be smart or stupid.

I don't worry about dying. I consider a dead body a piece of garbage, and if anybody wants any parts, fine. I don't care what they do with it, grind it up for chum or fertilizer. That's the way I feel about it. I don't want any tombstone, any ashes. I don't want anything. I don't think much of anything will be remembered about me. It doesn't matter at all, not in the least.

As soon as I am financially able, I'm going to retire and do the things I'd like to do. I wouldn't have any time on my hands. There are so many things I'm interested in. For example, I love antiques as well as building and refinishing furniture. It gives me a good feeling to hold a nice piece of wood in my hands. I'd also like more time to work around the place. Also, maybe I'd travel, go to Europe. I just want to do what I want to do when I want to. I know I could manage to live alone if I had to, but I wouldn't be too crazy about it. It comforts me to know that as long as I have the animals, my whole family is around me.

CHAPTER 18

Hope—An American Success Story

I was afraid of my daddy. . . . I never wanted to be alone with him. . . . I've come a long way from the backwoods.

Hope is blond and has beautiful, green eyes. Although she is unhappy about her excess weight, she knows that she is pretty. Her manner is forthright and confident. Her speech pattern reflects her uneducated, southern background. The undigested trauma in Hope's life was her father's sexual assaults. Her need to speak of it brought her to the interview.

A remarkable feat that Hope has performed is that, without denying the hideous shortcomings of her parents, she forgives them their limitations and is even able to take some strength from their positive qualities.

Hope married at fifteen and divorced at thirty. She is the mother of three, but her first husband has custody of the children. Now, at the age of forty, she is enjoying her second marriage of six years.

Hope has spent several years doing factory work and one year as a beautician. Work opened the world to her as college might to an eager student. Her story is evidence of the possibility for significant personal growth and social mobility in our society.

* * *

HOPE

THERE WERE EIGHT of us kids, and even though my daddy worked steadily in the mines, we never had much money because of his drinkin'. My daddy drank all the time, and I've always been bitter about it. I couldn't be a cheerleader; I couldn't be a majorette; I couldn't try for a beauty contest; and if I was nominated for anything, I had to decline because Daddy couldn't afford it. And yet he wouldn't let any of us girls work in the summer because he said, "People would think we were poor." The other girls I knew whose daddies worked in the mines wore nice clothes and their hair was well kept. I had to set my hair in bobby pins, and there's no way you can get a smooth pageboy with bobby pins.

The first memory I have of my father, he was buildin' or tearin' down some kind of a house, and I was sent to carry nails. I was about seven years old. He tried to handle me. When I was that small. I'll never forget it. It's the first thing I remember about him. He stood me up on these boards, and he took his hands, and he felt all inside of my clothes. From then on I was afraid of my daddy. I never wanted to be alone with him.

My next clear memory of him is a good five years later. My job, when I got home from school, was to wash the dishes and have the table set. Then after supper I had to do all the dishes again while Momma and Daddy went out drinkin'. One time I thought Daddy had left, and I got involved in the cartoon on the TV, and he came back in and started to take his belt off. I looked around and thought, "Nobody is doing anything wrong." He said, "I thought I told you to do the dishes." All I could do was let my mouth fall open. He gave me a lickin', but it was the only one I remember.

My dad was weird. I mean, he was touched. He had to be mixed up in his head. From the time we were little he always kissed all of us while we were in bed in the mornin', before he went to work. When he would come to kiss me, he would rest his hands on my breasts. I hated it. So I would tell Mother about that, and I know she said somethin' to him, because he'd never come to kiss us good-bye anymore. But then he would come to my bedroom in the middle of the night, and he would wake me up mashin' on my breasts. I would call my mother the minute I would wake, and then he'd go back to their room. The only way I could fight it was to tell my mother. She would get real mad and say, "It'll never happen again," like she was really gonna do something about it. Whether she ever said anythin' to him about it, I don't know, but she didn't stop it from happenin'.

One time when I was twelve I walked out the kitchen door, and my dad was out by the garage. He called me and I started over there and when I got halfway there I saw he had his "thing" out, showin' it to me. I stopped, and he said, "Come here." I said, "No," and I ran back in the house. I never talked back to my parents, but when my dad was alone, if he ever called me, I wouldn't go. I'd say, "No," and just get outta there fast.

I told my husband all about this on our wedding night. And I told him then, I said, "If we ever have girls, if you ever lay a hand on one of them, I'll kill you." I also told Danny, my new husband. I said, "You want sex, you go get a woman. Don't you go get a little girl." Not that I think he would ever. My first husband's not the type, and Dan's not the type, but I mean, when you've had that fear and you've been through it, you don't wanna see another little girl go through the same. I told them both, "I'll kill ya. I'll get somethin', and I'll kill ya, with all my strength I'll do it." And I would have.

My mother could read and write, but she never mentioned how far she got in school. My father couldn't read or write. I don't think Mother had any high hopes for any of us really. She made us go to school, but she never pushed homework. I liked school, so it was no problem. I think Daddy was her whole life and still is. She used to say, "When you kids get grown, I'm gonna leave your daddy. I'm not gonna live with him." And I used to think, "Why don't you do it now?" I was petrified of him anyway. So when all the kids were married, I said to her, "Why are you still with Daddy?" She said, "I'd be a fool to leave him now. He's retired; he's had a stroke; he don't demand much, just his beer and meals on the table; and I've got all his money comin' in." I think she would shrivel up and die without him. I saw her get deathly ill one time when she thought he wasn't comin' home. I think he was her whole life, and I think this was why she could never put a stop to what he was doin' to the girls.

I used to wish my aunt and uncle were my parents. They loved us and treated us like we were their kids. My mother didn't seem to love us. She never hugged or kissed us. But I remember a couple of times Mother used to play ball with us. She's heavy, about 260 pounds, and only about five foot tall—incidentally, that's my fear, bein' fat—but she'd run the bases and everythin', big as she was.

One of my mother's quirks is that she's just downright lazy, and she's a little two-faced too, which I don't go for at all. I heard her tellin' a relative how her house used to look spic and span, how she used to get up early in the mornin' and wash until dark. The truth is, she always kept a filthy house. But I remember that she could take a car engine apart and put the whole thing back together. I get that from her. I'm handy with gadgets, and I love machinery.

One thing I remember, when I was the oldest girl home and I was doin' most of the housework, I loved to read, and I'd be sittin' there readin', and she'd say, "Get in here and do the dishes," or whatever. I'd say, "Just a minute. Let me finish this paragraph." She would say, "One of these days you kids are gonna regret talkin' back to your mother." And so right away I'd close the book, but I'd think, "I didn't talk back to her. What'd I say that was wrong?" So I remember that with my own kids, when they say, "Just a minute," I give them a minute.

Mother and Dad used to go drinkin' all the time, so they really weren't with us all that much. It seemed to me that the reason they had a lot of children was so they would always have a baby-sitter. Maggie was a sister five years older than me, and I thought she was the most beautiful thing in the world. I wanted to grow up just like her. She took care of us all more like a mother than a sister. I didn't grow up sweet and meek like her, and now I'm glad, because now she just sits in a room crying. She's on welfare surrounded with kids, legitimate and illegitimate.

My sister Maggie got married when I was about twelve. She went for a walk with me, and she said, "I want to tell you somethin'. If you start datin', and a guy wants to do somethin' to you, say no." I didn't know from what she was talkin' about. "Even if he says he'll use something, you still say no, and if he wants to do anything to you at all, just still keep sayin' no, no, no." So I guess that I got some sex education from her.

I don't expect or want to end up like my mother. I don't want to be fat like she is. I don't want to be the dirty housekeeper she is. I don't want to be the back-stabbin' person she is. She drinks, and she smokes, and she doesn't care for her health. For years I hated my mother and daddy, but now I just hate what they did to me.

I see my mother as unsure of herself and her husband. She lived with the philosophy: If you don't think about it, it goes away. My daddy had some good character; with all his drinkin' he never missed a day's work. He supported us. He was a man of his word, and he could borrow any amount of money in our hometown bank, no collateral needed. My dad never beat my mother. He hit her once, but she told me it was her fault. She called him a "son of a bitch," and he told her when they first got married never to call him that. I know she loved Daddy, and I really felt that Daddy loved her in his fashion. Daddy's had a stroke, is retired, and drinks more than ever now.

When I was fifteen, I met Bob. My daddy wouldn't let me date unless we took all the younger kids with us. I dated Bob twice, and four months later we decided to elope. I thought Daddy would never let me get married. It was in my head, he's savin' me for himself. But Bob wanted to ask permission to get married. Daddy shocked me with his answer. He said, "On one condition. If you ever take a notion to hit her, bring her home, 'cause you better not lay a hand on her." I think there was love in that statement, but he never showed love.

The first meal I cooked for Bob was beans. I'll never forget it. He sat down at the table before I did, and I was still puttin' things on the table. When I took the first bite of beans, I gagged 'cause it was so salty. I went and spit it in the sink, and I said, "Why didn't you say somethin'?" because he was still eatin' the beans. He said, "Oh, it's not so bad. You'll do better next time." That's the way he always was. He knew I couldn't cook. That's why I always say Bob's a great guy. He'll make somebody very happy, but he's not for me.

He was a good husband. He helped me a lot. My housekeepin' wasn't filthy, like grimy dirty like my mother's, but it was sloppy, cluttery, like clothes laying all over, that kind of thing. But Bob was the kind that would help me with it rather than belittle me because of it. He helped me with the kids too, like a lotta husbands wouldn't. If I wanted to go someplace, like for groceries or shoppin', he'd watch the kids while I went.

I think when our kids were little, I wanted them to grow up believin' in Jesus and God, and I used Jesus and God to cope with a lot of problems with my kids. I'm sure Bob appreciated it 'cause he had more religious background than I did. I found that was a lot easier than spankin'. It worked one hundred percent better to tell the kids, "Jesus sees what you're doin' all the time, and when you're bad he knows it, even if Mommy don't." I still believe in Jesus and God and the Bible, the whole bit.

I'm stubborn. I get that from my father. Nobody tells me, "You're gonna do this," or "You're gonna do that." I found that out when I was sixteen years old. My husband told me not to wear shorts. It's one of his prudish ways. I told him I was gonna wear them, and he says, "You're not." I told him, I said, "If I'd a wanted a father I had one that was strict enough." "You're a husband," I said, "not a father to give orders." And I wore the shorts. Bob never gave me another order. He would always say, "I'd rather you wouldn't," and that went over bigger with me, bein' the kind of person I am.

When we were first married, we went to bed a couple of times in the night and then once in the mornin'. We repeated that almost every night, and even though I wasn't reachin' a climax, I enjoyed it. But during those first six months Bob kept tellin' me that he couldn't keep that up. I look back on that, and I think, "At twenty-two he was afraid of runnin' down?" Before the year was out sex changed to planned clockwork twice a week until we were divorced. It was never in the daytime. I told you he was old-fashioned. I think now, knowing what an orgasm is, that maybe twice I got close. It felt so good that I'd say I had two orgasms during my first marriage.

I was inhibited and Bob was puritanical. Neither of us knew anythin', but I thought there was more to it than what I was gettin'. I got sex books from the library and left them for my husband to read, but he wouldn't touch 'em. Maybe he thought that was belittlin' his manhood. He never improved. I don't think he even knew I was supposed to have fun too. After about eight years of marriage I talked to my sister about my sexual problems. She told me she at one time had been unable to reach a climax, but she found out she could enjoy it more if she was on top. So I tried that once, not sayin' anythin' because I was bashful too, and afterwards he apologized as though he had committed a very big sin. Anythin' he did with sex that was the least bit out of the ordinary Bob would apologize for. I wasn't forward enough to speak out and say what I was thinkin', although I've changed since those days. Bob's philosophy when anything was wrong was like my mother's—"If you don't talk about it, it will go away."

We were physically close in spite of our sex life. We were so close-seemin' to everyone that when we got a divorce, it was a shock to everyone, includin' my husband, because he hadn't known there was a problem. The whole fifteen years, any time we were together, we were holdin' hands. If we were just sittin', he had his arm around me. It was a very affectionate-type situation, and it didn't have to be in front of anybody. Just watchin' TV at home alone, we were cozy. Yet when we got to the bedroom, it was a different story.

At one point Bob hurt my feelings very much. During my third pregnancy, my mother-in-law lived with us. She was a super lady, and we got along fine. Then, I don't know if it was the pregnancy or what, but little things she did got on my nerves so bad. I said to Bob that since his mother was gettin' on my nerves so, maybe he could suggest that she visit another son until I could get back "on the track." He agreed, but he couldn't bring himself to do anything about it. I had worked at one point after my first baby, and Bob had wanted me to quit and never work again. So I told him, "I'm gonna get a job unless you ask your mother to go." I thought that would make him do it, but he said, "I guess you'll have to work then, because I can't ask Mother to go."

After I worked for three months Bob told me to quit, but I wouldn't. I worked that job for six years, and I paid a girl friend to watch the kids for us. He hurt me when he put his mother before me. It was the last straw. Any feeling of closeness was gone, even though we still held hands and maybe he still had feeling for me. We continued everythin' out of habit, but my feelings for him were gone.

I had one extramarital affair towards the end of my first marriage. I could have made love with that man all the time. It sure improved my sex life, but not with my husband. At first I tried to take what I was learnin' and teach it to Bob, but it didn't work. He was just as backwards as he had always been. Then after a while I didn't want to sleep with my husband at all. It made me feel dirty. I was in love with this man. I didn't ever marry him, but I wanted to divorce Bob.

Bob told me that I would never get the kids. He said there would be a court fight. Then he changed his mind and said he would give me everythin'. But I let him keep the kids, because by the time I was ready to leave, Bob's nerves were so bad that I was afraid he would end up in a mental hospital. Besides I didn't have anybody to take care of the kids, and if they stayed with him, his mother could help to raise them. I didn't want to take any material things from him either, like the house or the car, because I felt guilty. I felt that once he got over losin' me and I got settled, he would let the children come and stay with me. He was a great father with the kids.

I had about six or eight sessions with a marriage counselor who told me that I shouldn't leave my husband and children, and that at my age I shouldn't be looking for happiness or sex anymore.

I always felt Bob loved me more than I loved him. The things he did I didn't like were done out of ignorance, not because he didn't love me. I felt that from the day we were married. With me leavin' my husband, I was petrified. I wanted out, I didn't want to strip him of everythin' he had, and I didn't want to ask him for help. I was too proud, but I was scared to death because I didn't know if I could make it on my own. I would have starved before I would have asked him for help. I still feel today that I don't want to hurt the man. I hurt him enough, and I know I hurt him bad.

I would say that when I left my husband I was filled with a personal ambition that I didn't know when I was married. Part of my ambition was a determination to make it on my own, and some was to get ahead, to have somethin' better. What gave me ambition was seein' what Mom and Daddy could have had and didn't and also seein' Bob with that same attitude—"If you're makin' it now, why do anythin' more?" We just floated along, paycheck to paycheck. I wanted to take a step up, and I still do.

We were from the backwoods my whole life. In that first job I had, workin' in a factory, I saw how people really live. One of the women called me a religious fanatic because all I had to talk about was my kids and the church. Not that I was such a great Christian, but the only thing I did was I took care of the kids and went to church. So if you're sittin' across the table from somebody workin' and talkin', what else you got to talk about? I didn't listen to the news. I wasn't even interested in what was goin' on in the world. I didn't bowl. We didn't go dancin'. We didn't drink. I didn't smoke. I didn't cuss. It was because I didn't know nothin'. I was really dumb. That's what I mean by "backwoods." The first black person I had ever spoke to was at that job, and I was shocked the first time I ever touched her skin. Have you ever touched a black person's skin? Isn't it soft, and nice? And I used to say, "How come we didn't get soft skin like that?" I made a friend of Betty, the black girl, and we really got into some deep subjects, black and white-type subjects, you know? I guess I was honest, open with her, and she was the same way with me. She told me names they call us. She called us "crackers."

The actual work I did made me feel real good. I wanted to learn all I could about the job, and I thought I was good at what I was doin'. When a special job came up that only men had handled, I volunteered for it. It eventually led to more money, and I wanted to advance as far as I could. I worked at packagin' parts. Later I learned the numbers of all the parts and handled the paperwork too.

The factory where I work now has regular college courses which the company reimburses you for. If I stay with the job, I think I'll take advantage of that. There are so many things in this world to enjoy. I didn't realize I had a brain.

I'm very proud of supportin' myself after my divorce. In two years I had bought a used trailer and a new car to drive it. My income was helping to take care of my kids, and it really made me proud to know I could do that. My credit allowed me to borrow thirty thousand dollars for a home. I think that supportin' myself completely was the greatest thing in the world for me because now I know that if my second husband and I ever did split, I could take care of myself.

I've surpassed any expectations that I had about my life. I feel that I've come a long way from the backwoods. There was nothin' in my childhood that gave me any confidence. Even when my first husband told me I was pretty, it was unbelievable to me. I first felt attractive when I took a lover many years after I was married.

I learned to separate sex and love. . . . You can have sex with anybody to satisfy a physical need, but you can't make love with anybody. Between my marriages, I had plenty of sex, but I got uncomfortable and guilty having sex without love. I had sex with four or five guys and I felt dirty. I felt that I was turnin' into somethin' I didn't want to be, so I made up my mind, "I'm not gonna do it any more; there's not gonna be anymore bedtime." But then the next person I met was my present husband, Dan, and he was such a person! I don't even believe how we got married. It's like a fairy story to me. Everythin' seemed natural between us. Two months after we met we started livin' together, plannin' to get married. We lived together happily for eight months, and I kept tellin' him that if he had second thoughts to tell me because I didn't want another divorce.

Even today I can't separate sex and love. For example, if there's a little irritation in the house all day, then to go to bed with my husband, that's sex to satisfy his desire. If I'm really angry, I can't do that. But if there's love in the house all day, then I'm ready for love whether it takes the form of affection, an orgasm, or whatever. One of my girl friends told me that for bein' good in bed she charges her husband; if she wants a swimmin' pool, she's a good wife for a week. If she don't get the pool, that would be the extent of her sexual activity for a while. That to me is like bein' a prostitute, only you're gettin' paid off in things rather than money and from one man rather than ten.

Dan and I have intercourse more frequently than average. I'm satisfied dependin' on what's goin' on that particular week. If I'm tired, I'd rather satisfy him and be done with it and go to sleep. Sometimes I'm too tired, and I don't want to be bothered with the effort it takes, even though I know it's gonna be fun. And then there might be a week where we have intercourse every night, and where I have multiple orgasms every night. We've found with him and me that I can have orgasms with the help of his hand or with me on top. I've almost never had an orgasm with him on top, and when I have, the orgasm is so slight I almost don't know I've had it.

Dan didn't want me to work when we got married. He told me I was quittin' and that was the worst thing he could have done because I was determined, and I told him, "I was workin' when I met you and I'll work when I'm married, because I'm a workin' person and I intend to work." I always wanted to be a beautician so I put myself through school and went to work as a beautician. I'll go back to it. Dan thinks I'm good at it. He's got so much confidence in me he asked me to give him a permanent, and he's advertisin' for me, telling all his friends I give super "perms."

Dan didn't want for me to have anything to do with my single girl friends after I was married. Just even havin' 'em over for coffee and that kinda thing. He would rather have me spend my time makin' over him than doin' somethin' with a friend or with the kids and leavin' him sittin' on the couch. I tell everybody I got seven kids. I had to put a restraint on that. They're my friends, and they will stay my friends. Dan's better about it now. He's really changed a lot. And I expect him to restrain me when he doesn't like my behavior, 'cause you don't have much of a marriage otherwise.

Back in my first marriage I had wanted ten kids, but I learned I couldn't afford that many. When I was divorced, I couldn't have my kids live with me, so I decided I wouldn't take care of anybody else's children. But then after meeting Dan and falling in love with him and seeing how his kids were neglected, I couldn't find it in me to say no to takin' care of them. When we got married, I decided to have my tubes tied because we figured that his three and my three were enough.

My babies were the best babies, and they were all breast-fed. I was so proud of them. I feel that even though I'm not with my kids, I'm a better mother than the one I had. My greatest sadness is

that my kids are not living with us. My goal right now is gettin'
my kids to live here permanently, makin' them happy, and makin'
them understand why I had to leave them. And I want to help
Dan's kids.

Dan's kids were wild when they came to live with us. They had
been doin' what they wanted because their mother was never
around. They'd get on their bikes, and they could be gone all day.
My rule was: "You stay inside this neighborhood. You stop at
anybody's house, you better let me know, because I don't believe in
kids runnin' wild." So when we first got custody of 'em, it seems
Dan was trying to make the whole thing my job, maybe to get me
to quit work. But I was determined they were his kids, and he had
to help me with them. One boy, the oldest, had temper problems
so bad I was a nervous wreck by the time I punished him. The first
time I saw him carry on I just stood there with my mouth open. My
kids were never allowed to do anythin' like that. It's been two years
now since the oldest boy had a tantrum, so I think it's licked. Dan
saw that I couldn't handle all the problems alone so he helps a lot
more now.

No matter how fat I get Dan still loves me. He keeps tellin' me
how good a shape I've got, and I keep saying, "You're crazy. You're
supposed to be tellin' me how fat and ugly I am so I'll lose the
weight." To me, when you're too heavy, you're not sexy. A woman
should look like a woman. I do feel good that my chest is big. I like
my husband to be proud of me, and if I were flat-chested, it would
depress me a great deal.

In my first marriage it was an "I didn't know if I could survive
without him"-type thing. This one, it's more like "I don't like it
when he's away." I can't picture bein' without Dan and I like to
think he feels the same way. He tells me he does.

CHAPTER 19

Rosemary—A Radical

My father's rule was law, but after I was thirteen there was never anybody who could tell me what to do, no one ever. And no one will.

Rosemary, at forty-four, wears jeans, an undershirt, sandals, no bra, and no makeup. Her eyes and hair are pale brown, and her body is small and thin. Her voice and laugh are warmer and more forceful than her appearance.

Rosemary is a vegetarian, listens to rock music, and is open to everything new and youthful. In her kitchen above the jars of beans and rice is a poster that says "Fuck Housework." Since she was a child, she has been in angry rebellion against society, and she is proud to be a radical. "Unjust" constitutes her view of her father in particular and of society in general.

Rosemary was married at eighteen and divorced a year later. Her second marriage at twenty-seven lasted thirteen years and ended in divorce three years ago. She shares custody of her two teenagers with her husband. She lives on very little money, but hopes to have more income after she receives her graduate degree in social work. Her special interest and ability is counseling women.

Rosemary uses sex in a number of ways. Sex symbolizes her perpetual pursuit of love, her assertiveness, her mastery, her freedom from convention, her desirability, and her pleasure as well. It is Rosemary's paradox that, while independence is her god, so far she has "never gone a week without a man."

* * *

ROSEMARY

LOOKING YOUNG is very important to me. I make sure everybody knows I'm forty-four years old, because I love to hear them say, "Oh, you don't look a day over thirty." Unfortunately, they're not saying that as much these days. I was in a terrible automobile accident last year and, somehow, the result is that I look older. I'm getting lines on my face, and gray hair, and my body is all kind of sinking downward. The funniest thing is that when I do yoga and go up on my shoulders I see everything hanging down. Oh, I do hate that! I really want to learn to age gracefully and not lie about it or be unhappy about it. It's not good for my children to see their mother ashamed of what she is.

In spite of the aging that's going on I really like my body much better than I did years ago. When I was in my thirties, I began to realize that my body was OK, that I didn't have an ugly face, that my hips weren't too big, that my breasts weren't too small. I sort of came into my own sexually, and other men began to pay attention to me. I realized, all of a sudden, that I was attractive.

Until I read the Masters and Johnson book about ten years ago, I felt I was frigid, and that sexually I wasn't very good. But I latched onto that book like a leech, and it totally freed me. I found out I was perfectly normal. My feelings evidently showed, because I began getting attention from a lot of different men. That validated me. Fortunately or unfortunately, that's the way it was.

To show you how far I've come in ten years, let me tell you about a "feminist sexuality workshop" I recently attended. Here we were, twelve women sitting around in the nude. When you do that, I'm telling you, you lose any kind of skeptical feeling you ever had about your body. Everybody was completely disarmed. You undress and from then on you never worry about it again. Everybody talks so freely when there is nothing between you like clothes. We started out talking about body image, and then we got into masturbation, and then sexual relations with men and/or women— there were some bisexual women there. And we did massage: Five people massage one person; everybody had a turn. It was just fantastic, a tremendous experience. I attended this workshop because I'm going to be working with women in social work when I get my degree, and sexuality is a big part of my interest.

I don't know if it's good or bad, but I'm sure my background and childhood training is a little deficient in what it is to be a woman. I really tend to think it's good. I realized early that nobody takes care of you but yourself. I was mostly raised by my father; the aunts who helped raise me were distant.

My mother died when I was one, so the only parent I had was my father. He farmed me out to a number of different relatives until I was eight. It was during the Depression. He wasn't working, and he couldn't take care of me by himself. I didn't really have a substitute mother. There were all these different aunts, never a consistent other parent who said I was theirs. These aunts had kids of their own. Some were kind to me, but, you know, it's not the same.

My father would never quite give up control over me. I had to leave one aunt's place when I was three years old because of the arguments about how I was to be raised. My aunt said, "I'm not going to do differently with her than I do with my own, and if you can't accept that then you'll have to take her away." So he took me away. He had that kind of argument with every aunt I lived with. My father was always the most important figure in my life and I suppose he still is.

My father finally got a steady job, and I lived with him from the time I was eight until I was twelve. Those years I lived with my father were the happiest years of my life, but I don't attribute that to him. I attribute it to the fact that we lived in a little, tiny town in Kentucky, one thousand people, and I was absolutely free. He didn't pay very much attention to me and didn't feel afraid for me. If I was out after dark, nothing would hurt me in that little town.

I often didn't get home until ten o'clock at night; I knew everybody in the town; I had loads of friends; I was unfettered, allowed to develop; and I felt secure for the only time in my whole life. My father married a woman I adored. I wanted him to marry her. I had wanted a mother ever since I could remember, and now I was going to get one, so I was very happy about it. She tried hard to be a mother to me. Her failure was mostly my father's fault.

Sometimes he could be playful and nice, but when he disciplined me he became demanding and tyrannical. I have these visions of my childhood where I knew I was afraid of him, but desperate for him to love me. It was just awful. I used to ask him if he wanted me. "Am I satisfactory to you?" was one of the questions I used to ask. And his answer was always the same: "Well, we ordered you blond and blue-eyed, but we were very happy with you when you came as a brunette." Isn't that nice?

Maybe he resented me because of the burden I was to him, maybe because he didn't have my mother anymore. I know that I had a tremendous need for him, and he was never there for me.

When I was twelve we moved to another state, away from that idyllic town in Kentucky. It was a devastating thing, because my stepmother had lived all her life there, and she now had to move to a strange city with a baby and me, and she was pregnant again. It was awful for her. The house was an unhappy place. I had no friends and didn't know how to make friends in a new place. The new community was religiously different, and the kids weren't friendly to me. I was just becoming an adolescent and getting very rebellious, and my father couldn't tolerate that. He wouldn't listen to me. He wouldn't help me, and my stepmother wasn't allowed to. Every time she tried to involve herself, he said, "You just mind your own business."

My stepmother's situation was difficult. We never really had problems with each other. I admire her a lot. I never blamed her for anything. She's always been pretty unhappy. She came into some money a few years ago, and she told my father then, "Listen, you just watch your step, 'cause I don't have to stay with you anymore. I don't have to take your abuse anymore." I was overjoyed that she said this. He needs her enough that he might treat her better.

My father always wanted me to behave in some way that I wasn't. It was never clear to me exactly what he wanted. My father's rule was law. And for his wife too. Nobody was allowed to deviate from his law. I simply wouldn't stand for it. I realized when I became a teenager that my teenage years were going to be just hell if I stayed with him. I just wouldn't put up with it. He hadn't brought me up somehow *to* put up with it, isn't that strange? He didn't cow me, for some reason, as much as he wanted. I think it was because I wasn't with him enough.

My father disapproved of me from the day I was born. In everything I've done I think there was a measure of it that was meant to impress him one way or the other. Either to kick him in the teeth or to get his love, neither of which ever seemed to work. I was never really able to impress him. When I was thirteen I told my father I didn't want to live with him anymore. I went to live with two aunts. I guess they were sorry they offered, because I was rebelling against them, too. I was making my own rules. It was their house I left when I got married at eighteen. There was never anybody after that who could tell me what to do, no one ever. And no one will!

For many years I hated my father, and then I decided I loved him after all. I was trying to "make it" with writing letters, my kids were writing letters, and he was sending presents to them. Seven years ago he met my children for the first time in his life. He had never shown any interest. Even when he was in this area a few times, he didn't visit us, didn't even call. He's never been to this house. And all the time I lived with my two aunts, from the age of thirteen to eighteen, he didn't call or write once. So naturally I have felt tremendous rejection. During this letter-writing period I was trying to break through all that.

Well, when Kenneth, my husband, and I separated, I wrote a

letter to my father to tell him. He wrote me back and said that he thought I was really terrible, and that I had no character, and never had, and that he knew when Kenneth and I got married that it was never going to work, because how could anybody like me ever make a decent home? And so on. It was a horrible letter. I showed it to my counselor, and she has never given it back. She thinks I shouldn't read it again. I have never contacted my father since. I think I've given up the battle.

I've enjoyed more sex in my life than love. It's probably true that I've searched for love all my life because I couldn't get love from my father. Certainly if a Freudian got hold of me, that's what he'd say. But it doesn't seem to help me to know that. It doesn't matter. I have to deal with what I do even if I know where it comes from. I know I have to find my source of strength somewhere else than in a man. That's why I continually struggle to find myself.

My first marriage is so unimportant that sometimes I forget about it. I was with him so little, much less time than any number of men I've been with since. The real reason I got married was that I was living with relatives. It had always been made very clear to me that as soon as I graduated from high school I was to get out. I was scared shitless, to tell the truth, and getting married was finding someone to take care of me. It was security. But as soon as I got married, I thought, "Whew! This isn't what I thought! I don't like this!" My husband told me what to do, and it wasn't any fun. It wasn't like having a date all the time. He wasn't any good in bed; I wasn't enjoying it. I had an idea that I was supposed to so I complained to a doctor. The doctor got my husband into the office, too, and said that if he didn't try to satisfy me, he was going to lose me. My husband said, "Nobody's going to tell *me!*" And he wouldn't do anything about it. Besides I didn't like his trying to run my life.

I was married at eighteen, divorced at nineteen, and remarried at twenty-seven. My second marriage lasted thirteen years. I had quite a bit of sexual experience in between marriages. I learned a lot, but I still did not spontaneously enjoy sex, and I didn't yet accept the fact that it was normal to need external stimulation, manual or oral. I thought that women were supposed to enjoy penetration, and if they didn't have orgasms that way, there was something wrong. So I always suffered from a feeling of inferiority about my responses to both my husbands.

Kenneth, my second husband, was an excellent husband and

father and he never tried to rule me. He was also secure, safe, caring, and very dependable. But he was never a very good lover, and I was never attracted to him sexually. I was the only person he had ever slept with, and we just floundered around a lot. Sometimes we discussed sexual problems, but it was hard; we were embarrassed. Kenneth wasn't terribly responsive. Since he didn't know very much, he felt inferior. Sex became pretty ritualized, like every other night, or twice a week, or only certain prescribed ways and if it ever differed, it was unnatural to us. That's the way it was. In general, we became less close than at the beginning of our marriage. In fact I used to stay away from him as much as possible, and he seemed to accept that.

I started having extramarital affairs. I found that I did not know how to say no. I needed the men, not the sex, for my self-esteem. I felt free and as my sexuality increased, I found extramarital sex happy and satisfying, whereas, when I did get around to having orgasm with my husband, it wasn't all that good. I make my sexual preferences very clear at the beginning and if the man I'm with doesn't like it, he can leave. And that has indeed happened. I have never played the passive role in sex or in anything that I do.

I told my friends about my extracurricular affairs but I wasn't into having my husband find out. I really didn't want him to know. A lot of my friends were playing around too, and those who weren't probably wished they were.

I finally did tell Kenneth the truth as a result of my therapist, and I will never forgive him for making me do it. I said, "It would hurt Kenneth very much and I can't see the reason. Can't I rebuild my life without hurting my husband?" I came home from a therapy marathon full of fervor, very much under the power of the charismatic, sexy therapist who said, "Nothing is any good if it's built on lies." I did what he told me and was *instantly* sorry.

I never in the world wanted to hurt Kenneth that way, but it was too late. Kenneth started therapy too, but from then on it was just downhill. He could never trust me again and his own self-esteem was ruined. He did forgive me and he did want to continue the marriage, but I wanted to continue having other sexual relationships. Kenneth wouldn't accept having an "open marriage," which I understand. I don't think a marriage can work where one of the partners really loves the other and doesn't want to share that person.

It's unfortunate, it really was unfortunate because Kenneth was fine in so many ways. I don't like being divorced, I don't like having broken up the family for my children, but at the time I was very much into the Women's Movement and I wanted to be completely independent. I still do.

I remember that I idolized Kenneth. I thought he knew everything in the world and was the most brilliant, wonderful person that ever lived. There was nothing that he couldn't do. He took excellent care of us, and we had friends, and we had a fine relationship. We had no conflicts over anything. We were both Scroogey about money—socked it away and never spent it; we weren't religious, and we absolutely agreed on values. Politically, we've always agreed, always fought for the same things, and we weren't at odds about what we should do with our children or about how they should behave.

I always allowed Kenneth to comfort me and hold me and help me through bad times. I take more than I give. He's a nurturing kind of person, the kind of man I like, and I need a lot from the people who are close to me. Really, there was so much good in our marriage that I wonder, sometimes, why the hell I couldn't have just buried my sexual responses and made something out of my marriage.

I have to admit that sex was not my only problem.

When I got married, I was thrilled to quit work. I wanted to polish tables and stay home. But being a housewife and mother wasn't all that I had hoped. The roles didn't bring me the satisfaction and happiness I had expected. I was horribly disappointed. I was compulsive about the housework, and, being a perfectionist, I got no joy out of it. Mainly, though, my independence—so important to me—was threatened by constantly being defined in relation to my husband and children. I didn't really know exactly what I felt until I read Betty Friedan's book, and then I said, "My God! This is it!" I wanted what I had but it wasn't enough. I really had to have something for myself, my own accomplishment, that had nothing to do with Kenneth or the children. I've been struggling for that ever since. Being a mother is the most important thing in the world to me, but I want to have something else as important so that I'm not overwhelmed with that role.

I was always elated to have children. I'll always want to be involved in their lives. I couldn't not be. I know women who have left their children, but I could never do that. I don't pass judgment on them because I know I have a special circumstance. Not everybody was raised the way I was raised. I didn't have a mother, and I suffered enormously from that. How could I ever deprive my children of that? People who were raised with mothers don't necessarily feel that motherhood is some sort of sacred thing that subsumes their whole existence. If I had had to give custody of my children to my husband, I could never have left him. I could not exist, I could not be sane if I gave away my children. The guilt would just weigh me down. However, to be partly deprived of one's father, that's normal. I lived that way. Besides, Kenneth is a great father whether he's living here or not. He has never rejected his children.

I've never really been on the market as so many newly divorced women are, because I've lived for three years now with one man. I haven't had to go around trying to meet men. Since I was fourteen years old, I've never been without a man. As soon as one was gone, there was another. After each one was gone I'd think, "I'll never find another," and yet I would not be alone a week. When I think of that I wonder why that feeling is always with me. I know that if the man I'm living with now would disappear tomorrow, I'd have another man within a week. I don't know where I'd get him, but I'd get him. Maybe it would be just someone to sleep with for a while. That's why being able to have sex without love is fine with me.

I've broken down some of the prejudices women usually have about what sorts of men are suitable partners. The man I live with is seventeen years younger than I am. He's mature in lots of intellectual ways, so I don't lack intellectual stimulation. And certainly sexually we're just perfect. So I can't see that it matters.

I think I love him, but there are problems, like, he's not as knowledgeable and dependable as Kenneth was. He doesn't make any money; he doesn't support me in any way. He pays rent, and he pays for his food, and we share if we go out, and so forth, and he's a good friend to my kids. But in no way can I depend on him. I think that we're good friends and terrific lovers, but the thing that's sort of bad about it is that I lean on him, just as I leaned on my husband. If I have an emotional problem, and I'm very volatile, I scream and yell and cry a lot, and I lay that all on him. But he doesn't handle that as well as Kenneth did. He makes me take a lot of it back.

We decided that when my kids come back—they've been living with their father for a while—he will have to leave. There isn't room for us all. He is a writer, and he has been using my room as his study. During this whole time that he's lived here, I have never had a room. I've had nowhere to go to be alone. I use the kitchen table as a desk, but the whole house is here, you see. So I've never had anywhere private where I could go without chasing him out of the room. I decided I couldn't live with that anymore. I have to do this thesis to graduate as a social worker, and I'm going to have my two children again, and I need my space. And my lover needs his. He's getting his own place, and we're going to sort of go steady and see what happens. It's very shaky.

I know my neighbors think I'm just atrocious; part of it is the way I raise my children, pretty freely. And then, not only do I live openly with my lover, but there are always a lot of other people in and out of here, all colors and races and shapes and sexes. I've rented to gay people who were flagrantly gay. As a result of all this my neighbors won't speak to me. One of them built a fence so that they wouldn't have to have any contact with my yard. It bothers me for my children's sake. But they know that there are hypocritical people in the world, and they think more of me than they do of the neighbors.

My daughter has the hardest time accepting the way things are here. It's embarrassing to her sometimes. She doesn't really want to run into me downtown, looking like her, in jeans and work shirt and boots, which is the way I dress. With my long hair too, we look somewhat alike. We even behave a lot alike. What is she going to rebel against? I understand that that's a problem for her, but I also understand that she is going to have to deal with that somehow. I really believe that she and her brother are going to be stronger for having been raised by my values, rather than in some way that would be false.

I've never denied any of my values just because they were against what society teaches. Kenneth and I, in our whole political orientation, have always been against everything that's conventional. My thirteen-year-old son thinks it's perfectly wonderful. He feels so free. He says, "How many other kids my age are allowed to do this and that, and be as free as I am?"

I always felt that motherhood was going to be the most fulfilling thing. It took me a long time to admit that I wasn't feeling that way, that I wasn't being totally fulfilled. Everything wasn't just hunky-dory. And I was disappointed in myself for that. I felt the fault was in me for not being able to get everything out of this. I don't think I'll suffer from the "empty nest" syndrome because too much of me wants my children to be independent and out of my hair. I don't like anybody to be dependent on me. That part of motherhood has always been a shock to me; these kids hanging on me, needing from me when I need too much myself. I even need a lot from my children. My fifteen-year-old gives a lot to me, which I have to watch because she also needs more from me. That's one of the problems we have. Fostering independence in my kids is a very important thing to me. I don't want them to need me any longer than absolutely necessary. When I was married to Kenneth, I really expected him to take care of himself too. I thought my infidelities shouldn't be so important to him. I would say that my emotional life has been very much tied up with just me.

It helps to be able to live on very little money. I think that my entire life has prepared me for that, because I've never had very much and I've never asked anybody for anything. Since I was eighteen years old I've supported myself completely. I never asked anyone for a penny. And I feel that I worked for what I got when Kenneth supported me. Since we've been separated I've had hardly any money. And yet I really have everything I need and almost everything I want. I think it's a skill. I know how to keep my head above water.

Before I started in the school of social welfare one year ago I wanted to work; I wanted to make some money. So I just answered every ad I came across. I got a job as a secretary, but I lost it for opening my mouth. I don't think I can be a secretary anymore. I can't be that person who can be a secretary, subservient, but I would be able to find some job if I had to. I'll work, right down to the very lowest thing, which to me is either checking in a supermarket or housework. I'll do it if I have to. I just will, before I'll ask anyone for help. I wouldn't mind going on welfare either, if I had to. I think I've earned that; I've been a good citizen, paid taxes. But I don't want to give anybody any of this house—the Welfare Department takes a lien on your house—so I'll avoid welfare as long as possible.

The Women's Movement now is where I try to put my energy. So through these different groups over the years, I've touched an enormous number of people and areas. Whether or not I've been effective is hard to tell. It's hard for anybody to judge if they're effective because if you're a radical working outside the system you can't easily see the results of your work. But it's important to me to know that as a separate individual, not attached to anybody else, I am sought after for certain things.

As part of my degree this year, and I've gone to college for the last ten years to get that degree, I worked as a counselor in a family agency. I was really terribly effective. I found that I had a facility for listening and for helping people. The clients I had kept coming and they said they really liked it. I anticipate having trouble finding a job only because I always anticipate having trouble doing anything.

As soon as I alert my friends that I'm looking for a job, something will come to my attention. I have an enormous number of friends. When I had that accident I was overwhelmed by the numbers of people who were willing to just knock themselves out to help me. It makes me feel very good. So many women are afraid of loneliness, but I'm not. When I'm alone, it's fine. I don't really know what a lonely person feels. It's strange. I assume that what people mean is that there is no one who knows or cares how they feel, or that they even exist. But if something happens to me there are dozens of people I can count on. When I don't pick up the phone, it's because I choose not to do it, because I choose to be alone. I think I'm really glad that I have a lot of energy. When I don't have it, like in the past year, I feel really angry. I don't like to stop. I just want to go. I don't like to have to give in to physical infirmity. It probably frightens me more than anything in the world. I would rather die than have an illness that made me dependent on others. My independence is what I value the most.

I never wanted to be anything else than a girl. My father did me a lot of disservice, but I also gained something from being left alone. *What* I am was always OK. Now, *who* I am is the question. I've sometimes wished that I could be different, happier, more contented, less neurotic. I still wish for that.

CHAPTER 20

Hannah–Low Man on the Totem Pole

I had always thought I was capable, but my husband led me to believe I was an ass.

Hannah is a forty-six-year-old social worker who has three children ranging in age from twelve to twenty-two. Her husband was an aerospace engineer. They were married for eighteen years and have been divorced for the past seven.

In spite of her salt-and-pepper hair, Hannah looks young. Her skin is tanned and her figure is lithe and athletic. During the interview she spoke intensely and rapidly, often laughing at herself.

When Hannah was married at twenty-one she had a measure of independence and accomplishment that many young women lack. Her father had trained her to make decisions and to manage her own finances, she had studied nursing, she felt comfortable and confident around children, and she was knowledgeable about cooking and household management. She was also cute and energetic, but she came to see herself as inferior because her husband treated her that way.

* * *

HANNAH

IT MAY SEEM SILLY for me to say these things, but I think I wasn't ready to get married, and I just let my husband be the authority figure and decide everything. Then when you get older you see that it isn't what you want at all. He made me feel inferior in lots of ways, but I was too good a cook and too good a mother for him to put me down for that. He would put me down socially. We would be going through the door to a party and he would say, "Now don't talk too much." When I think of it now I just . . . oh! . . . But that's the way he was, very low key at putting me down. He was never overtly brutal.

Somehow my husband always made me feel poorly about myself. I was always in a downgraded position. I could never, sort of, match up to him in many senses of the word. He was so superior! You don't argue with your "employer" very often. He isn't really that forceful. It was something we set up. I needed an authority figure so he assumed the role. He is what most people would call a selfish person if you knew him. He gets his way about things.

And I had a similar father. I knew my father cared about me. It was a duty, not love. He was consistent as the devil. I knew *exactly* where I stood with him all the time. If he said, "You do that and you're going to get spanked," I got spanked every time.

He was very unyielding, very narrow-minded. For example, if I was five minutes late, I was campused for five days. He never gave me any leeway. The excuse didn't matter, it just didn't matter.

In other ways he promoted independence. He made us account for our allowances. If you wanted to get your next allowance you had to account for every single penny of the last one.

Since my mother had severe heart trouble, he spent a great deal of time with us. He took me and my two younger sisters to New York and to many cultural events. He wanted us to grow up and be something. We were expected to find a field, and all of us did.

My mother's heart trouble kept her confined at home most of her life. She died when I was seventeen. Although I was out of the house a lot enjoying sports, I could always talk to my mother about anything, and I learned a lot of mothering from her too. She loved her domestic role except that my father put her down in the same authoritarian way he used with me. She was a graduate dietician and believed in education too.

My mother had had heart attacks twice a year for many years. The last five years of her life we had oxygen in the house for these emergencies. I got used to seeing Mother in an oxygen tent. I'd come in all bouncy about a hockey game and I must have been exhausting to her. I still have enormous energy.

My middle sister, unlike me, was sickly. She was quiet, played the piano, and had a very close relationship with my mother. When I was fifteen and my sister was thirteen, my mother was hospitalized for a whole year. I was not allowed to see her, but my sister was. That was my first shock, real shock. I understood the intellectual explanations, that is, my excessive energy, but I couldn't understand it emotionally, and the hurt was deep.

I had a very, very deep relationship with my grandmother, and I miss that terribly. I really think that she loved me without a question. I could do no wrong. She did not feel that way about my sisters. She was *mine*. She and I were a lot alike, exactly the same in so many ways. Strong, mentally and physically.

Because my husband was raised by a very domineering father, he tends to be a nobody when he's with his parents. And away from them, he's Napoleon, like his father. And it's interesting. My husband's father does it to his wife. She's a very well-informed woman, and she would mention something she came across in the paper, poitical, financial, whatever, and they all laugh at her, I mean collectively. But she manages to say, "Well, you may think that, but I don't." She rises above it. She just pushes it by and seems to say, "The hell with you." But I wasn't able to do that. It destroyed me.

I had also been raised not to poke fun at and tease, whereas my husband's family all do that, supposedly to make you strong and tough. Of course none of them is tough and strong, it turns out.

My husband didn't help at all with the children, the house, parties, nothing. We had parties frequently, and I did everything. We'd go sailing. Sailing either breaks a family apart or cements it together. We would sail all day, close living, with the children on board. He'd sit at the helm, and I would do all the work on the boat. Then we'd anchor, and I'd take care of the children, do all the cooking . . . and this went on for years. I just assumed that was my normal role.

I chafed all the time, but I hardly ever said anything about it. I would get this cold shoulder from him, cutting me off from his emotional being; that's the way he'd do it, and I couldn't stand that. That's how he dealt with me, removing himself from me. I like to talk things through with a person, and I could never talk with him at all. He didn't choose to try to understand. I guess I wasn't important enough. And yet, the truth is he was far more dependent on me than I was on him. He didn't know how to cook. He didn't know how to fix his clothes. He didn't know how to pay his bills. He didn't take care of himself, essentially.

Then I had a very close friend who moved into this neighborhood. I absolutely adored Claire. She just opened all sorts of doors for me. I was at the right age to have them all opened, and she opened my eyes left and right. About the way I felt about my husband, the way I was raising my children, and everything else. She had six children of her own, and so we spent hours talking, and it was all fascinating to me. She was having many of the same problems. She was unhappy in her marriage for various reasons; mine were different. We hadn't done superbly well with our kids so we had things to discuss about why our children were doing certain things. So we became close friends.

I began to suspect my husband was seeing Claire. I'm sure I was the last to know, just classic, but I was. They were both so good at talking me out of my suspicions, and I cared so much about both of them that I believed them. I'm gullible and I wanted to believe them. I basically can't tell a lie. My suspicions bothered me so much that I mentioned them to Claire's husband, whom we saw regularly, and he totally rejected the idea; he laughed at me. So I just shut up about it now that I had three people working against me. But the undercurrent got worse and worse, and I had severe insomnia. For months on end I couldn't go to sleep. A couple of times I tried to follow my husband or Claire to see if they were together, but I never could find them. All this time she was my "good friend." Then it all broke. This was seven years ago.

I felt this great sense of relief that I wasn't going out of my mind. I truly thought I was. I just didn't know what was happening to me. And Claire was very understanding about me. We three went on seeing each other because her husband almost went "ape," almost lost his mind on it. She suspected he might. She had wanted to get away from him before and had never had the courage or help to do it. He was a very scary character.

So when it all happened, the three of us stayed pretty close; at least we talked. We talked about what we were going to do and how it was going to work out. At the time I didn't think I was going to get divorced. I thought we would all recover from it and go back to our normal ways. We had been married seventeen years and had three children. It was spring, and we were all lying out here on the lawn talking about it. In the meantime Claire's husband had left. He couldn't stand it. We were all very concerned about what he might do—suicide, murder; he was that bad. That was our main concern then.

Then we all decided to try to go back to our spouses and be everything everybody wanted. Claire was a very psychiatrically oriented person and wanted us all to go to "shrinks." So we all agreed, and crazily enough we were all going to the same one, all four of us. But Claire's husband and I, naturally, were against the whole thing. We didn't think that by unburdening ourselves we would learn anything. Claire's husband really put his foot down. He went once, and that was the end of it for him.

I would drive forty-five minutes because Claire thought this psychiatrist was so good, and the last time I went he asked me how I saw myself in relation to her, or what was different about Claire and myself. And I answered that I thought that if there was a party across the street and we both had sick children, Claire would go and I wouldn't. And then he asked me, "How do you feel about where you are in this foursome?" I said, "I feel like the low man on the totem pole." And he said, "Well, that's the way I see you, too." Big help! I don't know what I was paying, but I walked out of that place angry and crying at the same time, and I said, "This is ridiculous. I'm not driving forty-five minutes to be told that I'm low man on the totem pole. I know that!"

It was the best three months of my marriage that I had ever had. Unbelievable. My husband tried to satisfy me sexually, something he had never concerned himself with before. He was more than helpful; he talked more than he had ever talked in his life. We cried together, we laughed together, we did things together. I had never been so close to him as I was those three months. So I knew we could make it if Claire and her husband could. And if Claire couldn't make her marriage work, that was going to be the end.

And one day, nearly a year after the first discovery, I knew it was all over. But it was all right. The shock was gone, I was sleeping again, I wasn't going mad. I looked at my husband one day, and I said, "You're seeing Claire again, aren't you?" He said, "Yes." And I said, "They aren't going to make it, are they?" He said, "No, but I want you to know that I could have made it with you, but I just love Claire and I want to live with her." So he left, and that was when the really hard time began.

It was just about the hardest time I can possibly remember in my life—worse than when my mother died, much worse. And I had no best friend anymore either. It was just awful!

I had smartly gone back to school that year, as a junior. My nursing credits weren't accepted, and I had to do a lot of science courses over. That kept me going. It was a diversion at the time when Claire and my husband got married in Mexico.

The following year I was doing social work for the Health Department. I broke down a couple of times and had to tell my boss what the problem was, but it all began to get better, every single day. And then it got better and Better and BETTER!! For the first time in my life I was earning my own money, I was totally self-sufficient, going to Europe, and doing everything I had ever wanted to do with no one criticizing me.

For the first year after my separation, I didn't date anyone; I barely had my head on my shoulders. But when I did start, it was like when I was younger. I had more dates than I could handle. I got called by married men in this village, which threw me absolutely. I was really a very sheltered, naive person. One man tried to rape me—an older man I knew slightly who walked me home from a local meeting. He was drunk, I'm sure. But a lot of things were a shock. You find out when you become single again.

My two sisters and I were all divorced, and I sincerely believe that we suffered from the shame of divorce as much as anything. I could hardly say, "I am divorced." It was like saying, "Look at me, I'm a failure." It doesn't bother me at all now, but I remember it.

My father was horrified that my two sisters and I all got divorced. He was undone. He was very sick then. I tried to explain it, but he just couldn't hear anything. By the way, both my sisters married authoritarian types, too, right down the line. My middle sister has remarried a person who is just right for her, an equal. But oh, at such a cost!

As the years passed, my father got more and more narrow-minded, and I couldn't communicate with him at all. I tried so hard. I wanted to relive some of my past or talk about my mother, and he just couldn't conjure it up or get off the superficial level with me. He was always playing the father role. He couldn't let me in. My father died recently, and I've thought about him a lot this past year, but I feel no remorse.

After my divorce I tried to tell Claire over and over again how glad I was that this had happened. She would never see me. Even when she got very sick—she died of cancer three years after they were married and was severely ill the last year—she would not see me or talk to me; her guilt was so great. I believe that.

I talked to my ex-husband about it later—we are really as good friends as people can be under the circumstances—and told him that Claire really set me free. Claire *really* knew my husband didn't love me and that I was under this terrible shroud. She clearly recognized those things, and she went ahead and did things about *her* life, thereby making me do things about mine. My husband has truly had a hard time—her death and all.

But in contrast, *today I'm high man on the totem pole.* Claire is dead. Her husband remarried very quickly, and I suppose has some sense of happiness, but he never stopped trying to get his revenge on Claire through the children. He kidnapped the children. He was destructive. He forced the kids to make difficult decisions. He tore them apart. Claire thought he was a maniac and wouldn't let him have any of the children. Well, they all ended up with him. She couldn't prevent it.

My husband had a very rough time when Claire died, but he's all right now. He dates. But essentially he hasn't changed. He's all the things I lived with and fussed about and didn't like.

I also found out that I could take care of myself. I'm a very capable person. I had always thought I was capable, but my husband had led me to believe I was an ass. But I take better care of myself and my affairs now than I did when I was married, so I am really better off than he is. He was essentially a cold, reserved person. He's a little warmer than he used to be. I think Claire brought him out. He really loved her. I think he was happy for that short time. But I think she wasn't happy with him. She must have discovered all the things that I had said about him, for instance, that he never helped with housework. And I think he definitely did not really like women; they were inferior and he superior.

My husband and I didn't discuss sex ever in our marriage until that three-month period before the divorce, and then we did. I had told Claire that I had never had an orgasm in my marriage and that I was at an age now when I thought I deserved one. I had masturbated for a number of years and was perfectly aware that I could have an orgasm, and I was now ready to demand one. But the kind of comments I got I'll never forget. My husband would say things like, "You can't demand that. You have to earn it." He also said that about respect once. It's the kind of remark he'd make that would leave me in the pit of despair, with my pins knocked out from under me. So then I'd have to recover and get my courage up again. I guess I was trying to discuss it with Claire to make myself feel that I was within the norm in wanting to express it.

I must say, he did try harder. But then, he was having an affair with Claire, which is very interesting. Maybe they discussed it. But the sex *was* better. Certainly he made *her* have orgasms, but I believe he loved her. I think there's such an enormous difference if a woman feels loved. And I never did. I think it's much easier for a woman to have an orgasm if she feels loved. Some women have them more easily than others. It seems to be a mental thing. It's fascinating. I never had an orgasm in my entire married life. It wasn't until I had a man fall in love with me.

I had never before had sex with a man who really loved me. He just convinced me slowly but surely that I was going to have an orgasm. He spent hours. And then it got easier. We made love every single day of our lives, if not two or three times. He was much younger than I was; he was the best thing that ever happened to me. I thought I loved him at first, and we lived together for three months. Then I realized that the sex had been superb but I had confused the two, sex and love, and I wasn't in love with him. And I was hurting him. He was a very nice person.

The big problem was my intellectual pursuits. I was just about to graduate, I had a challenging job, I was very gung-ho about getting my master's, and my whole intellectual outlook was very different from his. He was not a reader. He didn't like music. He hadn't been raised the same way. It was a mismatch. But he was a gift to me, and I needed it desperately. He made me what I am today.

I began to have such a sense of myself that I wasn't going to live without it. If I went to bed with somebody, I was going to have an orgasm, too. And it got to be easier until I reached a point where I decided that all the men I knew were rats. They were perfectly willing to give in one way but not another. They were glad to make love to me, but they wouldn't come home and help—I had two children at home, my son having gone to live with my husband. So I decided to cool my heels for a while.

I was very happy with what I was doing, working hard and going to school, and I was beginning to get a little tired of all the sexual activity which was not particularly interesting to me because of the people I was having it with. I was annoyed with my jaded outlook on life, so I just cut all bridges. I still marvel at it. I stopped dating all these people I knew.

And then a man I had known for twenty years called me up and asked me to go to the movies. And I remember thinking, well here's somebody who doesn't want to get into my pants. It was the most different date I ever had in my life. He didn't touch me, he made no advances, and took me home and said goodnight. So I immediately became interested in him.

I had always resolved not to date a married man. I was not going to put any woman through what I had gone through, even if I knew the husband didn't love the wife. There are plenty of fish in the sea. His wife had recently walked out and left *him*. I was in no way responsible for their breaking up. So we went out and we talked. I knew his parents well, I knew his wife, his children—I had taken care of his kids when his wife was sick. I just knew so much about him that he was like an old friend. And *comfort* was there again. And that relationship just grew and grew and grew, and I haven't seen anybody else for the past three years. There's no fear in this relationship. It's a very equal thing. I believe I have found the man, and he, me. His name is Carl. We don't plan to get married, at least not now. We're afraid of spoiling it.

First of all, I'm attracted to authority figures, and Carl's a very strong person, although he shares everything with me and listens to me more than I've ever been listened to in my life. We have watched marriage as it exists in the United States today, and there are so few marriages we respect, so few that have anything like what we are living, that we don't want to jeopardize what we have. We want to protect it and guard it.

For instance, we have slept together with or without sex every day of the week for I don't know how long, EXCEPT we both take off from each other a day a week, a day that's totally ours. We don't intrude on the other person's privacy. You can't do that when you live in the same house. This is totally protected. We feel that it's titillation, it's excitement. We do what we want to do, even if it's to go shopping with a kid. It's a day when you don't have to worry about that other relationship.

Another thing about marriage; Carl *is* an authority figure, and I'm a little fearful that if I subject myself to being with him every single minute of every single day, essentially, under the same roof, that I will lose this sense of ME that I have so newly found. And I'm frightened of that. It's very easy to preserve that sense when I'm here at my house. I mean this is my domain and watch out! So although we share everything, and I believe our love is as true as any I will ever find, and Carl feels the same way, we really don't want to get married. And there isn't any reason to. We have everything we want: We live nearby, we can see each other anytime we want, we can spend weekends together.

And guess what? Carl always wanted to sail, and his wife wouldn't let him, and now for the first time in his life he has a boat, and for the first time in my life I love sailing. Also, because his wife has the children some of the time and my husband has mine some of the time, we can get away completely alone. Of course, it helps that in this community there is no stigma attached to being unmarried, or, if there is, I don't care about it. And my children aren't upset by it. In fact, all the children have benefited.

Carl and I are both planners, by the way. We look at property; we talk about trips we might make, places we might live in. We do expect to live together the rest of our lives and maybe if we were ten or fifteen years older we'd talk more about marriage in the future.

I am more active as a sexual partner now. I have learned to be assertive, too. If I feel like making love, I will go right ahead and try. And I never would have done that before, never. It's fun. It's just downright fun. It's so lovely to be able to try things and do things and not fear rejection and not worry about the consequences.

I never thought of sex as being a big thing in my life before, but it definitely is now. With my husband it was good sex even if not really satisfying. I guess I just accepted it the way it was. I didn't think of finding anyone else. I really loved my husband, and I wanted to make it sexually with him.

One of the things that is so wonderful in my new relationship is the honesty. We are friends as well as sexual partners. My husband was never honest with me. He didn't lie so much as not tell the truth.

Here's an example: When I was expecting my last baby, my two older children aged seven and ten were fascinated. And having been a nurse, I was enthralled with pregnancy myself. I enjoyed it. And I had pictures of fetuses and so forth. One morning they were both listening, feeling for kicks, with their heads on my abdomen. So I said, "Would you like to see what this baby looks like right now? I have a picture." But my husband said sternly, "They're too young for that." That's the sort of person he was. Here were two kids fascinated and ready to learn and I with the straight information . . . and he . . . oh!

I knew I was going to be a good mother. I loved nursing them. I had a ball with my kids. I wasn't one of those women who minded staying home. I was a very competent mother. I did so well with little kids when I was becoming a nurse I just knew that I related well to children. I was so confident about it that I am now convinced that it contributed to my husband's being a very poor father. There I was supreme and I don't believe I let him in. I cut him out. He probably felt that since he couldn't compete he'd stay clear, and he did. It was my mistake.

I'm very proud of the two oldest. My son is graduating from college this year. He persevered. And my daughter is a scholar; she's terrifically bright. She's not doing too well with men, though. I'm concerned about that. She puts all men off, and she does it in a destructive manner. Snide, sarcastic. I've talked to her about it. We've had a couple of real crying sessions about it. She had her first affair this year; it was not satisfactory at all. Carl has been more instrumental than anything else in getting her head straight about men.

When I first started seeing a lot of Carl, she was unbearable to him, insulted him, pushed him verbally. He had let it roll off his back, but I knew it was bothering him. Then one night at the dinner table she was being silly with a glass of milk. She gestured toward Carl, and the milk flew out of the glass all over him. So he picked her up and spanked her, humiliated her more than anything else. She went crying into her room. I knew she deserved it. Carl looked at me and said, "She must learn to suffer the consequences of her actions." So Carl went in and talked to her and solved the problem with her immediately. Their relationship changed overnight. They have been fast friends ever since. She wanted to be put in her place in the worst way. Her father never had. He had always ignored her bad behavior. Her father was never one to warm to her, either; he never held any of them, kissed them or anything. Well, the last one, yes. He finally grew up and enjoyed a child. The older two were just chores. The last one, the one he didn't want, is the one he's close to. She's definitely Daddy's girl.

I lead a very busy life now. I absolutely adore New York City. I love the tourist things. I must go to the opera regularly; I must get to the ballet, the theater; it's *exciting* to get to New York. I don't have to go with anybody. I love talking to people. I used to love bars, where you can talk to all kinds of people. Not so much any more.

I play tennis, I ski, I sail. And the thing I'm most proud of is earning money! And I'm going to go right to the top. They're going to have to pay me full scale within two years. I'm enjoying being a woman more and more and more—even a middle-aged woman, because even though my hair is getting whiter, and my skin wrinklier, I'm really younger than I've ever been in my life. I'm more comfortable, too.

And, finally, I'm not frightened of death. I've seen a great deal of it in my nursing experience. I held quite a few people who were dying. To me it's part of life.

CHAPTER 21

Brigit–Anything Goes?

I got to the point where I didn't want to carry another child around, not a forty-five-year-old man.

Brigit is fifty years old. She is a soft, roundish, feminine, sweet-looking woman with youthful skin and a warm, whispery voice. She was married for twenty-six years, and although she had three children during those years, she chose to work full time as a physical therapist. She was divorced three years ago.

The interior of her house, decorated by her children, is filled with beanbag chairs and pillows on the floor. The walls are painted orange and yellow and covered with posters.

Brigit herself, although she is competent and self-assured, is as casual as her furnishings. She was drawn to the interview to discuss her experiences of the last few years. A six-month exploration of the world of swinging was one of those experiences.

* * *

BRIGIT

THERE ARE TWO REASONS why I look the way I do, that is, fairly trim. I'm a diabetic, so I don't eat many carbohydrates, and I have a lover with the body of a twenty-one-year-old man. He's in such terrific shape that he's incentive enough for me to keep trim. It would be outrageous for me to be fat and flabby when he has a body like that.

It was hard for me to tell one of my best friends that I was getting divorced. I thought she wouldn't understand, but she said that I should have done it sooner. She tells me that I am more sure of myself now, less indecisive. I agree. I notice changes in me. I would never speak out at a public meeting before, but now even if I'm nervous I do it. Why? Well, for one thing I no longer have a constant battering that I'm a "dumb broad." I have a supportive relationship with my lover, plus my friends. I can go out on my own, relate to people on my own, not have to fit myself into my husband's picture of me.

For fifteen years I accepted my husband's evaluation of me. I think it played into my childhood feeling of being the youngest, the least accomplished, of my siblings.

I was the youngest child of four. Both my parents were in their forties when I was born. Ours was definitely a happy family, but, in spite of the fact that my mother was a very kind person, I somehow wound up feeling inferior to my sister. She was really lovely, and I, as a teenager, was twenty pounds underweight, gawky, smaller, and less talented. I was jealous of my sister until she became a diabetic like me. Then I realized that she wasn't as strong as she looked.

I was very close to my father especially. I remember him taking me out to gather wild flowers. My education was pretty well taken for granted. There was very high expectation for the boys, and my sister was a high achiever, too.

My mother was very impressive in terms of her faith and her ability to impress others with her faith. She made me feel good about myself, I'm sure. She was a very warm, lighthearted person, but I'd say her horizons were pretty limited. She didn't even drive a car.

When my father died, I was in my teens. I was the only one left at home. My mother had rarely even written a check in her life, so I was the one who managed things. I didn't particularly like being the manager, and I wanted to get out of it. But I loved my mother, and I felt guilty about wanting to abandon her.

Mother was wrapped up in family and seemed to feel that she was personally accountable for everything, including the diabetes in the family, and the nervous breakdown of her oldest son; he was diabetic too. The only thing my mother did, out of the best of intentions, that was bad was making the rest of us take care of my oldest brother when he had his nervous breakdown. He had to be entertained, taken along when we had dates or went somewhere. If he was fantasizing or seeming to get worried, we were to walk him, take a walk with him like a dog, cheer him up. It was a burden, especially for my older brother and sister. That poor brother has had the works, every kind of mental treatment there is. Besides psychotherapy, analysis, living with a family whose members have all been analyzed, he's had insulin shock, electric shock, lobotomy, you name it. He's living now in a sheltered environment and is doing OK. There is a theory that diabetes and this kind of mental illness might be related. My sister had a temporary sort of psychosis in her thirties, maybe because she's a diabetic. I wish my mother had heard that theory, because she always felt guilty about her son's illness.

One of the ways I survived as the youngest in the family was to go my own way. I didn't necessarily pattern myself after anybody in the family. I played by myself. I had my own friends and activities. I don't remember getting extra attention just because I was the youngest. My mother wasn't able to take care of me when I got a little older, because she was too involved with my oldest brother, the one who was ill. We had a series of cooks and housekeepers. So I was brought up by these strong women, who were, incidentally, black women. I don't brag about this—it's a mammy story. But I know it had a strong positive influence on me. I had a picture of women who were competent and strong and interested in family and church. Some of them were talented in ways other than domestic. I think I learned from them the ideal of working on my own, being independent and resourceful. It also made it very easy for me to have friends of many different races and backgrounds.

I met Sean, my husband, in college. He had enough education to get a doctorate under the GI Bill, if he wished. But he was a very nervous kind of person. He couldn't concentrate. He switched majors four times and actually never finished college. He wasn't happy with himself about that, I'm sure. He wasted all that time.

Sean had an immature attitude about money. Often he was out of a job, and even so, all of a sudden a new chair would appear. He had periods when he would get diarrhea of the pocketbook. He'd be out somewhere and just write a check. I tried always to manage the money. The one time my husband handled our finances, it took me six months to get the checkbook straight again. I'm very cautious about money. I don't do something unless I have the money for it.

So there were periods in our marriage when Sean was working and periods when he was not working. As a result, except for two years, I've always worked. I'm a physical therapist, and I have a very successful practice now. I always helped support us, and I was happy to because I loved my work. I remember quitting work two weeks before my first baby was born, and there was nothing to do at home! I went back as soon as possible. There were times when I felt sad that I wasn't staying home with my children, but I was fortunate in having a wonderful woman to take care of them. The children don't feel that I neglected them the least bit by working.

In fact, they feel enriched. The only really frustrating time for me was when they were old enough to be by themselves, and one or another would call me at work and say, "She's doing this," or "He's doing that." It was terrible to be on the other end of the phone, unable to do anything about the problem. But they weathered that period, and no one died.

Sean always laughingly said that when I was forty, he would turn me in for two twenties. And he did. But by the time we actually got divorced it didn't really bother me.

I'm honestly not a snooper, but about six years ago I came across a letter, and I realized my husband had been messing around. This was three years before our divorce. Things began to add up. We had been to a reunion, and he had cavorted around and stayed out all night. What really infuriated me was that he had taken our older daughter to this reunion to show her off, and she was a witness to all this cavorting around. So after I read the letter I called Sean and said, "Meet me for lunch." He said he was too busy. I said, "Meet me for lunch or I think I'll be in a lawyer's office." He met me, and he just sang like a bird. You can understand a momentary thing, a man being just carried away. But I eventually realized, after a few weeks, that he had affairs from the time my daughter was a baby. I thought back on those years and remembered that I was working then, too, that I was keeping a big house, that at times it was thirty-two below zero, and I was taking my children to the baby-sitter every day and going to work eleven miles over a hill and coming home tired every night, getting the kids, feeding them. And all that time Sean had a girl friend. He wanted to continue having other women. He said, "Well, this is the way I live." No apology. No anything. He said, "I'm just one of those people who has to have more than one woman." It made me angry, because I had had plenty of opportunities to see other men if I had wanted to.

I never accepted the double standard. Sean should have allowed me the option to play around too, not that I might ever have used it. I felt that it was dishonest of him. Still, at that time I felt that I loved him, and I didn't want to break up the marriage. At first I was crushed. I cried for two weeks, and then I said, "Well, what am I crying about?" Because really, you can never go back, you can never go back to the situation that you once had.

I was attracted to Sean partly because he was very different from my family. He was a party kind of person, fun, and always had a lot of people around him. In my family you were always supposed to work very hard, and if you wound up happy besides, that was extra, but not what you bargained for. I guess Sean was always looking for pleasure first. So it wasn't an absolute shock when I found out about his affairs. It fit in with his character. He did very well at superficial relationships, at parties and so on. At first I thought he had a great many friends, but he said no, that he just knew a lot of people.

I attempted to talk all through the years. I did try to get closer to him, but the reaction I would get, I guess when I was coming too close, was that he needed to disappear. He'd go away for a few days. I didn't realize then that he was going away with his girl. I just thought that he needed to be by himself.

I went to my pastor to talk about it and was told, "Go home and forgive your husband." I didn't think that was very appropriate advice at the time. I didn't take it.

I did not forgive my husband, but temporarily we reached a compromise where we each went our own way. More and more, sex became a pacifier for us, a way to soothe tempers and bury our real problems.

Sean had said, "Go ahead and enjoy yourself." I think it turned him on to know I was out with another man, making love. But it didn't turn me on to him. No way. What I had had with him was dead, and I just hadn't gotten around to burying it. I don't think I would have entered into another relationship if I still felt love for my husband. Whenever I came back from a date, Sean was there waiting for me. The theory is that going with another person turns you on to each other.

During this period of open marriage, a man I had known for years asked me out for lunch. This man, Nick, and his wife were notoriously miserable together, so I didn't feel that I shouldn't go out with him. I knew his marriage was a fiasco. I was in the mood to talk, and I just poured everything out. Nick knew my husband's girl friend of the moment. Lots of people did. Sean had taken her around and introduced her; he was outrageous. Nick and I were very sympathetic to each other's problems.

Sean had been asking me to go swinging, and I hadn't. It was one thing I resisted. But this last summer before our separation, I did. We always went with one other couple, not groups. At the time I was not happy. I was quite resentful. I was really trying to keep things together, and my husband still insisted on having his other women. I thought maybe swinging would work, maybe we could have an open kind of marriage. I really had no interest in it myself, because I've always connected sex with emotion, very much so. But I said to Sean, "OK. If this is what you want, I'll try it." One time after we had been with another couple in the same room, my husband wanted to make love after they left. I just threw up. It just didn't work for me. I make no judgment about other people. If they want it, fine. But as far as using it to solve a problem, I don't think it does. In fact I think it makes a problem worse.

I would never care to repeat the swinging experience. I was a flaming success, because I never stopped doing therapy even in bed. I could figure out what everybody's problem was. And each man had a problem. The way it works is you meet first for coffee or a drink and talk. Then if it's mutually acceptable, you meet later for sex. You don't just go in without having met the person. There are certain ground rules. You don't contact the person except as a couple. I must have done something right, because apparently everybody I had been with wanted to get back together again with us. But I was out of it before that could happen. It was a fairly brief adventure.

I think swinging was probably what killed things completely in our marriage. When I had had several experiences I saw what it was. It's a very depreciating thing. You feel like one more piece of meat. When I realized that my husband was willing to have me do this, turn me into a piece of meat, I felt, "Well, that's it. What was I ever crying for?" Anyway, during the course of that summer, while I was involved in swinging with my husband, I was really falling for my friend Nick, and he wanted me. When we did get together I quit swinging, and we've been together ever since. Nick was concerned about what swinging might do to me, and he was very relieved when I quit.

I don't separate sex and love. Sex to me is an expression of love. I'm not comfortable doing it without love. I have much more desire now than I had twenty years ago, and I'm much more comfortable with my body. My sex life has changed enormously. It couldn't possibly be more active than it is, and I feel so comfortable with it now. Nick and I are almost like children at play. If you love someone, it's wonderful to explore more things together. I think one drawback of the sexual revolution is that it makes sex too much of an acrobatic thing. That's how it was in swinging. I hated the feeling that everybody was chalking up scores. Now I'm happy that there is no one hanging over my shoulder saying, "Well, was that better or worse? How do you feel?"

The truth is I was very good at faking it. Even with Sean I didn't ask for anything, I just made him happy. I would say that he tried his best with me, but we didn't have the kind of communication where I could just explore and try things out. I always thought his ego was too fragile to sustain any sexual dissatisfaction on my part. My sexual experience with Sean over the years was not unpleasant— in fact it was certainly very pleasant—but it wasn't the peak of sexuality.

I've always been more or less a tuning fork. My husband was willing to listen to me, let me express my feelings, but not about my work, not about any serious subject. He always acted as if my opinion was either wrong or worthless. Even driving down the highway, if I would say, "There's the exit to so and so," Sean would categorically deny it. It got to the point where I didn't want to hear the term "dumb broad" again. And he interfered with my handling of the children. I would find something for them to do, and immediately Sean would find something different for them to do. It doesn't matter what his motivation was, whether he really thought my ideas worthless or whether he just had to do this sort of thing out of jealousy; the point is that it hurt me. It hurt me even though I knew that my husband told other people that he had a very understanding wife, that he was proud of me, that I was this or that. Sean's job required me to go to business meetings often, and he appreciated me as window dressing. I've always kept myself pretty much together. But then he would undercut me by telling a friend that he had "rescued" me, that he had done me a big favor by marrying me because there was so much mental illness in my family.

I think Sean was jealous that I was having a depth relationship with Nick. It was unlike the kind he usually had. While I concentrated on one person, he became more and more flagrant, went out more and more. He would take his dates to public places, introduce them to people who knew our kids. I'm sure it was done with some hostility.

Then all of a sudden Sean changed the ground rules and said that I was to give up Nick. There was a very bitter and very upsetting month. Then I went underground completely. Sean thought I had given up Nick. Actually, I hadn't. But I told Sean that he would have to deal with my being out a great deal because of my job, and that he was going to be upset every time I wasn't home. I did go lots of places, and it was very difficult for Sean. There were times when he followed me, when he camped outside my office. He was trying to tap my phone and all kinds of crazy things.

While our marriage was terminal, my husband went through the whole Jesus syndrome with the thong sandals, beard, long hair. I had four adolescent youngsters at home, and the minute he would hit the door the yelling would start. It was bad, just bad, and I didn't know how to deal with it.

It's interesting that Sean was the one in the final instance who pressed for the divorce. He became involved with one particular twenty-seven-year-old woman. He would be here during the week and over at her place during the weekends. He took her on a trip with him. So I finally said, "OK. If a divorce is what you wish, just be sure that when I start there's no turning back." Actually, I was feeling very nostalgic at that point. You forget the bad and go through a whole separation nostalgia. And I worried about practical things; there was that business of "What do I do about the mortgage?" and "I'll have to shovel my own snow."

But we did legally separate, and Sean went to live with this other woman. Then he lost his job, and he wanted to move back home. I was saying, "No, no, no. Let's at least see how things go with the separation." He was getting very bizarre with the spying and all, and I decided I had made my break and really did not want him back. It seemed ridiculous for him to say he loved this other woman and still wanted to come back and make love to me and live with me. Sean's answer was that he could always manage to love another one. I said, "Go live on your sailboat. It's beautiful weather." He did that, and a few months later he was living with a different woman.

During our separation Sean vacillated between being threatening and being friendly. Once he threatened suicide. I'm not sure how serious he was. He had a gun, but as far as I know, no ammunition. I would get phone calls: "You'll never see me again. You'll have to raise the children by yourself."

He also made terrible scenes with the children. He came over at four in the morning one time, got them up, and said, "Mommy's going to leave us. She loves somebody else. She doesn't care about us anymore." The kids were all crying and upset. I was angry because he could have contained himself. We had an agreement that we wouldn't do anything like that, that we would have a discussion before any kind of final announcement to the children. But Sean changed it all around. He said, "Daddy did something a long time ago, and Mother won't forgive him." Those years when we were trying to stick together were extremely difficult for the children. They all lost in different ways.

Sean never has talked as if he loved any of the women he was involved with. One of them he's been seeing for twenty years, but he tried living with her recently and couldn't stand it. Sean always said he loved me and still says it. But I can't live with it. I got to the point where I didn't want to carry another child around, not a forty-five-year-old man.

I think Sean did love me in his way. I was aware of a capacity for love that perhaps he didn't have. You can't pour a certain amount of water out of a pitcher unless the pitcher is large enough. He was always a very immature person. He needed me. He loved me in a very dependent kind of way. Whenever things got kind of hairy out in the world, he came running back to Mama.

There were very definitely areas of satisfaction in my life. I shouldn't be so negative in terms of my husband. There were times when we were very happy. I was very happy with my children. I felt good as a mother always, and even more now because they are good people, and their difficult times seem to be over.

It's hard to say what I'm most proud of. It's a mixture. I'm delighted that my children like me even though I'm a relative. I really enjoy being with them. I'm proud of my profession, and that I've gone as far as I have. I feel valuable there. I had no expectations when I was growing up. I just thought I'd get married.

I guess one of the best things in my life right now is the wonderful experience I have with Nick. Sexually it's just beautiful! I always felt that I could give pleasure to men, but I didn't feel that getting pleasure was so important. Now it's a different kind of thing. If you can do both, and you have someone who allows you and helps you to do both, it's a beautiful thing. Nick is a person who takes every kind of care. I feel perfectly comfortable, perfectly honest with him. He is interested in me as an individual. He has a high respect for me. He never, at the beginning or later, tried to push me into a decision to be his lover. He feels that my profession, physical therapy, is as important as his. He admires my work. My husband never had, that I know of. Plus the fact that Nick and I have never used sex to do anything: to make up for an argument, to mend fences. There is a different mood. I'm always as excited, when I see him, as I was four years ago, when this started, and I feel he is too. It's not just physical excitement. I can't wait to tell him everything. I have a list of things I want to talk about. I used to be this way years and years ago with my husband, but when I opened my mouth, I got cut off. He didn't really care to hear what I had to say. He was too interested in his own thoughts.

My children and my close friends know about my relationship with Nick, and his close friends, but not everybody, not his wife. I think eventually he'll get divorced, but I'm in no rush right now. His wife is content to stay as is. She likes the prestige of being his wife—he's fairly well known—and economically she's better off.

Once in a while, when I get depressed, I say to Nick, "I'm getting older," and he says, "Yes, of course, so am I. We'll do it together." I say, "I'm getting wrinkles!" "I don't see them." "But I'm deteriorating!" "We'll deteriorate together!"

CHAPTER 22

Wilma–In Wilma We Trust

I never wanted to be dependent on anybody . . . I don't trust anybody. More than anything in my life, I never wanted to be in a position where I had to. . . . As for femininity . . . I always equated it with sappiness.

Wilma has been a widow for two years. Although she misses her husband, she likes living alone with her numerous pets. She prefers cats to people.

She and her husband were glad to be childless. Wilma believes that her lifelong bouts of depression and her odd, twenty-five-year-long marital relationship precluded parenthood. She and her husband devoted their energies to other pursuits—her husband to drinking, and Wilma to self-education.

At fifty-two Wilma is big and overweight, but she carries herself well and is a striking woman, formidable in a handsome way. She is a curious combination of learning, literary taste, and brains, as well as tough, accented slang, including some dropped g's. She is a probation officer, one who deals realistically but sensitively with the misfits of our society.

* * *

WILMA

MY MOTHER was the most influential person in my life. I was very close to her. I was her confidante; she never treated me like a child. She trained me to have perfect manners when I was four years old, so that I was a pain in the ass to other kids. But I spent a lot of time with my mother and thought she was perfect until I was grown up. Apparently she envisioned my being her companion for life, so she was shocked and disappointed when I got married.

My mother was a very unfeminine woman, and she gave me a very negative view of males. As her confidante, all I heard was how disappointed she was in her marriage, how she'd really married beneath her, how men were bad news, selfish and self-centered, and sexually disgusting. My mother was positively quaint in some of her notions. She would make mysterious allusions to feminine indispositions. She was very vague and made me very anxious about menstruation.

When I was twelve, my father felt the need to tell me something about safety and sex, because there was a sex pervert around who had been murdering children. My mother wouldn't stay in the apartment while he talked to me. I realized afterward I was very angry. I really resented this and saved it up against my mother. My vibes told me that my mother couldn't hack it. Her sanity was a house of cards.

When I was young, I felt loved by my mother, but you have to understand something: The household was an extremely cold one. I never saw my parents kiss or be affectionate at all. Nothing. And when I had a friend who kissed her mother goodnight, my mother went on at great length, "How disgusting! People slobbering over one another, spreading germs." The way my mother conveyed affection was through food. She fed the world. She was a great cook, and I ate everything she cooked.

Although she wasn't demonstrative, my mother encouraged reading and conversation, especially political conversation, and I felt that she cared about my sister and myself. In view of her limited background, she came up with some fairly extraordinary ideas. I remember when everybody was raving about Ireland after seeing a documentary, her comment was, "Well, I notice the only fat one in that village was the priest."

When I was young, I was a tomboy. I was the leader of the games on the block. I ran faster, jumped higher, and I was very competitive. See, as long as I was a tomboy I wasn't threatening to my mother. But when I was sixteen, my aunt told us that some man she knew thought I was very good-looking. My mother got very angry and said, "Handsome is as handsome does." I said to her, "You sound like you're jealous of me." And what does she say? She said, "Well, why shouldn't I be?" I wish I could have stayed a tomboy. Among other things I never wanted to be a girl.

I've been subject to depression since I was about thirteen, but the first time I went to a psychiatrist was when I was twenty-six. Look, we were poor, we were lucky to eat. Who ever thought about depressions, or trottin' off to the shrink? That was too esoteric for working-class people. How was I to know that other people were feeling better? My mother attributed my depressions to a really rotten disposition, and I did too.

Although I have not gleaned much from off–on psychiatry, I am on medication. My shrink thinks my depressions are organic, but I associate some of my worst depressions with menstruation, an illegal abortion I had, and maybe with menopause, which started nine years ago. When I'm depressed, I fall asleep often, sleep too long, can't get up, eat too much, and am intensely irritable. Worst of all, I avoid people; I'm afraid if I start talking, I'll start crying.

My father played a very shadowy role in my upbringing. My mother manipulated my father. He was sort of a sad sack who wanted my mother's attention and affection. He never wanted children and he ended up forced into a competitive role with us. My mother sort of shut him out. She'd say, "We'll have this and that, but we won't tell your father." So he was cast as Simon Legree.

I don't quite know what went on in that house, but it must have been really bad, because I was so put out by my sister's arrival. I resented my sister with such an intensity! I was horrible to her. I remember coming home and seeing her sleeping in what I considered my crib, even though I hadn't slept in it for a while. And my sister, I thought, was a very ugly little baby with a red face who put lavender wool up her nose. She plucked the blanket and stuck it up her nose, or something. I hated her. Later on, I guess to get even with me because I was so nasty to her, she used to take my things and deny she took them and she'd break my roller skates. It was constant bedlam. We were just about the most inharmonious two, practically killin' each other. We even got to draw lines down the center of the sheet to separate us. I really blame myself. I was unrelentingly hostile to her. It was only when I grew up and came back from the army that I became friendly with her.

Let me explain something about my father. I was very friendly with my father until I was about twelve. We went places together, I went to soccer games with him, I went to Coney Island with him, we went to movies together, to the Armory to see the horse show and to the flower show. I didn't fall out with him until I was fifteen, and then I didn't talk to him for five years. I didn't talk to him until I went in the army, and then I said, "Good-bye." I'm just like him. If I had a grudge against you, I wouldn't talk to you for twenty years. I was so absolutely morbid about my appearance. That's what did it. It was some remark about my figure. It wasn't a very bad remark. I don't know what the man said. Something about my chest, which I didn't have much of. I was morbidly sensitive, I guess. I was so furious I called my father a dirty pig, and he got insulted. And I wouldn't talk to him, and he wouldn't talk to me. Two years later my mother asked me to wish him Merry Christmas, just to please her, she said. So I said, "Merry Christmas," and he said, "Thanks," and I didn't talk to him again till three years later when I said "Good-bye."

I don't know how I felt about my father really. I didn't feel loved by him, because he was so totally nondemonstrative and such a quiet person. Even in the conversations at the table he would be very quiet. I realize now what he tended to do, was, he put us down. It was very important for him. He had a terrible inferiority complex and very little formal education, and he just felt uncomfortable with people knowing more than he did, or even the idea that they might know more.

Now my father's eighty, and we don't really have conversations, but I sit and listen to him. I would say he's a very strange, very "schizzy" guy, and there's mental illness in his family, see, so it doesn't surprise me. His brother, sister, and his nephew were all institutionalized eventually. Believe it or not, he was eighteen when his mother died at the age of seventy-two. Those bloody Irish. No birth control. On my mother's side they were more neurotic than crazy. It's rather discouraging. My whole family, including my sister, is more than a little bit "schizzy." I suppose my parents did the best they could, considering hard times and their limited education. But my father was mean; he had mean streaks. For instance, our closet was right by where you walked in the door, see, and God forbid that you should make the terrible mistake of putting your coat on his hanger. He'd knock it on the floor and leave it there. Oh, really! And then you know, he had very eccentric tastes, the main center of which was that he hated the taste of anything that cost money. So he extolled the merits of macaroni until my mother told him, "If you really want to eat Italian food the way Italians cook it, it's damn expensive." When he found out the cost of olive oil, forget it. He loved things like boiled mackerel soup, which smelled the whole house out, and no one else liked it. Everyone hated it. Finally after eating this crap for years, with scenes at the table I'll never forget, one night my mother made him some boiled mackerel while she made us some fried fillet, and when we all sat down to dinner my father had his plate of boiled mackerel and we had the fried fillet. He looked at us and he looked at my mother, and my mother said to him, "We hate boiled mackerel!" He just meekly ate it, never said a word.

My father used money as a weapon. Like, my father would get tips at Christmas; for that period it was a lot of money, maybe five hundred dollars. Then he waited till the last minute to give my mother the money, so she had to go shopping on Christmas Eve when all the best things were gone. He did this on purpose. I saw this. I guess I stored it up, and I just never wanted to be dependent on anybody. And along with this, and it's a far more serious thing I suppose, I don't trust anybody. More than anything in my life, I never wanted to be in a position where I had to. I always wanted to have some leverage. Part of this must be a result of my parents' marriage.

Neither of my parents encouraged me to get married at all. My father thought a woman who gets married when she has a good job is crazy. I eloped with a man who spoke very little English and had no cultural interests, but my husband never interfered with what I wanted to do. He encouraged me to go back to school. I didn't get my degree until I was thirty-four. He encouraged me to learn to drive a car. He never discouraged me from doing anything. If I didn't do something, I never could blame anybody but myself and my own problems with inertia and depression, neurosis, etcetera. So I never had the put-downs that some women say they had.

My husband—he died two years ago—always had money for what *he* wanted to do. But he was very stingy. I didn't like this, but I would never ask him for anything. I spent my own money, and he spent his. He paid all the household bills, and for a long time he also bought the food. When we had been married two months I lost my job, and I asked him to lend me some money to buy a pair of stockings. He refused and said that if I wanted stockings to go and get a job. So you see, instead of saying, "Up yours and so long," I was so insecure I couldn't leave. I just got a job, and I never asked him for anything again.

My husband had such an incredibly deprived childhood, it's amazing he turned out as well as he did. Whenever I served him a meal he ate up everything in sight, like the grasshopper in the plague. Finally after we'd been married a while I said, "Listen, I'm here too." He was very embarrassed and upset, but it had never occurred to him that he wasn't the only one eating. After that he religiously left me my fifty percent, and at times it was ludicrous.

His mother died when he was nine and he was sort of sold for farm labor. Even when he was with his mother they were so poor they were starving half the time. His mother did cupping. Do you know how primitive that was? Cupping is, you know, bleeding.

When my husband and I were first married, we had arguments about everything. Finally I told him, "You are one of the most selfish people I have ever met, and the biggest cheapskate." He thought for a while and then he answered, "I agree." He was, and he didn't change. We were talking one evening, we'd been married sixteen years then, and my husband asked me, "What color are your eyes?" Can you imagine that? My husband and I had so little in common. He would go every Friday night to a bar, tie one on, come home loaded, sleep it off Saturday. What I would do, I went to the theater, I went to concerts, I went to the beach, I went with my cousins. We led concurrent lives. So actually, when he died, I had, you know, been doing all these things alone for years anyway. Not that I didn't miss him. I did. Because over the long haul we had become friends, despite our differences. We had a few things in common; we liked animals, we liked to go to the zoo, we liked to watch sports.

When we'd been married twenty years, we had a really violent fight. So we got separation papers. We were going to get a divorce. When we went to sign the papers, my husband was very drunk, and I was very angry. He gave the lawyer eight hundred dollars cash for a Mexican divorce. Then he sobered up and was very upset, but the lawyer wouldn't give him back the money, because he said he had already sent the money to whomever it was in Mexico. Who knows? But my husband was angry and brooded about this for days. He finally decided that he had to go through with the divorce even though he didn't want to, because, he said, that it was all my fault anyway, because I had been sober when it happened and he was drunk and that I should have known better, and all this jazz. I said, "If you don't want a divorce, why are you getting one?" He said, "I have to because no one's going to take my money and make a fool out of me." So he went to Juarez and got a divorce. So then he came back, and I said, "Well, I'm moving out and taking my things." And he said, "Why are you moving out? It's not necessary. We still like each other." So we stayed together for the next five years until he died. He arranged a new will and left everything to me and acknowledged that we were divorced.

I was pregnant once before I was married, and I had an abortion. I never used birth control and except for that time I never got pregnant. At one point early in my marriage I did go to a clinic and my husband went too, and we had tests, because I thought I would like to have a child. But no one could see what was wrong. I suspect part of the reason was that I could have done more than I did, and I think it's significant that I didn't. I think I've always been rather ambivalent about the whole thing. I could have gone and had my tubes blown. I was advised to do this, and I didn't. They felt that because of the abortion something had gone wrong. Well, my husband wasn't that gung-ho about raising a family, so I never pursued it. And he wasn't interested in adopting. And the other thing, of course, was I was an atheist and I wasn't going to tell the agency that I would raise the child to be a good anything, except maybe a good atheist. And that wouldn't cut any ice. Later on when the attitude toward people's religion had somewhat eased, my husband had such a drinking problem that I felt, well forget it! I knew enough to know it wouldn't be a good idea. Being fertile or not fertile never meant much to me, and I just didn't have this overwhelming need to be a mother.

My husband had been a boxing champion at one point in his life, in the army. He was a very powerfully built man, very strong. He could do two hundred one-arm push-ups. Incredible, right? And of course he was very vain and very proud about it. He had a very nice physique and was concerned about his looks. He wouldn't wear glasses. He was attractive to me. Asthetic men never did a thing for me. The more masculine, the better. Other women friends of mine thought he was quite handsome.

Nevertheless, the sex was no damn good. At first I didn't even know there was a problem. I was so inhibited that I couldn't discuss it with anybody else either. I didn't even know if there was something to discuss. It's incredible, but it's true. I gradually became aware of things. Also something interesting happened, and I understand this is not unusual. I read an article about a woman who was very enthused about sex, but who had never had an orgasm, apparently; and somehow I felt that this was my case, but I had no idea what it was that I was missing or anything about it or what to do.

I went to a doctor for a checkup. This was when I was about thirty-eight. And I said to the doctor that I wanted to talk to him about something because I really didn't understand what was happening. I told him that I just had no interest in sex at all, that I wouldn't care if I ever had sex. And you know, it was the strangest thing on his part, when I think of it now. He must have had his problems, because you know how he acted? As if I had never said a word. He didn't respond in any way. I just felt terrible, especially because I had never had the nerve to talk about this to anyone before. I wasn't one of those women who want to go around and discuss their sex life with everybody, or who run around getting exams because it turns them on.

And the damn doctor didn't say a word. This was the most total put-down I think I ever had. I was appalled. I went out of the office feeling there must be something wrong with me. I must be a leper or something. So I didn't get any help there.

A little later, about the time that I went into therapy, I suddenly became very interested in sex, which I'd never been in my life. My husband thought it was great. He had always complained at how disinterested I was. He told me I was the coldest woman he'd ever met. And all of a sudden here I was really interested. It lasted maybe two or three years, and then it all petered out again. The shrink said maybe it had something to do with glands. It's very strange. But during that time I enjoyed sex. I think I was becoming a nymphomaniac, for God's sake. I used to rush home with such enthusiasm. My husband, at first, didn't know what the hell was happening, and then he was very happy. It was very bizarre. Maybe as a result of my fling, I had evolved at least some concept of the things that I liked, and I was able at least to discuss this and achieve some sort of satisfaction for myself, which I hadn't before. My shrink, who hasn't helped me much, taught me to deal with anger by expressing it instead of totally withdrawing. So finally I got there. That was something.

I think the most common orgasm would seem to be clitoral. I myself have had two very minor vaginal orgasms, but they only occurred after really extensive sex, and it wasn't worth the effort. Of course this was something I wasn't anticipating, and at first I didn't know what was happening. I had read this book, *The Vaginal Orgasm,* which my shrink had given me early on. The book was written by a female analyst extolling the wonders of the vaginal orgasm, OK? If orgasms had occurred on a more increased scale, I would say possibly it would be really something. But they never did.

My husband was really more anxious for closeness than I was. During that time of sexual turn-on, we were more experimental and more active. But my husband had a peculiar problem: If I became more aggressive, he just immediately became totally passive. And this turned me off, 'cause I preferred somebody who at least met you halfway. When I cooled my interest in sex, my husband was older and was drinking more. And by that time I had moved into the guest room and was sleeping by myself. I didn't want to sleep with anybody all night. The shrink has explained it this way, that neither of us was really able to sustain intimacy for any length of time. And therefore our frequent blowups were sort of separations, and then we reconciled and things went along for a while, and then there was another one.

I feel that if my husband had to die, he at least died at a time when it was easier for me than it would have been ten years ago. Ten years ago I was in the midst of my sexual thing, and I'm not the kind of person who can just go and pick up a substitute.

Most of our difficulties began when he drank. He'd make sexual demands that I thought were excessive. I had learned to drive a car, and finally it got to the point when he came home bombed on a Friday night and wanted to have another sexual marathon, I just got in my little car and left. And he found himself with nobody to screw. Plain English. He went out and screwed elsewhere, but I didn't even care. He went to Denmark and had a ball. And the first thing he did when we went to London together was go off to a nude show. I thought to myself, "Who cares?" I stayed in the hotel and read the newspaper.

I don't understand the intense jealousy that sexual relations engender. I never had this. When my husband went off and had his flings, I just thought, "Good." I didn't want to know any details, and I didn't care. Maybe because I'm such a low-key person, it's not important to me. When we got divorced, he thought he'd try to find someone else, but then he decided the devil he knew was better than the devil he didn't know.

In our own way we were friends. If he had only been able to taper off the drinking. But the periods of being sober got shorter and shorter. I remember counting thirty-six bottles of beer in a twelve-hour period. I'm sure my husband was an unhappy man. People don't drink that way unless they are. But alcohol is really a drug, and it gets into you. My husband did go to AA, but the fact is that when he was drinking he was happy, more relaxed, and more sociable. The only thing is, he couldn't stop, and then he got obnoxious. He'd play that TV at a decibel level you could hear a block away, and he played German marches and drinking songs. I couldn't sleep, and I had to wait till he flaked out before I could turn the thing off. One reason I didn't leave was that I feared I would get intensely depressed. I view that as a weakness of character on my part.

My husband was really rather dependent. He learned to speak English and he could understand it, but he couldn't write it. I used to do all his contracts. Sometimes I would go with him and write the contracts on the spot, and I would look up the places on the map; I would talk to the people on the phone. I did all that. I suppose he appreciated it, but it's interesting about people: They may appreciate things you do for them but often to the degree that they're dependent, they resent you. And he resented me. My husband told his niece once, "That Wilma. She makes all that money and spends it on those fucking cats. Not a nickel left."

I used to be embarrassed because other people would say to me, "Oh, your husband has been telling me how smart and well educated you are." I guess compared to him and his friends, I was. But I'm not my idea of a well-educated person. I wish I were smarter and knew more than I do. I'm not a stupid person, I know that. I have a peculiar kind of temperament. I'm not a perfectionist; I'm certainly not worried about the yellow in my floor and all that jazz. But I've found that the more you try to learn, it's kind of depressing in a way, the more you become aware of what there is to know that you don't know. I think I was born under an unsatisfactory sign. I always think I want something that I don't have. It doesn't have to be material. I've spent years living in the future. But the future very rapidly becomes the present. So now I don't. I tend to live from day to day.

Even though sex wasn't all that important to me, it's interesting that I certainly am not an unfeeling individual. I love music. I really intensely love it. And I like eating, which I think has a large sensual component, especially for myself, since other areas are less important. I feel that perhaps, with a different background, things might have been different. I don't know. I have no sexual interests at this moment. I've realized since my husband died how much I really dislike men. I've thought about women. In the past, you see, when I was growing up, well, it's hard to say whether I had a homosexual attachment to this friend, or whether it was just one of these intense things teenagers have. Then, when I was in the army, I came in contact with homosexual women, but I had no more interest in them than I had in the men. I had no interest in anybody. I remember one woman I ended up sharing a room with quite inadvertently, when we were on detached service. I used to stay in and listen to symphonic music on the radio, and she went out. She used to get money from men to finance her homosexual attachments. She came in one night after having a few beers, and she said to me finally, "Kid, I can't figure you out at all." I had to laugh. I couldn't figure myself out. But she just looked at me and scratched her head. She didn't molest me, or make a pass at me, or anything. Maybe she thought I was sort of an asexual person, and to some extent I think I am. I think that in a sense I have sort of a writer's view. I'm an onlooker at life, not particularly a participant. I see my friends with their amours and their terrible griefs, and it's as if they're coming from another planet. I never could quite understand it.

As far as I'm concerned, if it really got to a situation where I found it intolerable, I'd go and invest in a vibrator. I like the idea of independence that it conveys. I think that's natural.

In a way I'm glad to be older. I feel people sort of respect me. I work with young people, and I get along very well with them. I think they regard me as pleasantly eccentric. They don't mess with me. They leave me alone. I can say things that maybe they couldn't. I rather like this. But my parole job is discouraging for a multiplicity of reasons. We deal with the people that everyone else has given up on, people with such a degree of pathology that it's really mind-blowing. There's no hope. The only thing I can do is get them through crises, try to hold their hand, take them to the doctor, try and console them. But you see, some of these people have, like, nobody and then I sort of get haunted by them. I start out with two clients and end up with the whole family on my back. Even those who aren't on probation are calling me up. I guess I get some satisfaction out of trying to help them, but mostly it's a very depressing scene. Part of the problem is the whole system. I think capitalism stinks. It generates all sorts of things that are negative, that is, the whole attitude toward poor people. Somehow, if you're poor in this society, it's your own fault. The kids never get a break in school—I won't tell you what I think of the school system—if you're poor, you get shafted everywhere. I've sat in the First District Court until I thought I was going to become a potted palm in the corner, because I've been there so many times, and on the same cases; they keep going back. And the way poor people get treated in the court, and the way women get treated, forget it! So being a parole officer is no good for a depressed person. I'm really hoping for a different job, and I'm looking forward to retiring.

I haven't decided what I'm going to do with my time, but I have enough interests. With my experience as a waitress and my love of food, I've thought of opening a seasonal restaurant. Real estate interests me too, but as for the work ethic, screw that. I'm tired of working. Before being a probation officer I logged nine years as a waitress, a couple of years in a bank, and I joined the army to find adventure. And where did I go? I went to Governor's Island. And what did I do? I pushed paper. And this may sound strange, considering what my job is, but I'm not that crazy about people. When I've had enough of people I just want to go away and not see anybody. I really enjoy living alone. I come home and close the door, and I'm relieved. I prefer my cats and dogs. Periodically I feel that I have to have a kitten. It's probably like a woman's need for a baby. I have twenty abandoned cats and three dogs to maintain and that's a lot.

When it comes to being masculine or feminine, I suppose I'm not very feminine, although I'm very unhappy about being so overweight. See, at one time I was rather pretty. I never had a great figure, but I was skinny, at least. When I went into the army I was five feet, eight inches and one hundred ten pounds. I looked like Katherine Hepburn in *Keeper of the Flame.* I liked being thin, but when men ogled me I was enraged. To tell you the truth, I would have been better off as a man. As for femininity, to put it in a nutshell, I always equated it with sappiness! All this business with vapors and fainting . . . and I loathe pink!

CHAPTER 23

Marcia–A Cockeyed Optimist

Maybe it's genes, but I picked up a lot of my mother's behavior. And I see it in my daughter, too. We're soft, we hardly ever get angry, and we just cope and make the best of whatever.

Marcia is an attractive, youthful, fifty-one-year-old widow with a low, quiet voice. Her husband died two years ago. She was married for twenty-nine years. She has two grown children. She dresses plainly, is modest and self-contained, and has a relaxed manner. She lives in a small cottage in a semi-rural area, the same one she grew up in. Her house is crowded with plants, books, photographs, and paintings accumulated over a lifetime.

Marcia was attracted to her handsome husband, but because of his alcoholism and irresponsibility she has had to work all her life to support both of them. Their financial straits were sometimes extreme. For fifteen years Marcia has been a bus driver. She is a high school graduate with an average income. She enjoys her job, her friends, the city with its innumerable offerings, books, music, exercise, and nature.

Marcia has freely chosen and lived by her values—commitment, responsibility, and tolerance—even though those values were not reinforced by her husband or her society.

* * *

MARCIA

I WAS BROUGHT UP as a sheltered child. My husband was the only person I ever slept with. I don't criticize anybody who did differently. In some ways they were probably luckier than I. It has run through my mind that maybe I wouldn't have been so crazy to get married if I had fooled around a little bit. I found sex a fine thing. I have nothing against it at all. I just didn't know anything when I got married.

My mother passed away when I was twelve, and my stepfather, who was quite an elderly man, raised me. I had no close relative to tell me anything about sex. I think my poor, dopey husband wasn't any better off than I was. I just thought that everything would be natural, and somehow we'd blunder along, and we did. We didn't have the problems a lot of other people have. I think people want too much, expect too much.

My husband always cared for me. He liked the way I looked, and he seemed to find me attractive. Other people do too. I think it's part of the reason that I'm satisfied with myself. We weren't very physically close, though. My family isn't like that. I wish we were. I would say that his sexual needs diminished somewhat with age. But it wasn't a problem. If I were interested, I could always let him know, and he'd try to cooperate, I guess you'd call it.

Now that I'm a widow I couldn't be sexually involved with someone I didn't care for, just for sex's sake. I'm not that much of a radical and besides, I'm shy. My mind is just not on finding a man. I don't dwell on it. It defeats my purpose. I have too many other things that interest me: my job, my friends, my hobbies. In fact, I don't think I'd ever want to be married again, tied down. I like my freedom. I can drop everything and take off any time I want. For a week or a month, if I feel like it. Until my husband died, I had always had someone to worry about. From the time I was twelve, when Mother died, I was in charge of the household—responsible for the cooking and cleaning and looking after my stepfather and my little brother. I was always very conscientious.

My father died when I was a toddler, leaving my mother in rather desperate straits. She married soon—I suppose to keep us together. I don't think she loved her second husband the way she loved my father, who, I understand, was a very warm, friendly person, big and jolly. My stepfather was a dour man. He spoke gruffly, and there was a lot of fear in my feeling about him. Mother always shielded us from him, and she made the best of her marriage.

My mother was rather liberal for that period. There was a girl in the neighborhood who was considered loose, running around and talked about, and I was having some kind of a party. A friend of mine said she wouldn't come if this "loose" girl was invited, but my mother said that I was not going to have the party unless the girl in question *was* invited. Mother was very kind and broad-minded. I'm tolerant too. Maybe it's genes, but I picked up a lot of her behavior. And I see it in my daughter too. We're soft, we hardly ever get angry, and we just cope and make the best of whatever.

My stepfather just wasn't a loving person. He had had a hard life and didn't know how to show affection. When we children were little, he took us places, but he never really played with us. In his later years he was ill and very dependent on me, and I felt that he liked and respected me. My family and I moved in with him, and he tried to thank me when he was able. When he died, he left this house and his estate to my brother and me. My stepfather was a very thrifty man, and I've grown up to be thrifty too. I never have to worry about going in debt, because I just don't. I save up and buy things for cash. I tried to teach my children this attitude, but my son didn't take to it as much as my daughter.

After I married and we were living in another state, my stepfather wrote saying that he was sick, that his housekeeper had left him, that my brother, still living with him, was drinking quite a bit, and he begged us to come and live with him. We did, but things didn't work out with three men and me in the house. Each one resented what I did for the others. They were like little boys; they all wanted my attention. They could never understand that there's enough affection in a person to go around. My brother left, but my stepfather came to rather like my husband. They could talk about the wars. My stepfather only lived four years after that.

I was only sixteen when I met Ben, the man who became my husband. He wasn't much older when he was stationed here. My girl friend induced me to get off the school bus and take a ride with these two soldiers from Alabama that she knew. I said, "OK, but if my stepfather sees me, I'll get killed." Ben was in the paratroopers, and he was a virile, dashing, handsome fellow. And the uniform . . . well, instantly I was head over heels in love with him. I wrote to him every day while he was overseas; as I said, I'm a very conscientious person. Ben was in the Normandy Invasion, and he jumped with the paratroopers into Holland. He saw many of his friends die. I'm sure Ben and his buddies drank a great deal over there, and their motto was "Live for today." Ben was only twenty-one when he came home and we got married.

Although I started out madly in love with my husband, I was soon disillusioned. He wasn't always truthful, he drank, often to excess, and he wasn't dependable. I think it was the army that caused these things. He'd say he'd be back at such and such a time, and he wouldn't show up. Since I was always the dependable kind, I just couldn't understand how Ben could be like that.

Ben and I had other differences. He was from Alabama and had a much narrower viewpoint about blacks. In many ways we had such different viewpoints it's a wonder we stuck together. Still, he was a lot of fun and had a tremendous sense of humor. He was a man's man, I'd say. He'd drop everything and GO, you know? Sometimes he'd just take off for Tennessee with a friend.

I remember when we lived out on a little farm for two years. It was a very primitive life, with an outside cistern for water. We had chickens, an outhouse, and a couple of coal stoves. It was winter and Ben went off in the car to get coal because we were out of it. He didn't come home for three days. We didn't have a phone so I went to a neighbor and called the hospital and the police, but they didn't know where he was. When he finally returned home, I said, "My God, where were you?" He said, "Oh, I went fishing with so and so." I said, "Well, we had no coal. The babies were freezing. I had to go out in the woods to find fallen logs to burn." Well, Ben had just wanted to go fishing, and forgot about us while I was worrying if I'd ever see him again. That's the kind of life it was. I don't dwell on these things.

Another day Ben came home, having had a few drinks, with a whole mess of stuff from the grocery store, including cakes and candy. There wasn't twenty-three dollars left for the rent. So I had to go back to the store with all these excess things and say, "Please, can I return these because I have to pay my rent?" And he never had his name on the checking account. That was always mine, because Ben would write a check without our having any money in the bank. He was totally irresponsible that way. I always made out the income tax, the school papers for the kids' financial aid, and even the savings account was only in my name. Ben always trusted me with it. Maybe he resented that I did all this, but it had to be, because he couldn't save anything. No matter how little we had, I was always able to save some. When we were desperate for money, I still kept five dollars in the bank. It was some sort of security for me. But that's all we had to fall back on. This was when I would go to the vegetable stand and for twenty-five cents get a basket of old apples and vegetables. I'd make vegetable soup and still have that five dollars. I guess I thought, "We'll get by somehow." And we did.

It was ridiculous when I think of what little money we had. When the kids were growing up they always wore hand-me-downs. Maybe that's why my son is so much more materialistic. He finds the best tennis racket, the best bicycle, and wants everything new.

He's a schoolteacher, so he can indulge himself. But my daughter is like me. She still likes to go to rummage sales and junk shops. I still pick things up from the side of the road that people throw out. To me, it's sinful.

When we came back here and moved in with my stepfather, we didn't have to worry about rent, and I was able to get a job. My stepfather was here for the children to come home to. My husband never worked steadily. He would quit his jobs, or lose them, or sometimes show up drunk. He did all kinds of work: He was a roofer, a clammer, a carpenter, a handyman; he worked in a factory, all kinds, but not all the time. I worked most of my life. For the last fifteen years I've worked as a bus driver. Before that I worked in offices and factories and I've been a movie usher and a waitress. I never made a large amount of money, but I could always manage on a little bit and keep a roof over our heads.

I think that Ben would, underneath, be contrite about his irresponsible behavior, but he didn't want to let you know. I was not supposed to scold. I was supposed to take things as they were. And I did. I never left him. I never had enough money, but really it was basically my upbringing—that down on a lower subconscious level you just stuck by the guy. And I *know* I felt that if I left him, he'd be lost. I mean that he couldn't cope. He'd be just a bum, as so many of the guys are, disheveled, living like pigs after their marriages break up. They don't eat a decent meal. I've seen some of his different friends.

Somehow I was Ben's security. He depended on me. He knew I'd take care of things, I guess. I think he appreciated me. I've heard from other people that he would brag about me on the outside. But if he were drinking, he could be very obnoxious. If he saw a spot on his food or something, he'd make a big fuss. Maybe it was his way of bringing me down to his level. I think I probably made it too easy for him. I just seemed to roll with the punches and did what had to be done. I don't think about it. I don't waste time resenting.

Ben was very good about letting me go for days. I could go into the city and visit friends, do all the things I liked. And he did *his* thing, which was fishing and hanging out with the fellows, and bullshitting for hours, which didn't interest me at all. So we had a compatible life. We had different spheres, a different circle of friends entirely. That's why I'm not so terribly lonesome. I'm not heartbroken. I'm used to doing things alone.

In his last years he wasn't well, and he drank much less, just a few beers. He'd come home about two in the afternoon and watch television. I bought the color TV for him because he enjoyed it so much. I go a lot to concerts and lectures and classes, and he's home watching TV, so why not get a good set that he'll enjoy?

I try to think about the good aspects: Ben was not basically unkind. He was always fun. He was a very warm, generous person; he'd give to anybody, and he was a very good-looking, handsome man, always sexually attractive to me, definitely. He never aged. His hair was blond and curly, really attractive. Kids and animals loved him. Dogs would follow him home.

His own children loved him in certain ways, but they also resented him. They knew that when he was drinking, they had to watch out. They were afraid of him then. Ben probably did things he was later sorry for. I remember one time he slapped my son because my son wasn't fast enough in helping him spackle. And he was sometimes rather unkind to my daughter because she was never the student her brother was. I remember a few times Ben would call her stupid and have her in tears. I know she resented it. In many ways she rebelled against him. She isn't married right now, but she is living with a black fellow and has a baby. Ben didn't know about that relationship, but he knew she was friendly with blacks and that was one thing I don't think he could accept. My daughter's a fine person. What she has done isn't what I would choose, but I don't think marriage is necessarily a piece of paper and a blood test. My daughter and her guy are committed to one another, they're both working, they're happy, and they're taking care of their baby. If you go against society, I know it's difficult. But I know they don't give a damn what the rest of the world thinks.

I have a good relationship with my daughter's fellow. It's a shock when you first meet him, but you'd be surprised, you forget about a person's color when you get to know him. He's a much finer father and husband than her father was, in many ways. You can depend on him. He doesn't drink, and he will take care of the baby as much as she will. To me, those are the important things.

My job is very secure, but no matter what, I know I could get a job that would keep me going. It's not that I have a mortgage or little kids. I do a little volunteer work, I like going to the city, I read, I enjoy music, I take art classes, I love to walk on the beach and to ride my bike. I love my friends, and I'm always amazed that much better educated people than I am seem to enjoy my company.

I go out of my way to keep my friends. Once I'm your friend, you're stuck with me. I have a friend who is twenty years younger, and she invites me to go places with her and her boyfriend. I forget that I'm so much older. I think it's great. And I have a friend who is in her seventies, and *she* thinks well of me. I switch back and forth between the ages.

I don't worry about death or the future. As long as I'm independent, and enjoying my freedom, what's the use of worrying? When my son left, after my husband's funeral, I really got the blues. But I went to the city for the day, enjoyed myself, had dinner out, took a long bicycle ride the next day, and felt better. I don't sit and mope. I'm not a religious person, either. I guess my life could have been better and it could have been worse. Whatever happened, happened. I guess you could call me a "cockeyed optimist."

CHAPTER 24

Nancy–Larger than Life: White

My mother's a tough old lady. . . . She's going to be the last woman on the beach. My mother and I are alike in being strong, independent, stubborn, and mean.

Nancy is forty-seven, formerly beautiful and currently handsome. She is blond, has translucent skin, and stands five feet, eleven inches tall. She makes it clear immediately that she is a character from Texas. She has had two marriages, two divorces, and countless lovers. Her first marriage at nineteen lasted three years. Her second marriage at twenty-six lasted fourteen years. She has lived with her three children from that marriage for the last seven years.

Nancy is a college graduate. She has been a nurse, worked in show business, and sold cars. She is currently selling real estate. She has a great deal of energy and devotes much of it to political and humanitarian causes.

Nancy brought to the interview a short story she had written that personifies woman as nature: rich, bountiful, eternal yet changing, and existing to be explored and enjoyed in all her variety. The story portrayed man as an explorer who drinks in all the wonders of nature, enjoys all that he can, and then returns abruptly to the hustle of city life. She spoke quite passionately about the ruthlessness of men and how much they could learn about tenderness and permanence from women. Then, once the tape recorder began running, Nancy launched into the rough, tough persona of the interview.

* * *

NANCY

GIVING BIRTH to three big kids wore out my uterus, but I still have a virgin belly; I can wear a bikini. I drink a quart of wine every night, but I'm not an alcoholic; I'm too mean. At this moment in my life I don't know any man that I'd walk across the street for; I don't even masturbate.

There was a time when if I didn't get enough sex, I would get frustrated and horny and start looking for somebody. I used to tell people that men reached their peak at nineteen, but I didn't know when women did because I hadn't come to it. I think I did last year when I broke my neck. Had a spinal fusion and that slowed me down.

My dear, I didn't know there was a chair in the house while my daddy was alive. I always sat on my daddy's lap, bathed with my daddy, and climbed on my daddy's shoulders. My life just revolved around that big, tough, Texas, outdoor man. I loved animals, and one time my daddy brought me a nest of wild rabbits and helped me raise them in one of the bathrooms. I decided there and then that if I had kids, they would have every kind of critter to raise. He didn't let Mother know about it; he was pretty sneaky. When I was six years old my daddy got spinal meningitis and died within forty-eight hours.

When Daddy died, I went to bed and didn't eat or speak for six weeks. My mother was sitting next to me with some broth, and my first words were, "Well, the one who loved me died." Mother and I always pulled against each other from then on.

My mother has ice water in her veins and she still tells me what to do. To stop our verbal battles my brother used to say, "Nancy, why don't you hush; don't you know that Mother has never changed her mind?" And I would say, "But there's gotta be a first time," and I keep battling.

As long as Daddy was alive, my mother stayed in bed and was frail and delicate. I don't think she liked sex. But the minute he died, she got out of bed. She didn't want anyone telling her how to raise her kids. She was stubborn.

When I told my mother that I marched with the Montgomery, Alabama, civil rightists she said, "Don't tell anyone." I said, "Mother, I'm not coming home until you tell everyone in your club that I went on this march." As a result, I didn't go home for four years.

I see so many things in myself that are just like my mother. We are alike in being strong, independent, stubborn, mean, and unbending. I sure do see her as a good survivor. She's going to be the last woman on the beach. She's a tough old lady. She was the first woman driver in Texas. She has leukemia, and she has broken her neck twice in the last four years. She is supposed to be dead by all medical calculations, but she's planning to move to a retirement village where they have promised to let her teach a Sunday school class and left-handed knitting. She just turned eighty, and she will not wear her glasses and will not use her cane.

Back in my high school days, the rule was you could tease a boy until he was about to die. My girl friend and I kept a notch on the door for every boy we had kissed, and at the end of our freshman year in college the door was about to fall down. I was known as "hot lips," but I was also extremely pious. I remember when we found out that one of our friends was no longer a virgin, we stayed up until three o'clock in the morning discussing what our attitude towards her should be, and how we could guide her in the paths of righteousness. Should we or should we not associate with her. Unbelievable. Virginity was your "flower." Times have changed, and if I had ever lived for one month with either of the men that I married, I never would have married them. When I got married at nineteen, I had only had intercourse with my husband.

My first husband was a gigolo, and I was the first chick whose pants he couldn't get into immediately. He was a twenty-seven-year-old musician who played the violin. Making love to women was his specialty. He was a master. He played *me* like a violin. He cheated all the time. He believed in spreading culture by injection. It was two years before I found out about it, and it took me another two years to get over him. He thought I had more money than I did, and when we got to New York, I found out I had to earn a living because he was studying conducting. He had to pay child support from a former marriage; he was making payments on a violin and a car. I didn't know anything, but I wasn't afraid of anything either. By the time I was divorced I could have sat on a burning cigarette and dangled my feet. I never gave myself Brownie points for earning a living. I do volunteer work now for the visiting nurse service and that requires just as much effort as earning a living.

Not once have I regretted my divorces. When I finally got over my Hungarian fiddle player, every "t" was crossed. If you don't know the depths of despair and loss, you don't know the heights. If you feel that your intimate self is kind of super, you don't have to armor yourself against people. Even though I get ripped off occasionally, I'd rather trust people.

I had to find another man after my divorce to take care of my bruised ego. It took me a couple of months, and I did. I fell in love with an international tennis player and spent a year with him. He was very much like my first husband: They both had driving ambition; they were in constant need of people to build them up. I have never been that deprived.

When I met my second husband, I was in heat to have babies and I never slept with him until we were married. I spent the dullest honeymoon with him that anybody ever had. I would have gone home except I couldn't say, "Oops, I've made another little mistake here."

My second marriage was fourteen long years of boredom. He would get frustrated and beat on me. He was an impossible, sentimental father, a very shallow man. I was twenty-six years old and had just run away from my tennis player when I married him. My second husband always felt so inferior to me, and it was true. He is inferior. He didn't need a complex; he was just plain inferior. He couldn't do anything, so he'd flake out on weekends with a migraine when things needed doing around the house.

After my second divorce, when I was forty, I had a three-year affair with a married man. I should have known better, but I can forgive myself for almost any stupidity that I get into. I went to a party the other night, really tied one on and made a complete jackass of myself. I said to myself the next day, "Well, I'll never do that again." But I probably will. If you think you're pure shit and you can't do anything, you're in trouble.

A few years ago I played the twenty-six-year-old route for a while, like the men do. For some reason I'm attracted to younger men. That was good sex and kind of interesting for a while. But if you talk to these young men about civil rights or the problems with your children, they have no idea what you're talking about.

With me, I think sex was just a very strong desire for intimacy. With one young guy his fun was to make love, and we made love every place there was: in a tree, underwater; we just ran all over the countryside, skinny-dipping, snowball fighting, always ending up with a good fuck. It was sheer idiocy and fun. Technique has very little to do with it. I get as much just sleeping next to the man I love, with my foot on his calf, as I would screwing the best lay in the country. Perhaps a man's sexuality is less tied to his general feelings. They can have a wonderful sexual experience without remembering the girl's last name, whereas, with a woman, it has to be a culmination of many things, whether it be joy, play, or empathic understanding. Most women are jealous of my sexual experiences.

We all have masculine and feminine traits. I would like men to be more like us. I don't see any reason why men should not become more gentle and warm. That is what society has done wrong with our little boys. The little boy will fall and skin his knee, and his dad will say, "Don't cry. Act like a man." And at the age of four he'd *act* like a man, but he never turns into a real one. I like a man who can cry, who can be gentle and support himself, too.

I have excellent friends, male and female. In fact, if I pride myself on anything, I pride myself on my friends. It's an achievement to have good, intimate, long-lived relationships. But I don't feel the necessity of being in daily contact.

I have never been discriminated against as a woman. I learned early that it was dumb to learn to type, because then that's all you get to do. I sold fleets of Oldsmobiles in Dallas one year. I made twelve thousand dollars selling cars in the summer while I made three thousand working as a nurse in the winter. But I preferred nursing. Really, I don't have much respect for money. I was born in a town where there were more millionaires per capita than anyplace in the world. My very best friend was left forty-five million dollars. But money doesn't mean much to me. Just because a dollar is attached to something doesn't make it of value.

I can't say what I've accomplished. I know what I've tried to do, but there's no direct path between my efforts and the results. It looks right now like I've done a pretty fair job of raising my kids, but who knows? There's no pat answer. I once told my mother-in-law who was interfering, "Look, we've seen what your methods have produced; this is my turn." I liked being a mother, especially as the kids got older. My kids just tickle the hell out of me now. I like their ideas and projects. I don't like them to be dependent on me.

I hated my daughter when she was thirteen, and she seemed to be thirteen for two or three years. My children are all different. I expect more of my daughter and less of my boys because they are their father's sons. They have no mechanical ability, and they have many incompetencies. I am afraid I am passing on to my daughter my lack of expectations for men in general.

I don't think I have any failed ambitions. I've lived pretty much to the hilt. I aim to do a lot more traveling when my youngest is in college. I'll be really free. Right now my ex-husband takes the children every other weekend. You have no idea what a complete delight it is to have a whole weekend to yourself. Sometimes I camp out by myself and sometimes I just have to have people. I'm extremely gregarious. I even prefer to read a book with someone else so we can discuss it.

I took up skiing when I was forty-four; I play tennis, swim, dance till dawn, and still tire most people out. I love to entertain on a grand scale. I built this big house to give parties in, and now that I'm going to sell it, I'm not sure anybody else will want it. I'm fixing it up to put it on the market. It needs work; there's some screech-owl shit on the eaves.

CHAPTER 25

Ruth–Promise and Fulfillment

My husband always has assumed that I could do anything, absolutely anything, and I've knocked myself out to prove that he was right.

Ruth is forty-eight, petite, ash-blond, good-looking, and proud of having kept her youthful figure. She speaks with animation and unusual directness. Often patting the table and moving about, she told her story with authority. She also expressed her deep religious convictions.

Ruth has been married for twenty-six years. She has four children whose ages range from sixteen to twenty-five. Ruth spent many years as a devoted mother and as a helpful wife to her husband, who is president of a small college. Their home is informal, attractive, and bulging with books.

Although Ruth set aside her early dreams of a career in order to be a mother, she managed to make a second career out of her social and religious volunteer work. Now she intends to put her many skills into paid professional work.

Ruth is twice blessed. Both her past and her present were smiled on by fortune and circumstance. And Ruth never takes her blessings for granted and always holds her values dear.

* * *

RUTH

WE HAD OUR twenty-fifth wedding anniversary last year and had a reaffirmation ceremony. I had suggested it to my husband, and although he thought it kind of pretentious, I said, "I'd like to do it. Let's do it." We might not have if it hadn't been for the encouragement of our oldest daughter. She's an artist with a magnificent sense of celebration of all kinds of occasions.

I wore my wedding dress, and I think more people were impressed by the fact that I could still get into it than they were about anything else. The reaffirmation ceremony included all the kids. I had the florist make a bouquet with removable flowers, so that I could give one to each of the kids with a statement as to what love represented in our life. Our pastor worked with us in redoing the wedding ceremony, so that it fit a renewal of vows.

Dave and I shared and still share similar intellectual interests. We talked and talked and talked, and still do. When he returns from a trip I go to the airport, and we're both hoarse by the time we get home. We can talk up a storm, even after twenty-six years.

My husband always has assumed that I could do anything, absolutely anything, and I've knocked myself out to prove that he was right. He is one of the few men to whom I could show something I made, and he'd say, "Gee, that's great." Or I'd say, "Look, I waxed the kitchen floor," and he'd admire it. Whatever I did, he appreciated. He loved my cooking. At the same time he assumed that he had the right to call up at five in the afternoon and say, "I'm bringing three people home for dinner." He did that constantly. Usually I didn't mind, but a few years ago I felt it was taking too much out of me, and I said, "No, I can't cope." He was rather hurt and somewhat shocked by that, but he's been a little more careful since to check it out first. I should have put my foot down years ago, but I assumed that that was part of my job, and I wanted to be the best damned housekeeper, wife, cook, mother, the whole schmere.

I got married in my senior year in college. My husband and I never discussed the possibility of my continuing my education. We both basically assumed that he would be the breadwinner, and I would raise the kids. There were a few times while I was changing diapers that I shed a tear over the fact that I hadn't gone on and had a career, but I knew I wasn't about to let someone else raise my kids. So it has kind of evolved that I am going to start work when the kids finish school. That's right about now.

I used to wonder how people got divorced after twenty years. I thought that if you could make it that long, you could make it the rest of the way. But now I understand one of the things that might happen. When the kids reached adolescence, at least in our experience, suddenly the division of labor that we had worked out wasn't working anymore. My husband did his job, and he had left the majority of the child-raising chores to me, the emotional responsibility, anyway. But then the time came that when I said "no" to the kids, Dave said, "Why not?" This was very divisive. I realized we had to make some changes. We had to talk out what position we were to take on a particular issue, so that when I said to the kids, "These are the limits," I wouldn't get the ground cut out from under me. I couldn't handle that.

So this was sort of a period of forced growth. It meant learning how to discuss feelings and things with Dave. He's a very level-headed person, calm and unflappable. For twenty years I couldn't win an argument, because I would get excited. I couldn't be reasonable, and he just shot holes in my balloons. Finally I learned I had to approach him in a very certain way in order to get him to discuss anything at the feeling level.

He gets along very well with people, but he's not emotionally vulnerable to anybody much beyond me. I don't know why, but I'm the only one on the face of the earth who can blow his cool. I know that. Even the kids can't. It's rather awesome sometimes, because it leaves me with a big responsibility not to abuse this power.

I did it once, deliberately, calculatedly, and I don't think I'll ever do it again. It was the major crisis that precipitated greater involvement on Dave's part.

When our oldest daughter went to college she was being sort of rebellious. Julie moved in with her boyfriend and was planning to go spend intercession with him. I discovered this when I called to talk to her and was told that she didn't live there anymore. I was really upset when I found out that she had told her father when she was home at Thanksgiving and that he hadn't said anything to me about it. I absolutely hit the fan. I left. For twenty-four hours I ran away. I left a note, rented a car, and disappeared. Well, he was off the wall until he found me.

I insisted on a showdown. I said to Dave, "Do you really want your daughter to live this way?" He said, "I don't know as we have a choice. And I don't want to antagonize her." But I insisted, "Do you want her to live this way? This is one time in my life I'm giving *you* a choice. You risk antagonizing her or you damn well antagonize me." I made it that clear. Dave said, "Well, let's wait and see. Meet the boy. Maybe she loves him." But I wasn't willing to give even that much of a benefit of a doubt. I said to him, "Why can't you be an indignant father once in a while? You always stay out of the emotional scene. You're always cool." This time unified action was necessary. Dave went along with me, and it proved in the long run to be right.

Our daughter came home for Christmas, and I said to her, "Julie, you're not going back to that school. If you want to live that way, you're not going to do it on our money. You'll have to support yourself." There were five days of agony over her boyfriend. There were multitudinous phone calls. Finally one night we had dinner guests, and she came around the corner, and I excused myself and went back in the other room and looked at this stricken kid. She looked at me, and she said that she had just talked to him and that he had said, "Stand up to your parents. Don't put up with this business. Make a choice. Me or them." And she said to me, "Mom, I had to choose between one person and six. Will you forgive me? I feel like such a fool." I was really awed that she included the rest of the family in her choice.

So she stayed home that semester and went to another college in the fall. She came to understand that that kind of casual relationship was not acceptable. She had actually considered breaking it off before we blew the whistle. She knew she was being exploited and didn't know how to handle it, how to get out of it.

I'm afraid that a lot of gals now who are saying that what's sauce for the goose is sauce for the gander are being terribly exploited. They're saying that they have to sow as many wild oats as the guys used to be free to and the women weren't. But in the long run they are going to find themselves damaged by this kind of thing. There's no reason for them to say no. They don't have the crutches that we did, and unless they have strong characters it's a lot tougher to resist the pressure. I haven't come across any young girls who say that sex is great or wonderful. My pastor said, "I wish I had a nickel for every young woman at twenty-six that I've counseled who at age eighteen thought she knew what she was doing." They've had a series of "meaningful relationships" one after another, and now they are incapable of trusting. They see no hope for themselves as human beings. They feel destroyed by this series.

I can't separate sex and love. I can't even envision going to bed with somebody I didn't really care about. In the last five years my husband and I have been much more able to discuss our feelings about sex. This came about as a result of the necessity to discuss other things, specifically the children. In the early days there was basically a lack of understanding on both sides, and neither of us knew how to discuss it in a way that would be helpful. There was a time when, sexually speaking, Dave felt that he was on a diet and I felt overfed, let's put it that way. But we learned.

There was a cartoon I saved several years ago: It shows the wife in the kitchen with the pots boiling over on the stove, with a baby in one arm, another one pulling on her skirt, the dog and cat fighting in the corner, and the husband coming in the kitchen and ardently embracing her, and she says, "For Pete's sake, why can't you come home exhausted like other husbands?" I love that, and it was almost our situation sometimes when the kids were little.

Probably I have more sexual desire now than I did before. I was sort of slow developing along this line. I was twenty-one when I was married. It took quite a while for me to learn to develop a response. So now the quantity is about the same, and the quality is a lot better than it was a long time ago. And it took a while before I was able to say, "Hey, it doesn't have to be that kind of a response every time to be OK." That has been an educational thing. It doesn't have to be there for me. It can still be possible for Dave, and for him, it's essentially necessary to have orgasm. I tell him not to worry about me. If it happens, it's great, and if not, it's not all that traumatic. If the interval between that kind of response gets very long, he'll notice and be concerned, but I try to put his mind at ease. I don't feel that sex or my sexual image is a great problem.

Neither of us has had an affair. I never accepted the double standard and neither does Dave. He says, "Why should it be any different just because the plumbing is hooked up differently? If I expect someone to live up to my standard, I should be able to apply the same standard to myself."

I think I expect equality because my parents treated each other as equals. I was born when both my parents were in their late thirties, and I was the only child. I got both the male and female expectations.

I adored my father. Dad did a lot of work with the Boy Scouts, and he taught me all the knots, camp building, how to split wood, how to handle a jackknife, and how to climb trees. He definitely encouraged me to be a tomboy until I was a teenager. He was also the one who gave me sex education books and made sure I knew what that was all about. I remember getting my first lecture at six, walking along the river. Instead of birds and bees, it was fish. He used to write me letters separately when he was overseas during the war. I treasured the fact that he wrote letters to me separately from those he wrote to my mother. He taught me how to dance. My parents still put on records at night and dance. So he made me feel good as a girl, too. I wasn't just a female Boy Scout. There was some ambivalence and some confusion, though, because his stories didn't always come out the same way. When I was thirteen he said, "Don't ever let anybody kiss you on the mouth." Period. And when I was eighteen or nineteen he said, "Well, a little necking never did anybody any harm." "Why didn't you tell me that five years ago, Daddy?"

It wasn't just my father who was passing on the rules of life to me. I was with my mother a lot more because my father was gone a great deal. And we moved many, many times. I was in the eighth grade before I had a whole year in the same school. My education was a little choppy, but I didn't seem to suffer. I know there was a lot of input from my mother, but my main focus was on my father. He was always loving to my mother, too. He called her "my sweetheart" and "my best girl."

My mother would have been women's lib for her generation, had she the opportunity. She was the town's old maid before she got married. She was a business woman and a strong individualist. She made sure that her child would not be prevented from doing things, as she was as a child. So I learned to do all kinds of things, both masculine and feminine. I darned socks, and I mowed lawns. I've always prized the fact that my mother knew when to keep her hands off, when to let me alone to learn by myself.

My parents have lived with me for four years now. It has worked out very well. It's good for them to be around the grandchildren, and it's good for the kids. I know it could be difficult, but this setup is ideal. They have their own telephone, their own thermostat, kitchen, and TV. They join us for Sunday dinner and holidays. Of course they have each other, and if my father were not living, it would be hard for me, as my mother is physically weak now. She needs a lot of small things done for her, and she can be a demanding taskmaster.

My parents aren't financially dependent on me. They don't live with me because they can't afford a home. We gave them the choice, and they chose to live here. They definitely are emotionally dependent on me, however. My mother will ask me frequently, "Now that you look back on it, what do you think were the things your father and I did right or did wrong?" I'm apt to mention something she can't even remember. For example, just one comment from my father about maybe having a few more A's on my report card. I worked my tail off to get all A's. And for all the tomboy bit, when I got to high school, he said, "You can't beat the boys at their own game. They don't like it." I didn't know how to handle that.

I'm very proud of the work that my husband does, and I'm glad that he likes it. It was only about five years ago that I discovered that mixed in with all this pride in who he is and what he does that I was jealous as hell. Although I intended to devote my main energies to motherhood, I found after a few years that I had to have something more, something sort of intellectual. I couldn't cope with just the four kids. I needed something of my own. I've been active for years now in volunteer social work—race relations, psychiatric and drug counseling, for example. I work through the interfaith council in this city. Then I went back to college and got a degree. Dave used to say to me, "Why can't you just take courses?" But I said, "No. I have to have a real purpose, a goal. I can't just sit around and take courses all my life."

Dave has come to accept in me this very strong drive to do something at the professional level, which I've set aside for twenty-five years. But I don't think he understands why it's so important to me, and I think he's concerned that he won't be as well taken care of.

I'm ready right now, if I can find a job, to be a paid professional. I'm not going to be somebody's secretary. I want a job where I have a secretary. That's the important thing. And I don't want a job just to earn money. I'm looking for job satisfaction.

I'm a high-risk person, and I've just got to try, even if I fail. I've been successful at most things in my life, although there have been times when I've been acutely aware of failure. Usually it was when a person did not respond in a way I had hoped for. Many times I've been in a position, working with these kids, where I laid my feelings on the line, reached out, and was not accepted, or was brushed off. In that sense, I have had to cope with failure.

I do believe that love has been very good to me, and I feel that that puts an obligation on me to share it with people who need it. It's been a long time since I've even had to worry about being loved. Dave may not get emotionally involved with the things I do, but when I do get upset, he's always there for support. It has allowed me to risk a lot more of myself as a person without feeling completely wiped out if things don't come through.

I hope I know my weaknesses: that I'm not always sensitive

enough to people's feelings, that I tend to hit things head on, and that I've got to learn to soft-pedal it a bit more. Although I'm very religious, I'm not a single-minded zealot. The fulfilled life is a full life. I love to dance, play tennis, and garden. I'm a sprinter, though, not a marathon racer. I like to have something I start, I do it, and it's done. Most of my frustration with housework is that it never stays done.

I have some wrinkles and some gray hair, but they don't bother me. I'm a lot happier at forty-eight than I was at twenty-five or thirty-five, definitely. I wouldn't want to be sixteen again for anything. I've generally been content with whatever age I was at. I don't think about my age. I'm not panicked by the fact that I'm forty-eight. So what?

CONCLUSION

WE STARTED our interviews with middle-aged women with a few assumptions that proved false. The first was that the physical fact of menopause would be a significant problem. Although all the women we interviewed felt assaulted in varying degrees by the physiological effects of menopause or aging, they did not consider these effects of major importance.

The second assumption was that childhood is destiny; that is, that a woman's character and behavior are largely derived from her childhood experience. This assumption proved to be only partially true. The child is mother of the woman, but adult experience can be equally formative. Many of the women we interviewed were able to make remarkable changes even late in their lives.

Some women came from the worst possible circumstances; they had no consistent person to provide tenderness. These truly abandoned women have found their self-esteem from external sources—their personal accomplishments, their sexual assertiveness, their independence, their earning capacity, and, above all, their survival. They are all forceful personalities who know that they have survived against the odds, developing character and pride in the process.

Other women were handicapped by the rigid demands of their parents, and, as a result, much of their energy was consumed in trying to gain and maintain approval, rather than in manipulating the physical world. They were trying to "figure the teacher" and seldom tried to "figure the task."[1]

The third assumption was that many women we talked to would be suffering from the "empty nest" syndrome, that is, from feelings of loss and uselessness with no children to care for.[2] Actually none

---

[1] Jerome Kagan, "Acquisition and Significance of Sex-Typing and Sex-Role Identity," *Review of Child Development Research*, eds. M.L. Hoffman and L.W. Hoffman, vol. 1 (New York: Russell Sage, 1964), p. 158

[2] Pauline Bart, "Mother Portnoy's Complaints," *Transaction*, vol. 8, Nov.-Dec. 1970, pp. 69–74.

were. Most of our women found pleasure and self-esteem in the role of mother, but motherhood had never been their only source of meaning. The mothers whose children were handicapped met the difficulty of caring for those children with touching and quiet courage, but even these women never defined themselves solely as mothers.

It was the role of wife, not mother, that turned out to be the primary source of self-esteem for the women we interviewed. Even women whose careers held the promise of financial and worldly success before marriage happily exchanged them for marital status. Marriage, not menstruation, was their puberty rite and performing it conferred status. Only Meg, knowing herself to be homosexual, refused the honor.

Marriage turned out to be limiting for many of our women. It left them too dependent on loving and being loved. They did not anticipate the need for "a room of one's own" from which to develop a separate identity. For example, Phyl, assessing her considerable musical skills as a selfish preoccupation, gave up the violin. She agreed with her mother's dictum that her husband should be her "whole life." Ironically, Phyl's divorce was the trauma that forced her to change her priorities and to put her own needs first. Through full-time work, new friends, and a joyous return to music, she is building a separate self.

Many of the women we interviewed resemble Phyl in that they were also trained to please their prince. These trained-to-please women lived vicariously through their husbands, and marriage became their "declaration of dependence."[3] When confronted with criticism from their husbands, they could not use "fight or flight" as a defense; they accepted the blame, denied their anger, and then clutched or clung to ward off their feelings of helplessness.[4]

These traditional, trained-to-please women are good purveyors of what our society teaches them: namely, to be a successful woman you must find a husband and place his needs above your own. Unfortunately, most of them were divorced by their husbands. Clutching and clinging worked against them.

---

[3] Alexandra Symonds, M.D., "Phobias after Marriage: Women's Declaration of Dependence," *American Journal of Psychoanalysis* (1971), pp. 144–152.

[4] Willard Gaylin, M.D., *Caring* (New York: Alfred A. Knopf, 1976), p. 179.

All of our women took some part of their self-esteem from their desirability and their sexual behavior. Being attractive and desirable to men has always been part of the feminine mystique. Even Cinderella needed beautiful trappings to win the prince. For some, however, this mystique became the major measure of their worth. These sexually obsessed women use sex primarily to undo the past and to control the present. For example, Lillian, following society's prescription for women, never developed any of her powers other than coquetry and, at forty-eight, is still asking only one question: "Am I desirable to a man?"

In the best of circumstances our women identified sex with assertion, intimacy, and pleasure. They are women with high self-esteem whose emotional security allows them to enjoy more intimacy in their personal relationships. Because the love and approval they received as children were subject to fewer, more reasonable conditions, they were freer to take risks and to choose their own values. It is noteworthy that they also value friendship more than do the women with lower self-esteem.

All of these women are more inner-directed and assertive as well. They do not turn themselves inside out to please their husbands or lovers; they maintain an identity that gives them the power not to please.[5] They can acknowledge and express their anger, they are less afraid to question the demands made on them by our society, and, although they face an uncertain future—our society has not cleared a path for middle-aged women—they prefer the trauma of change to the "trauma of eventlessness."[6]

For example, Irene, who was a nurturing but dependent wife, saw that her husband was unloving and cruel to their children. At forty, with trepidation, she went to college, became self-supporting, and ended her marriage. Irene's desire to please others has never left her, but this desire is a result of having *been* pleased rather than *having to* please and therefore has its limits. When her prince turned into a toad, she left him.

The women with the greatest sense of fulfillment happen to be those who have jobs or careers or avocations. Over half of them

---

[5] Elizabeth Janeway, *Between Myth and Morning: Women Awakening* (New York: William Morrow, 1974), Chap. 13, "The Weak Are the Second Sex."

[6] Robert Seidenberg, M.D., "The Trauma of Eventlessness," *Psychoanalysis and Women*, ed. Jean Baker Miller (New York: Brunner/Maxel, 1973), p. 353.

developed their careers or consuming interests in mid-life. Most significant, every one of these women is fully occupied and excited about what she is doing.

Judging by the twenty-five middle-aged women presented here, quite a lot has happened to Cinderella since she left the ball. She married the prince, but more often than not she is divorced. There is a less than fifty–fifty chance that she is presently enjoying regular sexual intimacy with her husband or lover, but when she does, it's better than ever. Almost all would be receptive to sex now, but, unfortunately, most of the widows and divorcées have not as yet found a "suitable" partner in their middle years.

After forty years, not a single Cinderella would choose to relive her youth, with its attendant uncertainties and humiliations. Although she still wishes for a man, she no longer requires a prince, and she recognizes that "living happily ever after" is an ending exclusively for fairy tales. What she does require is the reality of friendships, some emotional flexibility, mental and spiritual enrichment, and, of course, good health. Above all, she requires faith in her own values, a degree of control over her own destiny, and the opportunity to exercise some of the powers that are uniquely hers.